The Socratic Method of Psychotherapy

THE SOCRATIC METHOD *of* PSYCHOTHERAPY

JAMES OVERHOLSER

COLUMBIA UNIVERSITY PRESS *NEW YORK*

Columbia University Press
Publishers Since 1893
New York   Chichester, West Sussex
cup.columbia.edu
Copyright © 2018 Columbia University Press
All rights reserved
Library of Congress Cataloging-in-Publication Data
Names: Overholser, James C., author.
Title: The Socratic method of psychotherapy / James Overholser.
Description: New York : Columbia University Press, [2018] | Includes bibliographical references and index.
Identifiers: LCCN 2018016928 (print) | LCCN 2018021790 (ebook) | ISBN 9780231544832 (e-book) | ISBN 9780231183284 (cloth) | ISBN 9780231183291 (pbk.)
Subjects: LCSH: Psychotherapy. | Questioning. | Socrates.
Classification: LCC RC480 (ebook) | LCC RC480 .O94 2018 (print) | DDC 616.89/14— dc23
LC record available at https://lccn.loc.gov/2018016928

Cover design: Mary Ann Smith

Contents

Preface vii

ONE Introduction to the Socratic Method 1

TWO Psychotherapy as Therapy for the Mind 5

THREE Integrating Science and Practice . . . and Philosophy? 16

FOUR Systematic Questioning: If You Do Not Know, Just Ask 32

FIVE Inductive Reasoning: Learning from Personal Experiences 53

SIX Universal Definitions: What Do You Mean by That? 68

SEVEN Socratic Ignorance: Accepting What You Do Not Really Know 87

EIGHT Guided Discovery: Searching Together as a Team 102

NINE Self-Improvement: Helping Clients Grow and Mature 114

TEN A Focus on Virtue Ethics in Psychotherapy 129

ELEVEN Wisdom: Can You See the Big Picture? 146

CONTENTS

TWELVE Courage: Are You Brave Enough to Be Yourself? 162

THIRTEEN Moderation: Learning to Tame Your Desires 173

FOURTEEN Justice: Is It Possible to Be Fair to Everyone? 186

FIFTEEN Piety: Do Spiritual Beliefs Have a Place in Psychotherapy? 198

SIXTEEN Psychotherapy from a Socratic View 210

SEVENTEEN Conclusions: Where Do We Go from Here? 219

References 231

Index 253

Preface

Where does an appreciation for the Socratic method begin? How can a historical figure from more than two thousand years ago have a potent influence on psychological treatments today? Is it possible to integrate ancient philosophy with contemporary psychotherapy? For more than thirty years, these issues have played an important role in my life in terms of my scholarly writing, the clinical services I provide, and my own personal growth.

I believe that my interest in self-guided discovery started young. When I was a child in the third and fourth grades, I struggled to complete basic homework in arithmetic and reading. Simple mathematical formulas and the dreaded word problems would frustrate me, and I would quickly feel upset with myself. I could not see the need for such nonsense, and I could not anticipate a time in my life when these skills would be necessary. After dinner, I would ask my parents for help. My mother always deferred to my father. However, my father worked long days as a manual laborer, leaving for work at five-thirty every morning. He would promise to help with my homework, but after dinner he read the evening newspaper (back when major cities published a morning edition and an evening edition of the daily paper), and this took most of his evening. As kids, we often joked that my father spent so much time reading the paper that in reality he wasn't just reading it, he was memorizing it. When my bedtime arrived, he promised to look over my homework and leave a note for me in the morning. The next morning, the "note" from my father was in the form of corrections marked on my

PREFACE

homework, with no explanation or guidance as to what I had done wrong. I would always get good grades for my (er, his) homework, but I took no ownership for it and, even worse, I was not learning. I eventually stopped asking for his "help." Even as a child, I could see that, as nice as it was to have the answers handed to me, it was important for me to struggle and learn. My father was a good man, honest and hard working. He was not a great teacher, and probably I was not a great student during those early years.

I had a similar experience when I developed an interest in assembling model boats and cars from hobby kits. I enjoyed the *idea* of making a massive model ship or even a ship in a bottle. However, as soon as I opened the box and saw the number of tiny pieces, I felt overwhelmed by the project. My father enjoyed detailed craft projects, so he would step in to help. But again, it was easier to work late into the evening, when my little hands no longer got in the way. Within a week, I had a beautiful model ship, completely unassembled by my own hands. I took no pride in the ships (except for the one I did finally assemble on my own, a small trawler made from twelve parts).

Perhaps the third time will be the charm. When I was seventeen, I purchased my first car, a 1968 AMC Javelin, for seven hundred dollars. It had a 350cc engine and a four-on-the-floor stick shift. However, it already had 92,000 miles on the odometer when I bought it. Over the first few months, it needed a new starter, new radiator hoses, a new muffler, and new shocks. I was not mechanically inclined, but I thought I could learn both how to drive stick and how to make repairs on a car, two feats I had never before attempted. My father was a skilled amateur mechanic who could fix anything with a screwdriver, a wire clothes hanger, and some duct tape. I had hoped to learn the basics of auto repair, but that went differently than I had anticipated. I would be out back, working on the car, winter or summer, struggling with my simple box of tools and even more simple understanding of auto mechanics. He would point me toward our *Chilton's* manual, the five-hundred-plus-page tome that contains detailed schematic diagrams of every part disassembled into a mixture of bolts, gaskets, and springs. However, without understanding how the part moves or functions, the diagrams were no help. After two or three hours of frustration, lying on the concrete floor, my father would come out, give a few instructions that meant little to me, and quickly become exasperated by my ignorance. After I went in to do homework (I was now doing *all* of my own homework), my father would take over, make the repairs, and my car would again be drivable. I experienced hours of frustration followed by the shame of my ignorance and still didn't learn much about auto mechanics.

Looking back I can now see the shadows that influence my interest in teaching. I still never learned what a binomial is, but I did learn some things. I learned that teaching is not about lectures or scolding. I learned that learning is by doing, not by listening to someone else. I learned that there can be a sense of pride when developing new skills. I learned to do things for myself. I believe these early moments of ignorance and frustration laid the foundation for my interest in the Socratic method.

During my undergraduate schooling, I registered for a course on criminology. The professor held joint appointments in sociology and the law school, and he favored a teaching style characterized by one version of the Socratic method. He would pose questions to the class, and when no one would answer, he would read from his class roster, select a name, and call on that student. The professor liked to call on students in the back of the room as likely candidates for not having done the homework. If the poor student stumbled, could not answer, or gave an incomplete response, his standard reply was, "Why don't you continue reading on this topic. I will ask you the question again in our next class." He would write down the question and the student's name to ensure he carried out his promise/threat. Such a response terrified every student. I quickly learned to raise my hand to answer any question I thought I could answer so I was more likely to be skipped over when he posed a difficult one.

In graduate school, I thoroughly enjoyed reading a book chapter on attitude modification methods (Johnson & Matross, 1975), which mentioned the use of questioning and inductive reasoning as the key components of the Socratic method. In that chapter the authors referred to a more detailed overview of the Socratic method in counseling and psychotherapy, but when queried several years later, one author couldn't locate that earlier unpublished report (Ron Matross, personal communication, October 10, 1989). I felt this was an exciting strategy for therapy, and without that mythical unpublished report on hand, I began exploring on my own the philosophical foundation behind the Socratic method.

As a young psychologist still in graduate school, I was aligned with the theory and ideals of behavior therapy. In the early 1980s, the cognitive revolution was underway. The work of Aaron Beck and Albert Ellis was already reshaping contemporary psychotherapy. The cognitive approaches expanded the role of behavior change and helped the effects generalize beyond situations that allowed for strong environmental control over antecedents and consequences.

In one graduate seminar, the professor relied on a somewhat distorted version of the Socratic method. He would frequently use questions to explore topics related to psychotherapy, expecting students to confront and explore their own beliefs and values. However, if the professor liked a particular student, the questions were relatively simple. If the chosen student stumbled, the questions became even easier. And for a few students disliked by the professor, the questions started out hard and became impossible to answer. As a member of the elite group of chosen students, I sensed the bias and quietly shared my concerns with the students who were being picked on in class. Despite the misuse of his exploratory questions, I retained my appreciation of the Socratic method and how it could be used to guide a sincere educational exploration through dialogue.

As I read Plato and studied contemporary philosophers' interpretations of his dialogues, I continually asked myself how this information could help me become a better psychotherapist. This was a slow process, not only because reading philosophy often means wrestling with obtuse language and pedantic writing styles, but because I had many other responsibilities: classes, field placements, and conducting my own research projects. However, I kept up my study of philosophy whenever I found some spare time. Over the years, I developed a rhythm: Read books and articles that examined ancient philosophy, write about the Socratic method, think about my ideas and how they guide my therapy, conduct my own sessions with clients, and continually ask myself what works in real therapy sessions instead of what may have made sense in the isolated, pristine, naïve view of my mind. While on my predoctoral internship, I wrote my first paper on the Socratic method as a component in the treatment of clients with a dependent personality disorder (Overholser, 1987). I then started to develop the more complete model of the Socratic method as a framework for psychotherapy (Overholser, 1988), and I have continued to explore and expand these ideas.

After I joined the faculty at Case Western Reserve University, my priorities shifted to starting an independent program of clinical research and preparing lectures for my graduate and undergraduate courses. My work on

PREFACE

the Socratic method took a back seat. While much of my time was focused on collecting data and publishing research studies, I remained active with a small clinical practice. I always felt that my best sessions had included core elements of the Socratic approach, and I continue to believe that I am a much better therapist when I am focused on the Socratic method. As my interest and focus endured, my view of the model expanded. I looked at the various components that make up the Socratic method. I had intended to write one paper on the use of questions to guide therapy, but while I was writing it, I kept seeing the need to link that idea up with the use of questions and their application using inductive reasoning. I found myself working on both these topics, in two separate papers, in the same year.

I would invest in each paper on the Socratic method approximately two years (and often longer) working through various drafts, revising the ideas, and adding case material. I was intolerant of abstract ideals that did not translate into clinical technique. I was equally intolerant of raw case material that lacked a sound theoretical basis. It has been a challenge, over the entire course of my career, to integrate the philosophical core of the Socratic method with strategies from contemporary psychotherapy while also being grounded in actual case material. The process of thinking, applying, and refining these ideas has taken decades, but I feel the process has helped me grow as a person and as a professional.

I feel it is important to include a cautionary note about using client scenarios and case examples in a professional text. Throughout this book, I use case material from clients with whom I have worked over the years. I find the cases guide my thinking and clarify the ideas covered in this book. I have been a practicing clinician for more than thirty years, and I respect the many insights I have learned from work with my clients. However, I also respect my clients and consider confidentiality a cornerstone of effective psychotherapy. Many case details have been omitted, disguised, or otherwise modified. I follow three guiding principles whenever presenting case material in published form. First, if the client background is described in detail, I solicit the client's written permission allowing the release of confidential material, to be used for professional presentation and educational purposes. Second, in most situations, I have tried to ensure that no true client identity can be revealed through the material presented in the text. In the case vignettes, I avoid presenting background information about the client's life, problems, or family. Background material and specific details have been shifted in ways that protect the client's identity and personal information. I have tried to present each case vignette using a compilation of summaries and quotations to capture my style of psychotherapy, though I have also tried to ensure that all clinical material is presented in such a way that the description remains true to the actual dialogue that occurred in our therapy session. I keep the spotlight centered on my role as therapist and on the specific exchange that occurred during an actual therapy session. I sometimes blur the details of a case by blending notions across multiple clients, creating an amalgamated reenactment that maps onto actual psychotherapy sessions but cannot be directly tied to one moment in time. By adhering to a mixture of these three principles, I believe that client confidentiality is protected securely and anonymously. I aim for a level of secrecy such that even if my former clients were to read this book, they could not be sure whether they were being discussed.

At my professional core, I am a licensed clinical psychologist with a strong background in cognitive-behavioral psychotherapy. Today, there is a strong emphasis on research support for any psychological intervention. However, there is little research to support the Socratic method as a form of psychotherapy. This dearth of empirical support might be unfortunate, but it makes sense. Throughout his life and dialogues, Socrates relied on theoretical ideas and common sense. Socrates trusted a network of beliefs only when all of the various ideas were intermingled in a compatible manner, such that there were no internal contradictions across a person's beliefs. When Socrates discussed a topic with an individual, he would look for incompatible, clashing ideas. When such inconsistencies were found, Socrates helped the individual see the disagreement, and then he strongly encouraged the person to discard at least one of those beliefs. According to the historical Socrates, there was no need for research—true knowledge could be uncovered through reason and dialogue alone. Furthermore, too many of the ideas he was interested in grappled with major life issues and moral beliefs such as courage or justice. These notions were so abstract that empirical research into them was not possible. In a similar manner, many of these same strategies appear relevant to the Socratic method as a form of psychotherapy today. The process of exploring ideas and looking for a rational basis through reason and dialogue plays a central role in cognitive-behavioral therapy and its more recent spinoffs.

PREFACE

Throughout this book, I have tried to articulate ideas originally espoused in ancient philosophy and temper them by the realities now being confronted in contemporary psychotherapy sessions. Over the course of my career, I have seen too much emphasis placed on "new" ideas, but when I have examined these "innovations" in more detail, I often find they are simply old ideas revived or repackaged in new terminology. Thus, I continue to respect many older sources, and I am pleased to cite older references throughout my writing. The abstract concepts explored in philosophical works remain important issues to be confronted in society today. Too many current publications chase the latest fad and risk moving away from important topics and lasting ideas.

The present book strives to help mental health professionals approach psychotherapy sessions from a broad and philosophical vantage. The goal is to approach each client's struggles from a perspective that promotes growth and maturation, allowing for a range of ideas and strategies that can guide the therapist's plan for effective change.

This book will cover the theoretical foundations of the Socratic method, as espoused by Socrates and captured by Plato, and will discuss how they can inform strategies that can help guide psychotherapy sessions. Each of these strategies comes from the dialogues of Plato, but I have examined them over thirty years of clinical practice.

As I complete the writing of this book, there are many people I want to thank. I am deeply indebted to my loving wife and my darling children. Without them, it is likely I would have led a life of addiction and misery. I would have had no understanding of a meaningful life, and I would have wasted the past thirty years on nonsense, whether in the form of extreme academic productivity or excessive partying with friends. Instead, I feel that I have found my reasons for living and the personal values to which I am happy to devote my time and my life.

I am equally indebted to my clients. I feel honored to work as a psychotherapist, which I believe is the highest level a psychologist can ever reach. My clients have trusted me with their thoughts, dreams, worries, and private concerns. I wish I could identify specific people by name, but that would not be proper. I am thankful for the time I have spent with my clients and remain hopeful that my words as a therapist have been helpful to some of these wonderful people. I know their words have enriched my life.

PREFACE

I also want to thank my students and colleagues. For many years, I have been fortunate to discuss these topics in classes I teach at both the graduate and undergraduate levels. These classroom discussions have provided innumerable opportunities to share my opinions, sharpen my views, test my ideas, and refine my thoughts. I am always impressed with the background knowledge and perceptive insights my students have shared in the classroom environment.

Finally, I am forever thankful to my friend and colleague Dr. Görgen Göstas, who gave his time and wisdom to read carefully the chapters and share his thoughtful comments. He consistently shared his ideas and constructive feedback during the prolonged process of my writing this book and kept me motivated to continue writing the next chapter.

I am happy to thank the CWRU Baker-Nord Center for financial support in preparing the index for the book and all members of the Case Western Reserve University community for tolerating my style and supporting my academic endeavors. Without the help of a sabbatical semester, I would not have found the time finally to focus on the Socratic method in a book-length treatise.

The Socratic Method of Psychotherapy

ONE

Introduction to the Socratic Method

THE SOCRATIC METHOD facilitates learning and discovery through a process of collaborative exploration, and it can be applied to many situations. The method dates back to ancient times and is derived from the discussions led by Socrates in Athens.

In psychological writings, a variety of authors, including Aaron Beck and Albert Ellis, have endorsed the Socratic method as a useful tool for teaching and psychotherapy sessions, and this has reignited a scholarly interest in the method. However, discrepancies continue to exist across the various authors who describe "the Socratic method," a "Socratic dialogue," and "Socratic questioning" (Carey & Mullan, 2004). A Socratic dialogue can take many different forms (Carpenter & Polansky, 2002), and scholars even disagree about whether Socrates had a distinct method (Scott, 2002). Even worse, most authors mention the Socratic method only in passing and rarely provide useful details about the ideology or procedures undergirding the Socratic approach. This book will try to clarify the ideas and procedures of the Socratic method within psychotherapy sessions. However, I will not bother with trivialities in terminology. Instead, "the Socratic method" will be used interchangeably with "a Socratic dialogue," "a Socratic discussion," and "the elenchus."

The translation of a few terms requires explanation. In classical texts, *sophia* is wisdom, which is only found in those people who seek a life of thoughtful contemplation. In contrast, *episteme* is knowledge that has been supported from a scientific viewpoint. *Phronesis* refers to practical understanding. *Techne* refers to technical expertise. *Aporia* refers to a state of puzzlement or confusion, which often comes as a result of Socrates's questions, when people become aware of their own ignorance. Perhaps the central term to confront is the *elenchus*. This refers to a process of cross-examination and refutation. In a general manner, the elenchus captures the traditional view of the Socratic method. In its simple version, it is the interrogative exchange aimed at clarifying and refuting the questionee's beliefs. In its more complex version, the elenchus is a lifelong strategy for remaining thoughtful and objective (King, 2008).

The historical foundation for the Platonic dialogues has largely remained within the provinces of philosophy and the classics. There have been a few authors working in education (e.g., Whiteley, 2014) or applied philosophy (e.g., Howard, 2011) who refer to Plato. However, most if not all scholars who discuss the Socratic method within the field of psychology fail to cite any publications either from antiquity or from contemporary philosophy. I have tried to remain true to the historical figure of Socrates as portrayed in the dialogues of Plato. Whenever possible, I attempt to remain anchored in the words attributed to Socrates, citing the classic two-volume source, *The Dialogues of Plato*, translated and edited by Benjamin Jowett (1892/1937). I remain surprised and a bit disappointed when I see authors attribute their personal values and opinions to Socrates and Plato without any evidence that they have ever read these important texts. To understand the Socratic method, I had to step outside of my own field and explore authors from classics and philosophy. This strategy has posed an endless series of challenges for me as an academic and a scholar. I struggle with the disparities of epistemology and method across the fields and with the vastly different writing styles endorsed by psychology versus philosophy. Furthermore, the Platonic dialogues can be engaging at times, but they pose their own challenges in my attempts to follow the narrative, learn from the dialogue, yet still translate the material into contemporary clinical psychology.

In philosophical writings, "the Socratic method" is usually synonymous with "the elenchus." I will generally avoid this latter term because it remains beyond the lexicon of psychology. However, it is useful to recognize the elenchus as a discussion aimed at confronting, challenging, and refuting beliefs held by a client if the client cannot provide strong logical support for those beliefs. This notion is quite compatible with contemporary cognitive therapy. The elenchus helps a person move, slowly and gradually, toward discovery and new insights that can be trusted and valued (Seeskin, 1987). In true Socratic fashion, we will emphasize logic and examples. It makes sense to view clinical work and the case examples it provides as a natural laboratory for inspiring and exploring new ideas (Westen, Novotny, & Thompson-Brenner, 2004).

In the historic dialogues of Plato, the term *interlocutor* is used to refer to Socrates's participant in the discussion. When discussing examples and trying to keep the material anchored in references from philosophy, I sometimes blur the line and refer to the discussant as the "client" or the "other person," instead of interlocutor. Likewise, instead of constantly referring to Socrates and to dialogue exchanged centuries ago, I sometimes cautiously replace Socrates with "therapist" as the speaker in the discussion.

* * *

The present text cites a wide range of sources, giving credit to many pioneers in the fields of psychology, psychiatry, and philosophy. Because of the philosophical foundation that supports the core of the Socratic method, many of these references are from older sources and philosophical journals. There is less need to hype the latest research findings when the underlying ideas are ancient. Also, I have included many citations to support the philosophical foundation for the Socratic method. I have not included a wealth of citations for psychological views because my list of references was becoming rather extensive. I feel that psychology underlies everything I do, and I can support claims made within my home field. However, I feel obligated to provide support for statements that come from philosophy, classics, or virtue ethics.

To facilitate the dissemination of these abstract ideas, I have written this book in a conversational style rather than as an academic tome. As noted by Beutler and colleagues (1995), the standard format for academic journal articles is not appropriate for recommendations pertaining to psychotherapy. Instead, a single-authored book allows the freedom to discuss, explore, and present novel ideas that may be beneficial to the practicing or aspiring psychotherapist. I hope that graduate students, clinicians, and university professors will find value in the ideas expressed here and be inspired to integrate the Socratic method into their approach to psychotherapy.

Finally, relying on the Socratic method requires an important conceptual shift. There is much less focus on empirical support. Instead, the strategies are guided by comprehensive theories of human functioning combined with frequent involvement in clinical practice. The notions are influenced by hermeneutics as an improved strategy for the study of human behavior (Packer, 1985). Empiricism involves the examination of observable data collected without bias. Unfortunately, the empirical approach is a poor fit for the abstract concepts central to the Socratic method. In contrast, hermeneutics involves scholarly attempts to describe behavior without relying on abstract terms or theoretical assumptions (Packer, 1985).

The Socratic method has strong ties to rational support for ideas, relying on hypothesis testing to examine various beliefs (Packer, 1985). Hermeneutics, by contrast, relies on the evaluation of practical activities used in everyday work. Thus, the Socratic method as applied by psychology relies on a rational analysis of historical ideas *and* on a practical review of work performed in weekly psychotherapy sessions.

In describing the Socratic method of psychotherapy, this book will cover the primary active components of therapeutic dialogue: (1) the reliance on a series of questions to gather information and explore topics in detail, (2) the use of inductive reasoning to learn from specific examples and apply the new knowledge to the client's life situation, (3) a focus on broad terms or universal definitions to ensure that the discussion moves away from a narrow focus on specific problems or trivial events, (4) a willingness of therapist and client to accept the limits of their knowledge and approach all situations with an open mind and a willingness to learn, and (5) the use of guided discovery to move the dialogue forward with a sincere search for new ideas. When these five strategies are combined, they can be used to focus on several large goals for therapy, including the development of self-control, with an emphasis on self-improvement and on the willingness to explore virtue ethics as a guide for major life decisions and a positive focus for future goals. Thus, psychotherapy according to the Socratic method builds upon long-established ideas but integrates these ideas with the contemporary practice of psychotherapy.

My goal in this book is to provide new ideas that may be helpful for novice and seasoned experts in mental health counseling. I also readily admit that more ideas and research are needed. The book covers ideas that have been found useful, from the perspective of one therapist, and it welcomes new voices to share in or challenge these ideas.

TWO

Psychotherapy as Therapy for the Mind

THE LIFE AND philosophy of Socrates underlies the Socratic method. Socrates (469 BC–399 BC) was a philosopher who lived a modest existence in ancient Greece. He enjoyed talking with the people of Athens, where he lived his entire life, engaging them in thoughtful conversation about the perennial metaphysical topics that provide the foundation for philosophy and ethics in society.

Socrates's father, Sophronicus, worked as a sculptor or stonemason. Socrates too was a sculptor of sorts, a sculptor of the mind. He used his questions and dialogue to chip away at the surface to reveal the true image, the essence of an idea. Socrates's mother, Phaenarete, worked as a midwife, and Socrates likened himself to his mother, as he served as a midwife to the mind (*Theaetetus* 157). The midwife metaphor captures the Socratic view of teaching (Hansen, 1988). Like a midwife, Socrates was not pregnant with ideas but was helping others, often younger and less experienced people, give birth to their own ideas (Reale, 1987). Just as the midwife induces labor through the use of drugs, the Socratic method first induces confusion, instigating a search via questions that expose the person's ignorance (Versenyi, 1963). *Elenchus* refers to an interactive dialogue that explores an abstract topic and reveals gaps in logical reasoning. The goal of the Socratic elenchus is to deliver a new idea into the awareness of the client's conscious mind (Scraper, 2000).

Socrates valued the life of a philosopher. He denied ever being a teacher and even opposed being described as such. According to Socrates, a teacher held certain bases of knowledge and shared that information with students. Instead, Socrates viewed himself as lacking knowledge but interested in *learning*. He saw himself as a fellow explorer, searching for knowledge that could be trusted. Socrates never wrote down his ideas, because he did not trust the written word (Seeskin, 1987), and he distrusted the written word because he believed that reading encourages one to memorize ideas that then become "carved in stone." A written document cannot be customized to fit the level of the student or adapted to the unique interests of each person (Kraut, 1992a), and it cannot clarify any misinterpretations or misunderstandings in the reader (Howland, 1993). A written exposition is like a longwinded monologue (Seeskin, 1987). There can be no question-and-answer exchange with a book (Despland, 1985). Socrates argued: "Writing is unfortunately like painting; for the creations of the painter have the attitude of life, and yet if you ask them a question they preserve a solemn silence. And the same may be said of speeches. . . . And once they have been written down they are tumbled about anywhere among those who may or may not understand them" (*Phaedrus* 275). Because it is not possible to cross-examine a book (White, 1976), the reader assumes a passive role.

There is a bit of irony here. I am writing a book about a historical figure who opposed books and using words attributed to Socrates, written in an ancient text, to explain why spoken dialogue is so valuable. A lively exchange of questions and answers can force a person to defend or cast aside his or her beliefs and encourage true understanding (Kraut, 1992a). In the *Phaedrus* (275d–e), Socrates complained that an idea put into written form can be distributed inappropriately and used in ways unintended by the author. In contrast, Socrates believed that useful ideas were generated through the contact between two minds, like steel striking flint. I hope to do the same, to stimulate ideas in a field that is falling flat in the age of documentation and repetition.

Throughout his adult life, Socrates spent time in the agora, the open marketplace of Athens, where he would engage locals in thoughtful dialogue. The dialogues focused on the person's understanding of abstract concepts. Protagoras was a popular instructor in the Sophist style, which employed persuasive lectures that relied on uncritical acceptance by a passive learner. In contrast, Socrates preferred a more interactive style, one guided by lively exchange and a rational exploration of ideas (Versenyi, 1963). For this he was accused of and tried for impiety and corrupting the youth of Athens.

Socrates was considered impious because he opposed the Greek views of the gods and goddesses, believing that they must be entirely good, with no anger, lust, spite, or jealousy, unlike the typical characterization of the ancient Greek gods of mythology (Irwin, 1992), who had supernatural powers but often used them in harsh and harmful ways. These radical views went against the mainstream thoughts of Socrates's day. He was accused of corrupting the youth of Athens because some of the young men who listened to his dialogues later imitated his style of questioning people in authority. Such rebellion angered the leaders of the city, and they directed their anger toward Socrates, punishing him as their scapegoat (Waterfield, 2009). In short, Socrates was unpopular because he distrusted popular opinion and had offended local leaders and damaged their pride (Tredennick, 1969).

Socrates was tried, found guilty, and sentenced to death, and, despite opportunities for an easy escape, he remained incarcerated until the time came for him to drink hemlock poison and suffer a quiet death. During his final moments, Socrates was surrounded by his friends, and he accepted his execution with dignity.

Plato, a friend, follower, and colleague (not a student) of Socrates, took on the role of biographer and recorder of Socrates's dialogues. Almost everything we know about Socrates has been filtered through the writings of Plato (with some additional insights shared by Xenophon). Plato was born in 428 BC into a wealthy family. Over his lifetime, he developed wide-ranging interests in philosophy, politics, and government. After the execution of Socrates, Plato wanted to capture his memory of the dialogues and preserve the legacy of Socrates.

The dialogues were written in reverse chronological order, beginning with the trial and execution of Socrates, depicted in the *Apology*. It is commonly believed that among the dialogues, the *Apology* is most historically accurate, describing the events taking place during the last month of Socrates's life. As the dialogues proceed backward in time and Socrates gets younger, the writings become less dependent on Plato's memory of actual events and most likely are more products of Plato's imagination. However, the ideas of Socrates and Plato have become intermingled, and there is little value in searching for the original author behind them. Nonetheless, the dialogues of Plato are often regarded as a semihistorical record of the life and lessons of Socrates.

Generally speaking, Plato's writings are collectively called "dialogues" because at the center of each is a dialogue between Socrates and one or more citizens of Athens. (There are, however, two of Plato's dialogues, *Laws* and *Sophist*, in which Socrates does not appear and one, *Statesman*, in which he plays only a minor role.) Although there is some debate as to the order (Allen, 1984), the early dialogues were written sometime between 399 and 388 BC (including *Apology, Crito, Laches, Ion, Charmides, Euthyphro,* and *Protagoras*). The middle dialogues were written around 388 or 387 BC (including *Meno, Gorgias, Phaedo, Parmenides, Phaedrus, Symposium, Critias,* and *Republic*). The late dialogues were written between 367 and 361 BC (including *Sophist, Statesman, Philebus,* and *Laws*). There are several other dialogues whose authorship has not been adequately verified (including *Eryxias, Menexenus, Lesser Hippias,* and *Alcibiades I* and *II*). Because of the time spent recreating each story, over time they most likely became more about Plato's ideas and less about Socrates's dialogues (Rogers, 1933). Thus, it is generally considered that the *Republic* captures views held more by Plato than were ever expressed by Socrates. However, Socrates's search for knowledge as captured in the dialogues of Plato are considered much more historically accurate than anything found in the writings of Xenophon (Godley, 1896).

After Socrates's death, Plato was able to purchase a plot of land on the eastern edge of Athens. Sometime between 388 and 385 BC, he established the basis for a school of sorts, in a park that had been dedicated to Athens's hero Academus. This land became a community where other scholars could gather and share their experiences in philosophy, mathematics, law, and geometry. The area became known as the Academy, and it is generally considered to be the first university. Plato lived and worked at the Academy until his death in 348 or 347 BC. The Academy remained in existence as an educational institution until 529 AD; it is now an empty field on the outskirts of Athens.

"The Socratic method" is the general term used to capture the type of discussion used during Socrates's inquiries, which were often aimed at identifying clear definitions of ethical terms (Hackforth, 1933). The form of a Socratic dialogue is often referred to as a *dialectic* or the elenchus, although there are subtle differences between the two (Matthews, 1972). In the elenchus, Socrates uses a series of questions to examine all of the ramifications of a person's statement, often in the process detecting and refuting the invalid and unsupported beliefs underlying that statement (McKinney, 1983). The examination and refutation of erroneous beliefs plays a central role in the elenchus (Renaud, 2002). Questions often aid the search for a valid definition of key abstract terms (Matthews, 1972). A series of questions examines the meaning and likely truth of the client's beliefs (Robinson, 1971a). The removal of mistaken beliefs, created along with a state of ignorance, sets the stage for a new search for valid information (McKinney, 1983). In a dialectic, the discussion aims to explore ideas, confront different views, and eliminate false beliefs.

During the time that Plato organized and led the scholarship at the Academy, Aristotle came for eighteen years of study. Aristotle went on to write his own important works and to tutor Alexander the Great. For our purposes, we will not discuss his encyclopedic overview of ethics so as to remain true to the ideals of Socrates (and Plato). Throughout the present book on the Socratic method, we will maintain a clear and dominant focus on the ideology espoused by Socrates and captured by Plato. Other important scholars in philosophy, logic, and ethics will also be largely ignored in an attempt to remain true to Socrates as the eponymous originator of the Socratic method.

Moving from Ancient Dialogue to Contemporary Psychotherapy

This book hopes to explore contemporary psychotherapy, both its strengths and weaknesses. As a researcher and clinician, I have more than thirty years experience struggling to balance the importance of science and practice in clinical psychology. The book will be grounded in cognitive-behavioral therapy, which is considered an effective and well-documented form of psychotherapy today. At an even more essential level, effective psychotherapy highlights the psychology of the mind or, even better, the treatment of the mind. In all schools of psychotherapy, there is a clear emphasis or an implicit focus on the client's cognitive processes. Cognitive therapy focuses on confronting and modifying the client's interpretations, attributions, and expectations. However, other aspects of the Socratic method appear compatible with an array of theoretical models. The therapist may attempt to modify the client's beliefs, promoting insight and self-awareness about personal motives and neglected past events. Therapy promotes a balance of energy within the individual and aims to increase a person's interest in others. The therapist remains genuine, honest, and self-motivated while nonetheless addressing and challenging different facets of the client's personality. Finally, the discussions may confront broad issues related to life goals and a person's sense of meaning in life.

Throughout the Socratic dialogue, two or more people exchange ideas, challenge beliefs, and remain open to new perspectives. Whether confronting, for example, political views, religious beliefs, or opinions about drug use, the goal is to analyze the validity and utility of one's preexisting beliefs while keeping an open mind to new learning opportunities. The Socratic method aims to promote new insights and shifts in perspective in everyone involved in the dialogue. This type of dialogue can be useful in a classroom setting, and I have found it especially central to my career as a clinical psychologist and a psychotherapist.

The Socratic method is closely aligned with cognitive forms of psychotherapy, especially cognitive therapy (Beck, Rush, Shaw, & Emery, 1979), rational-emotive behavior therapy (Ellis, 1962, 1994), narrative therapy (Meichenbaum, 2003), and constructive therapy (Anderson & Goolishian, 1992). Clearly, cognitive therapy as developed by Beck has a strong foundation in the Socratic method (Moss, 1992). A Socratic dialogue is a primary tool in cognitive therapy, providing an elegant method of conveying empathy, fostering collaborative relationships with the client, and aiding the process of guided discovery (Rutter & Friedberg, 1999).

At the center of all forms of cognitive intervention lies a focus on the client's mind and attitudes. Thus, at base, the Socratic method is a psychology of the mind and mental processes. Put simply—perhaps overly so—many cognitive factors can be categorized as pertaining to one of three processes: *interpretations, attributions,* or *expectations.* This basic taxonomy helps therapists and clients focus on simple changes, guided by the view that negative thinking will create negative moods.

Interpretations guide our understanding, creating meaning from ambiguous events, including social encounters and performance evaluations. For example, when traveling in Asia, I ate dinner at a street market. I was served an exotic meal with a strange type of meat. If I believed the meat was octopus, I could quite happily eat it, even if it tasted a bit chewy. However, if I had believed the meat was boiled rat, I would have found the taste repulsive and been likely to vomit. If I expected the meal would make me sick and could disrupt my travels in an exotic country where I knew no one, I would have skipped the meal entirely and gone hungry. Interpretations influence our emotions, our behavior, and even our physiological reactions.

Attributions refer to a person's estimate of the most likely cause for past events in his or her life, whether successes, problems, or failures. Attributions relate to our view of causal factors and determine the allocation of blame for negative events, whether blame is localized in our self or in others. For example, attributions of blame are commonly noticed when conducting couples' therapy, as the partners express their frustration and anger over minor events.

In contrast to attributions, which typically look to the past, *expectations* look toward the future. Expectations refer to a person's estimate of the probability that certain events are likely to happen in the near or distant future. Expectations underlie our reactions to many events and can determine the amount of time and effort we invest in projects ranging from job applications to personal relationships. For example, when a client does not expect to be hired, he becomes less likely to apply for a new job. However, when a client views himself as well trained and competent, he is more likely to apply for a job and will approach the interview with excitement, enthusiasm, and confidence.

Cognitive-based theories of therapy were originally derived from clinical practice and experience. Aaron Beck, Donald Meichenbaum, and Albert Ellis were all actively involved with the direct provision of psychotherapy sessions, and through these sessions these founders of the discipline developed and refined their ideas about what makes for effective therapy. In contrast to the current push for research on psychotherapy outcomes, where large research projects are coordinated by professors who write the grant applications but no longer work directly with clients, the Socratic method relies on an inductive approach and places a higher value on clinical examples than on statistical significance.

As a form of treatment for depression and other psychological problems, adherents to the Socratic method are strongly opposed to the use of medication. The cultural climate underlying modern society emphasizes rapid-result approaches for the treatment of mental illness and accepts quick and superficial explanations instead of thoughtful and theoretical descriptions which might take time to formulate (Bemporad, 1996). However, it can be helpful to retain a strong focus on psychotherapy as a treatment for the *psyche*, that is, as a treatment for the mind and mental processes (Overholser, 2003a).

In some ways, the medical model has been helpful. A medical model reduces the stigma and helps mitigate the blame often associated with mental illness. Those suffering from mental or psychological issues may be seen as lazy, disrespectful, or rude, deliberately deviating from expected social norms in a slothful or socially inappropriate manner. However, when family members are given a biological explanation, often the focus shifts from anger and accusation to understanding and treatment. It is much more acceptable to inform friends or coworkers about an appointment with a physician for a renewal of one's prescriptions. It can be much more difficult to request time off from work for an appointment with a psychotherapist to discuss internal struggles.

Despite its advantages, the medical model is not without its problems. Over the past thirty years, there has been a proliferation of medications advertised as effective treatments for mental illness. In fact, there has been an artificial creation of psychiatric labels, that is, *a medicalization of normal emotional struggles*. The higher rates of incidence and prevalence of most forms of mental illness may be driven by economic forces, not by true improvements in medical taxonomy or discoveries in biological science. The intentional manufacture of mental illness can be seen clearly in the history of depression (Greenberg, 2010). Over the past fifty years, there has been a substantial increase in the rate of diagnosis, and this higher incidence aligns with the expanding sales of antidepressant medication. When depression is labeled a disease instead of an emotional reaction, it will be approached via a medical model and treated with biological interventions (Greenberg, 2010). Because of the primarily profit-driven nature of the pharmaceutical industry, there is a major financial interest in "selling sickness" (Moynihan & Cassels, 2005). Thus, in modern society, common worries and normal emotional struggles have been labeled mental illness and medicated (Moynihan & Cassels, 2005). Common forms of shyness or social reticence are labeled social anxiety disorder. When diagnosing a client, occasional periods of distractibility or weak performance on academic exams are labeled attention deficit disorder. Some of these labeling issues date back to changes made in the diagnostic system, and the business side of psychiatric diagnosis is being exposed. The financial basis that underlies modern psychiatric diagnosis has become such an important issue that it is being confronted in both popular culture (Lane, 2016) and more scholarly outlets (Breggin, 2016). In this age of psychotropic medication, it remains important to focus on each client's cognitive processes and how they can be changed.

Psychiatric diagnosis provides an assortment of terms that can help identify and label various emotions and life struggles. The limits of labeling have been discussed by Thomas Szasz (1960), who argued in favor of less stigmatizing language. In Szasz's approach, it is more accurate and helpful to view most psychiatric patients as struggling with assorted "problems of living" and with personal difficulties adapting to the demands of modern society. Instead of labeling people with a psychiatric diagnosis, more people can be helped if they are viewed simply as individuals with struggles in living. Furthermore, there is an extensive history behind the problems with labels that stigmatize those with mental illness (Szasz, 1970).

As the field has changed over the past thirty years, it can become a bit troubling to ask "What would their reactions to brief therapy be if the pioneers of psychotherapy—Sigmund Freud, Carl Jung, Alfred Adler, Viktor Frankl, Fritz Perls—were alive today?" How would they react to the push for short-term therapy, treatment sessions guided by structured therapy manuals, and the curtailment of sessions because of limited insurance coverage?

Prescriptive approaches that rely heavily on psychiatric diagnosis and a medical model essentially ask: "what is the problem, and how can I fix it?" However, clients are not broken. Instead, they are people struggling with adjustment and coping. Likewise, with the push for empirically supported treatments, it is important to focus on the relationship that underlies effective psychotherapy. It is not the therapist's job to lecture to clients, under the naïve belief that a client's problems can be resolved by being given facts about mental illness or its treatment.

Therapy often benefits from a collaborative and patient interpersonal style, one adapted to the unique needs and style of each client. Although remaining supportive, the therapist does not just quietly sit and listen to the client ramble about recent struggles. The therapist aims to confront longstanding issues and promote lasting changes. It can be difficult to confront dysfunctional behaviors and challenge negative thoughts while still trying to remain tolerant and respectful, protecting the supportive bond with the client. As noted by Leonard Nelson (1949), explaining the Socratic method is similar to a violinist trying to describe the act of playing music; it can be demonstrated much more easily than it can be described. The therapist should not expect clients to accept a statement or a belief they do not really believe (Seeskin, 1987). Unfortunately, this dogmatic style is evident in many examples presented by Albert Ellis and drawn from his own clinical work. Instead, the Socratic method relies on a gradual process based on shaping (Frojan-Parga et al., 2011).

Over the years, many authors have explored the importance and functions of the Socratic method. According to Benson (2000), the Socratic method can interpret the other person's statements, examine the validity of the person's knowledge, help both parties appreciate the limits of their understanding, and guide a process of self-examination and exploration. In the age of short-term therapy, perhaps a gardening metaphor can shed light on the different perspective I am advocating for here. The therapist may try to prune negative beliefs and critical attitudes while also planting the seeds for more positive views of life, self, and other people. But gardening is a slow process. The proper conditions for healthy growth are sunlight, fresh water, and fertilizer. These conditions can be viewed as analogous to a positive and supportive attitude in therapy that aims to support positive growth in each client.

Conclusions

There is a rich history that provides a strong and diverse foundation for the Socratic method. Its origins lie in ancient philosophy, but this book will attempt to integrate these ideas with contemporary efforts to refine the art of psychotherapy. The goal is to learn from these historical documents that inaugurated the fields of philosophy and ethics while keeping the focus on useful strategies for guiding psychotherapy sessions.

Dialectic means the method of conversation (Taylor, 1953) whereby Socrates discussed important issues in an inquisitive style. Socrates (as recounted through Plato) made important and lasting contributions to the field of philosophy. Two of his primary contributions are the use of inductive reasoning and the search for definitions (DeVogel, 1963). The dialogues focus on abstract ideas. Although Socrates aimed for universal notions, it can be difficult to bypass phenomenology—that is, each client's emphasis on their own subjective experience. Reality is reality as perceived and actively constructed by each individual (Moss, 1992). Furthermore, there is typically a reciprocal influence; once a person creates an interpretation of "reality," the perceived reality has a powerful effect on emotions and behavior (Moss, 1992). Psychotherapy according to the Socratic method is heavily focused on cognitive change. If a person's beliefs change, then the way the individual lives is likely to change (Waterfield, 1994). According to the Socratic method, psychotherapy emphasizes five processes and two primary topic areas (Overholser, 2010a). The five processes are systematic questioning, inductive reasoning, universal definitions, a disavowal of knowledge, and the use of guided discovery to structure the flow within sessions. The two main topic areas include self-improvement and virtue as it can be displayed in everyday life.

Upcoming chapters will explore each of these components in detail, addressing both theoretical foundations and practical applications. Overall, the Socratic method aims to cultivate positive life views in the client and to help clients improve their adaptive living while moving toward important life goals (Overholser, 2015a). There is minimal focus on removing acute distress or managing specific problems. Instead, the overarching goal of the Socratic method is to help people see trivial problems as minor hassles and common nuisances that may distract them from the importance of lifestyle changes and a lifelong goal of self-improvement.

THREE

Integrating Science and Practice ... and Philosophy?

THE PRESENT CHAPTER will explore the roles of *science* and *practice* as the dual underpinnings of effective psychotherapy, striving for a sincere integration of these sometimes opposing sides of psychology. The acumen of researchers can be greatly enhanced when they remain active in clinical practice. Likewise, the careers of clinicians are improved when they remain active in scholarly activities. The field of psychotherapy is enhanced through the combination of and dynamic interplay between the science and the practice of psychology.

The Making of a Psychotherapist

Practicing psychotherapy is an odd skill. To become an effective psychotherapist, one needs a combination of academic credentials, personality traits, and a sincere motivation to help others. I have come to appreciate just how critical it is for a psychotherapist to care sincerely about every client while at the same time maintaining a professional distance and objectivity so as to be able to view the patterns in the ongoing struggles of each client. I believe that I grow, both personally and professionally, thanks to the moments I have been fortunate to share with clients.

The academic credentials of a psychotherapist begin in graduate school. Throughout graduate training in psychology, there is a heavy emphasis on scientific methods. Students are immersed in the theory and technique of research design, control groups, and hypothesis testing. Students learn about basic psychometric properties and the central importance of reliability and validity. This grounding in science paves the way for conducting research, which the student eventually will present as a master's thesis and a doctoral dissertation. These skills in objectivity and rational approaches provide a strong foundation for all work as a psychologist.

During graduate training, students begin by learning the theories underlying personality development, psychological assessment, and psychotherapy. When first starting out as a therapist, graduate students are closely monitored in placements and practicum settings. Eventually, they complete their schooling with a full-time internship that focuses heavily on the direct provision of clinical services. After completing their internship or postdoctoral training years, some psychologists discontinue their involvement with psychotherapy. Furthermore, some academic scholars have openly admonished clinicians, emphasizing the need for clinicians to study recently published theories (Baucom & Boeding, 2013) and empirically supported treatments (Hofmann, 2014), while disregarding the potential importance of the reverse: scholars appreciating the subtle nuances of clinical practice. When it comes to public pronouncements and scholarly publications, it seems that full-time clinicians may not have as strong a vocal advocate for their side.

A skilled psychotherapist possesses several personality traits. An effective therapist can remain calm, supportive, and caring toward each client even when discussing difficult or traumatic topics. Furthermore, patience and a focus on nurturance are helpful in most psychotherapy sessions. Many clients appreciate a therapist with a sense of humor and who can tolerate ambiguity. Skilled therapists are attentive throughout every session, are not easily distracted, and can keep their mental focus on the client's struggles without allowing their mind to wander.

The Socratic approach requires patience to avoid the impulse to rush during a discussion (Seeskin, 1987). The therapist remains somewhat unflappable, expressing emotion only when it fits the goals of therapy. However, it is difficult to remain genuine while also focusing on the plan and goals for psychotherapy. Too often, clients may share a casual remark or a personal story, and if the therapist reacts in common social parlance, it could be detrimental to the client or the course of therapy. For example, when a client informs the therapist, "I'm pregnant," there is a natural reaction to respond, "Congratulations!" However, in some cases, the client may be upset about the pregnancy and congratulations may be unempathic toward the client. Likewise, if a client says "I am a real nerd" or "I know I'm ugly," it feels natural to respond, "No you're not," out of social convention instead of deliberate therapeutic intent. Every word and action in therapy must be guided by intentional therapy goals.

To become a skilled therapist requires ongoing clinical practice and many years of experience. To become good at any complex task, practice is essential. A professional cannot become a skilled therapist by reading books and journal articles or even a daunting library of scholarly works. Instead, clinical expertise requires years of ongoing clinical work combined with superior clinical skills, visibility in the field, and possibly advanced credentialing. A professional cannot claim expertise in a specific type of disorder without having had years of experience working with clients who have been diagnosed with that disorder (Overholser, 2010b).

To develop expert skills requires frequent deliberate practice distributed across ten thousand hours (Ericsson 2014) or a period that may persist for ten (Ericsson, Krampe, & Tesch-Romer, 1993; Ericsson & Towne, 2010) to fifteen years (Skovholt, Ronnestad, & Jennings, 1997). Such extensive effort is necessary for a professional to refine the skills needed in the particular domain (Ericsson, 2008), even in fields like psychology. For professors to become expert in their field, they typically need years of practice (Skovholt et al., 1997). The same goes for psychotherapy.

The Scientific Foundation for Psychotherapy

Currently, there is a strong emphasis on empirical support for psychological treatments. However, the field may be emphasizing the research realm at the expense of the nuances of therapy sessions. With the current emphasis on integrating technology into therapeutic practice and on the production of manuals to guide psychotherapy, the quality of treatment has been reduced (Woolfolk, 2015). Effective therapy is likely to benefit from an idiographic approach guided by theory but that remains fluid within each session. An effective psychotherapist brings a flexible and creative approach to guide the client's process of self-exploration and personal growth. Ideally,

INTEGRATING SCIENCE AND PRACTICE ... AND PHILOSOPHY?

therapists can provide therapy that remains sensitive to each client's unique needs while remaining true to the ideology of the approach (Kendall & Beidas, 2007). Over the thirty years that I have served as a psychotherapist, I have come to place more value on the therapeutic relationship and less on technical skills or book knowledge. A strong working alliance provides the necessary (but perhaps not sufficient) foundation for effective psychotherapy (Overholser, 2007b).

The field of psychotherapy has evolved tremendously over the years. Despite the invaluable contributions made by the early pioneers, few people today have read the original published works of Jean-Martin Charcot, Pierre Janet, or Paul Dubois. This is not so for the pioneers of psychoanalysis. There are still many psychotherapists who adhere closely to—or at least read and study—the works of Sigmund Freud, Carl Jung, and Alfred Adler. It can be useful to read the original works published by the pioneers and use these foundational texts to appreciate the long and varied history of the field.

The behavioral approach became popular largely thanks to the research and theory proposed by Joseph Wolpe. Originally described as an objective psychotherapy for the neuroses and presented as a theory of reciprocal inhibition, Wolpe explained therapeutic strategies that were found effective in the elimination of neurotic behavior. Wolpe's ideas and his clinical recommendations evolved into systematic desensitization as a treatment based on reciprocal inhibition (Wolpe, 1958). Even though the theoretical underpinnings of reciprocal inhibition were refuted, the core "active ingredient" remains helpful. Clients benefit from various forms of exposure therapy, and the treatment of anxiety disorders has been guided by exposure-based treatments.

From behavior therapy evolved forms of cognitive psychotherapy. The treatment of depression (Beck, Rush, Show, & Emery, 1979) and general states of dysphoria (Ellis, 1994) can be improved through changes in attitudes and expectations. Important studies have documented the benefits of CBT for OCD that obviate the need for prescription medications (Franklin et al., 2002). Today, empirical support for psychotherapy can be observed in a meta-analysis across a range of studies (e.g., Malouff, Thorsteinsson, & Schutte, 2007). However, short-term reduction of symptoms does not necessarily translate into long-term remission from the disorder (Westen, Novotny, & Thompson-Brenner, 2004).

INTEGRATING SCIENCE AND PRACTICE ... AND PHILOSOPHY?

As a struggling scientist-practitioner in the field of clinical psychology, it is important to be actively involved with research and to remain thoroughly updated on the latest developments in the field. The therapist might read many research articles each week and appreciate the value of well-designed studies that are occasionally conducted on clinical samples. It is extremely difficult to conduct well-controlled research on clinical samples, but the published reports can still shed light on many interesting clinical issues. It is also useful for a scientist-practitioner to design and coordinate an ongoing research project examining clinical issues such as depression and suicide risk in psychiatric patients.

Ideally, there can be a unified approach where clinical practice and clinical research work in tandem to stimulate ideas that advance each other (Kazdin, 2008). I, however, have cultivated a critical eye whenever reviewing research studies. I have served as a journal editor, associate editor, and ad hoc reviewer for many years. Because of my involvement with more than thirty academic journals, I would estimate that I have personally reviewed more than six hundred published or rejected research studies. In my opinion, there have been too many weak research studies that have somehow survived the peer-review process and been published in high-quality journals. Too many studies in clinical psychology rely on a cross-sectional assessment of normal individuals as evaluated through a packet of self-report questionnaires. Many of these studies rely on samples of convenience, especially college students currently enrolled in an introductory-level psychology course. Can this heavy reliance on analogue samples weaken the empirical foundation for clinical psychology? Some research studies have emphasized the internal validity of the methodology, yet they appear low on external validity or the ability to generalize beyond their structured research environment (Green & Glasgow, 2006). Even medical research studies often rely on "surrogate outcomes" as easily measured analogues that might reflect the real desired outcome from the intervention (Rothwell, 2005). To be valued, generalizations beyond the experimental situation must be clear and adequately justified.

It can be difficult to examine the findings from research conducted with college-student samples and generalize the results to guide the assessment or treatment of psychiatric patients (Henrich, Heine, & Norenzayan, 2010). When authors describe their sample as a group of "young adults," they might be trying to gloss over the fact that the participants were recruited through a college course and are unlikely to capture the demographics or life experiences reported by the average psychiatric patient. Other studies use subjects recruited via online surveys, which can be completed quickly and anonymously. The latest methodology makes use of the Amazon MTurk system, where anonymous participants are recruited from anywhere in the world and paid a very small fee for completing a few questionnaires. Often, the participants receive twenty-five cents for their involvement in the study, which places very little burden on one's research budget. However, a bit of cautious skepticism is warranted. If participants are paid only twenty-five cents to complete five questionnaires, they may try to complete them as quickly as they can, so they can move on to the next project. Some participants might not care about being honest, accurate, or detailed in their replies. They may not bother reading the questions any more than needed to get a sense of how to complete the form. Perhaps I am projecting my own sense of being lazy or greedy onto the thoroughly honest members of the MTurk population. Still, I worry about the validity of findings raised from any anonymous survey completed online. It seems too easy to provide falsified data. Researchers may need to take steps to ensure they are not analyzing random answers that were provided in order to complete the requirements of an online survey quickly (Kraut et al., 2004).

In too many cases, the participants, measures, and procedures do not align with the question under investigation. In some published research studies, no clinical samples are examined, no diagnostic interviews are used, and no longitudinal designs are attempted. Even more importantly, some faculty members never leave their campus; that is, they never make connections in their community, failing to develop clinical or research bonds with local mental health treatment centers. Many psychology faculty members now conduct research on convenience samples. These same faculty members are often promoted, asked to serve as ad hoc reviewers for similar studies, and join the ranks of journal editors, where they can process, respect, and publish other analogue research studies conducted by their peers, colleagues, and former students. I worry about the future of the field of clinical psychology and the integrity of the empirical foundation upon which it is currently being (re)built. Pardon my diatribe, and I apologize to the many readers I may have just offended. Please take this as a warning and a wakeup call. Knowledge for the sake of knowledge makes little sense; research must aim ultimately for promoting improvements in people (Navia, 1985). I hope that young faculty members trained in clinical psychology might ask themselves a few key questions: Did I go into clinical psychology in order to study normal processes in normal individuals? Did I envision that research would entail handing out packets of questionnaires to college students so they could earn a few extra-credit points in an undergraduate course? Do I believe that my research on college-student samples really sheds light on important topics pertaining to mental health and mental illness? These can be difficult questions, but answering them honestly may redirect the faculty member back to the front lines of clinical work.

When I interview applicants who hope to be admitted into our graduate training program in clinical psychology, I often ask about their career goals. Over the years, I often hear the same view: Students see themselves working in a setting where the core of their work is focused on the direct provision of clinical services but that allows time for research conducted with patients as their subjects. Some students will also briefly mention their interest in teaching or supervision, but most applicants emphasize the importance of clinical work, with some lesser emphasis on applied research. Many students comment that they would like to spend many years working in the field as a psychotherapist. Then, after gaining a substantial amount of clinical experience, they would hope to teach, believing that a good instructor benefits from years of applied hands-on clinical experience. Unfortunately, the average faculty member follows a very different career path and often sets aside all other priorities to protect a narrow focus on campus responsibilities and the ultimate goal: promotion and tenure. Again, I worry about the field of clinical psychology and its corrosion from within. From a purely Socratic view, it would be interesting to interview some of the established experts in the field to see whether they really have a mastery of the topics upon which their reputations have been based.

Despite the apparent potency of cognitive-behavioral therapy, it may be losing its effectiveness. A meta-analysis has found that the established treatments for depression are not as effective as earlier studies found (Johnsen & Friborg, 2015). The effectiveness of CBT has been steadily declining since these early studies were published. The declining effects are seen in patient self-reports, clinician ratings, and lower remission rates. Meta-analysis revealed two factors. First, therapist competency was a significant predictor of treatment effects, revealing that beyond the structure of the therapy and the format for each session, the skill of the therapist remains important in determining the effects from treatment. Second, patients were more likely to benefit from treatment led by an experienced psychologist than by a graduate student just gaining their early experience. Thus, clinical experience and clinical competence are essential ingredients for successful therapy. There is a risk that second-generation therapy is being watered down. Therapy seemed effective in cases when cognitive therapy was conducted by Aaron Beck and in rational-emotive behavior therapy (REBT) sessions led by Albert Ellis. However, the newest generation of therapists was taught by trainees who studied under Beck, and now trainees are being trained by that second generation. As many of these "academic grandchildren" are not involved in the weekly provision of therapy but merely conducted therapy during their own graduate training, it makes sense that instruction in how to work clinically would become diluted or distorted. Furthermore, high levels of therapist structure and demand will produce fast but temporary changes in client behavior, accompanied by a high rate of relapse and dropouts (Rachman, 1976).

There are several possible reasons for the reduced potency of CBT treatments. In some cases, a novel approach is more effective because of the change and excitement surrounding a new intervention. Because of the novelty of new approaches, healthcare professionals can tend to chase the latest fad treatment. However, over time, as the initial excitement fades, so does the effectiveness of the new approach.

Structured therapy manuals create problems because they impair the creativity and restrict the flexibility needed for idiographic treatment (Davison, 1998). Manuals may help the novice learn basic therapy skills, but they do not reflect clinical practice. Most practicing therapists rely on theory or clinical experience rather than empirical research and treatment manuals (Gyani et al., 2015). Manuals ignore the process of therapy (Schulte & Eifert, 2002). Imagine a novice trying to learn how to play tennis from a manual (Nussbaum, 1986)!

Clinical expertise plays the pivotal role in translating empirical findings into recommendations for clinical practice (McCracken & Marsh, 2008). Expertise develops over years of practice in the field, years spent conducting the basic activities involved in effective practice. Unfortunately, academic researchers sometimes prescribe various treatment recommendations that are unrealistic and fail to match the realities of clinical practice (Beutler et al., 1995). Socrates recommended that people, especially experts, aim to know what they know and admit what they do not know. Thus, it is vital to appreciate the vast differences between psychotherapy as described in its idealized form in textbooks and the clumsy realities of clinical practice. For example, in the spring of 1989, I wrote a thirty-page manual to guide the research-based treatment of chronic depression. I spent five months preparing session-by-session guidelines for my graduate students to administer cognitive-behavioral therapy with adult psychiatric outpatients. I was pleased with the manual and eager to begin the research project. After gaining approval from the internal review board, I led the way, providing therapy personally to several clients diagnosed with dysthymic disorder. By the second session, I had discontinued the project: I could see the manual was impairing my ability to serve as a competent therapist. It is not good for the client if the goals for therapy have been established before the start of therapy sessions and imposed on the client (Ryan & Deci, 2008). I had become more intent on following my own rules than on relating to each client as a unique individual. I had stopped learning from each client. Instead, I was focused on teaching the clients the skills I had predetermined were essential for managing their negative moods. Unfortunately, I was acting as an expert in a context where expertise is not helpful. As a young professional, I learned a lot from this aborted research project—though it was not at all what I thought I was going to learn.

Research studies often avoid the complex issues that arise from the diagnostic comorbidity common in many clinical settings by selecting clients with a single diagnosis, and the research protocol commonly excludes a sizable portion of clients from the study (Westen, Novotny, & Thompson-Brenner, 2004). In fact, one investigation revealed that roughly one-third of adult patients with depression seen in an outpatient clinic would have been eligible for antidepressant drug trials (Zimmerman et al., 2004), while another study reported even higher rates of patients that were rejected from drug trials (Keitner et al., 2003). Too many studies focus on "pure" treatments delivered to "clean" samples, but by doing so these findings lack external validity and are of little use to practitioners in actual treatment centers. Psychotherapy has been pushed into a pseudomedical format aimed at confronting supposed disorders of the brain (Woolfolk, 2015). Research on psychotherapy has adopted the approach used in medical studies, adding to the chasm between research protocols and treatment-as-usual practices in most mental health clinics (Goldfried & Eubanks-Carter, 2004). Unlike the services provided in the typical mental health clinic, most treatment-outcome studies focus on the rigid application of therapy conducted for a fixed number of sessions in a theoretically pure manner (Goldfried & Wolfe, 1998). Research studies typically rely on pure forms of psychological treatment, while the clinical practice of psychotherapy uses the best available mixture of ideas and strategies (Goldfried & Eubanks-Carter, 2004). Therapy is less likely to be successful when the focus is on structured treatment packages and when process issues are neglected (Ablon & Marci, 2004).

Finally, despite the interactional nature of psychotherapy sessions, research studies often minimize or completely neglect the client's contribution to therapy (Ablon & Marci, 2004). In research studies, clients are treated from a nomothetic perspective, whereby all clients who meet criteria for a specific psychiatric diagnosis are viewed as similar. However, an idiographic perspective admits that each client is unique. Thus, in my own practice, I may have back-to-back-to-back sessions scheduled with different clients who have all been diagnosed with major depressive disorder. Despite the similarities in diagnostic presentation, each client has his or her own unique struggles, concerns, and psychological patterns. My therapy was different for each client and adapted to his or her needs, not my own preconceptions.

Integrating Science and Practice

In most professional circles today, there is agreement that psychotherapy is best conducted through an integration of science and practice. Dating back to the Boulder conference (Raimy, 1950) and the Detroit meeting (American Psychological Association, 1947), the *scientist-practitioner model* has served as the template for graduate training in psychology. The belief is that a person cannot truly understand what has been learned through reading books or listening to lectures. Likewise, no amount of teaching can help a student reach the same level of understanding as a person who has lived the actual experience (Burnyeat, 1990).

The scientist-practitioner model is the cornerstone of clinical training in psychology. Unfortunately, it has become rather worn and risks being discarded—not because it lacks value but because very few professionals can live up to its ideals. Some psychologists (e.g., McFall, 2006) have openly rejected the clinical side of psychology, arguing in favor of a scientific approach that puts research at the core of the field. However, the scientist-practitioner model remains essential for the advancement of the field and the improvement of clinical services.

Professors and researchers are encouraged to remain active in the clinical practice of psychology (Jones & Mehr, 2007). Although it can be difficult to conduct research with clients as participants, this type of research is more likely to shed light on the true nature of psychological disorders and on what can be done to help clients. Unfortunately, it can be difficult to work as a faculty member at a research university and remain active in clinical practice (Overholser, 2007). There are numerous demands on a faculty member's time, and too often clinical work is relegated to a historical footnote in the life of an academic. Some faculty members become involved with clinical supervision or consultation experiences, thereby having less time for face-to-face contact with clients (Overholser, 2012a). When faculty members have discontinued all clinical work and their skills have begun to fade, it may be difficult for them to teach graduate courses on psychotherapy (Overholser, 2012a) or supervise graduate students in their clinical work (Overholser, 2007a). Unfortunately, this lack of ongoing clinical experience is disrupting the fields of clinical psychology (Overholser, 2015b) and psychiatry (Guidi & Fava, 2014).

When a person has direct experience, they develop *personal knowledge* of the events (Burger, 1981). However, when one *learns* about events through a lecture, readings, or other secondary sources, they may develop *beliefs* about the events (Burger, 1981). There is a risk that some professionals may become limited to secondary sources about psychotherapy, reading books and journal articles while neglecting the direct experience of working with clients. One who writes and publishes while handling administrative responsibilities that preclude time for clinical work is humorously dubbed a "Sir Grantsalot" (Westen, Novotny, & Thompson-Brenner, 2004). In some situations, a professional's beliefs, whether correct or incorrect, may nonetheless lack practical knowledge about the strategies that are most useful for guiding psychotherapy sessions.

Psychotherapy is an odd field within psychology. It is not really an artistic expression, but good therapy can be creative. Psychotherapy is not a technical skill, although many contemporary writers have focused on developing structured treatment manuals. To be effective as a therapist, a mix of elements, including the personality of the therapist, must align with the theory, therapeutic style, and type of clients being treated. When all these areas combine in a fruitful mix, therapy can be a powerful counterbalance to the stress and demands of modern society.

Research and practice can blend together in an exciting, dynamic interplay. When a psychologist remains active in scholarship and clinical practice, a powerful synergy can develop (Overholser, 2008). Research is enhanced by clinical practice, giving the investigator a better appreciation for the central problems experienced by most clients. Alternatively, clinical practice is enhanced by scholarship because it remains informed of and involved in new ideas in the field. There are limited benefits when work is restricted either to science or practice alone. The combination of theory, research, and clinical practice can evaluate or generate new ideas for psychotherapy.

The Structure of Psychotherapy Sessions

Therapy sessions benefit from a modest degree of planning and structure, within an individual session and across a series of sessions. Consider the training advice from the legendary family therapist Salvador Minuchin (Minuchin & Fishman, 1981), who described the goals for training someone to become a family therapist. Minuchin claimed that too much emphasis had been placed on the memorization of basic technique, causing technical skills to be applied in a rote manner. These technical skills help the novice pay attention to basic details. However, to become skilled as a therapist, it is essential to move beyond the application of rules and techniques. An effective therapist must rely on spontaneous interactions, working within the confines of the context created by the patient or the family. This advice has been ignored for most of the past thirty-five years.

It is essential for a skilled therapist to appreciate the big picture as a comprehensive plan for the client's therapy. Too many novice therapists struggle to see the goal of a single psychotherapy session, let alone goals that extend across multiple sessions. Minuchin and Fishman (1981) also explained psychotherapy through the metaphor of an artistic painting. If you look closely, you will see the individual brushstrokes. Taken out of context, each brush stroke is a chaotic stripe, an apparently random mix. However, at a distance, with the proper perspective, you can see the bigger picture and understand how the individual stripes blend into a coherent whole. The same applies to psychotherapy sessions: individual statements appear much too narrow, but when the full picture is visualized across multiple sessions, the skilled therapist can envision the plan for change and growth.

Structure is helpful for the novice therapist, who often struggles to convert theory into therapy. Even for a seasoned practitioner, it is difficult to understand the abstract concepts and adapt them to an individual client. Several other approaches to psychotherapy have suffered because of their vague clinical guidelines. Consider, for example, the interpersonal psychotherapy (Klerman et al., 1984) of depression. Depression is seen as a direct consequence of problems in social functioning, and these problems can be captured in one of four domains. Despite providing a taxonomy and framework centered around these four areas, interpersonal psychotherapy offers minimal guidance as to how to work with these domains as a clinician. Likewise, existential analysis has struggled to derive a structured methodology that could be used to produce a treatment manual that could help a novice therapist (Overholser, 2005c).

The present work aims to lay the foundation for the conceptual understanding and practical application of the Socratic method. However, no attempt will be made to articulate this application in the format commonly found in published treatment manuals. Throughout the remainder of this book, there will be a heavy emphasis on the Socratic method as it can be used in contemporary psychotherapy. The Socratic method will be described in terms of its four essential components, which can also be considered as the four strategies that can help guide the psychotherapeutic process. First, throughout most therapy sessions, there is a clear and dominant use of a systematic series of questions to explore important topics in a thoughtful dialogue. Second, there is a reliance on inductive reasoning to guide the search for new information. Third, there are persistent efforts to define important words and phrases in a manner that could apply broadly. Fourth, there is a willingness on both the part of the therapist and client to acknowledge their personal ignorance. These four strategies structure a therapeutic process of guided discovery, working collaboratively with each client as a unique individual. The focus of psychotherapy sessions aims for two main themes: self-improvement and virtue ethics. These broad topics move beyond a focus on acute symptom reduction and promote broader aims for personal growth and life values.

INTEGRATING SCIENCE AND PRACTICE . . . AND PHILOSOPHY?

Philosophical Foundations for Psychotherapy

The field of psychotherapy benefits from a sincere integration of science and practice. However, it can be difficult to conduct well-controlled studies in most clinical settings. Likewise, it can be difficult for most clinicians to remain active in scholarship as it is traditionally portrayed in books and journal articles. Nonetheless, whenever possible, the field is improved when new developments in psychotherapy are based in scholarly work. Historically, the founders of the field were all clinicians. Most innovations in psychotherapy come from clinical practice settings (Westen, Novotny, & Thompson-Brenner, 2004). It has only been recently that a solid research foundation has developed to support some types of psychotherapy.

Important decisions and evaluations (such as pertaining to fairness or equality) cannot be based on the senses but must be based on reason (Gosling, 1973). According to Socrates, a wise person should not trust the world as experienced through the senses: too often sensory experiences can be fooled (Ahrensdorf, 1995), and perceptual experiences are too easily changed (Gosling, 1975). Information obtained through the senses is usually fragmentary (Kaplan, 1977). According to the Socratic view, personal experiences can produce incorrect views and misleading evidence because sensations and the physical world are always changing (Ackermann, 1972). Thus, one person may view a stone as cold while another person may rate the same stone as warm, depending on their own conditions, and both perceptions may be deemed accurate (Crombie, 1963). In contrast, Socrates was interested in exploring ideas that were stable over time and generalizable across situations. While science begins with a hypothesis and moves toward a specific test, reason uses dialectic to move from a hypothesis to a general principle (Wilbur & Allen, 1979). Ideas are important to confront, examine, and potentially change. Important issues like equality, justice, and beauty are ideas that cannot be captured through the senses (Irwin, 1995).

Just the same, empirical research is not without its limitations. Throughout the past century, research on topics related to psychology, psychiatry, and mental health treatments has expanded. However, there remain disagreements across the theoretical and practical approaches within these fields of mental health. Psychiatrists rely on the importance of medications to treat many forms of mental illness. However, some studies have revealed the power of the mind, as we see in placebo and nocebo reactions.

The placebo effect is typically stronger with new treatments (Johnsen & Friborg, 2015). Furthermore, many studies have been overturned when later research reaches the opposite conclusion. Take, for example, the benefits of daily consumption of alcohol or the health risks posed by various food groups. Each year, a new study adds to our understanding, but in the process, the findings sometimes contradict prior research findings.

Limitations of an Empirical Approach to Psychotherapy

The Socratic method is aligned with contemporary psychotherapy, especially cognitive therapy and rational-emotive behavior therapy. However, there is extremely little research to support its use as a form of psychotherapy. Thus, the strategies and goals of the Socratic method are deficient in empirical support and should not be considered an empirically supported treatment. However, remaining true to Socrates, empirical support is not essential and really not even very important.

According to the Socratic approach, objectivity goes beyond the limits of sensation and perception (Burnyeat, 1990). Important broad concepts, ranging from beauty to justice, cannot be perceived through the senses (Vlastos, 1991) but only processed at a higher cognitive level (Burnyeat, 1990). Therefore, knowledge is not obtained through the senses but through more complex mental processes (Burnyeat, 1990). Instead of a focus on empirical evidence, an inductive review of case material allows the accumulation of evidence and a search for commonalities across diverse examples. Furthermore, a coherent network of theories and ideas provide the philosophical foundation for the Socratic method. Socrates and Plato relied on an intuitive and experiential approach, supporting their ideas through analogies and examples (Reale, 1987). Additional support can be found in anecdotal evidence derived from many years of psychotherapy sessions. Although many researchers will deem this support inadequate, it is helpful to approach the Socratic method with an open mind and a bit of modesty. There have been a wide range of treatments for mental illness that have demonstrated effectiveness in research studies, but these same treatments would now be considered outdated (Overholser, 2002). Today, many people have forgotten innovative treatment strategies such as malaria therapy, insulin shock therapy, prefrontal leucotomy, or lobotomy.

Conclusions

Today, experts in psychotherapy try to develop treatment protocols through the use of analogue research, and some publications provide detailed instructions for clinicians in the form of treatment manuals (Westen, Novotny, & Thompson-Brenner, 2004). Clearly, step-by-step manuals conflict with the basic tenets of the Socratic method (Brickhouse & Smith, 1994). It is helpful to assume that the average clinician is a competent professional who is eager for a few helpful ideas, rather than an ill-trained novice who will remain faithful to a published manual (Westen, Novotny, & Thompson-Brenner, 2004).

Psychotherapy is shifting to a focus on symptoms management and discarding the empathic understanding of the person in context of his or her life. It is a mistake to believe that psychotherapy can be effective by teaching new skills through a lecture from an expert therapist (Graybar & Leonard, 2005). Current forms of therapy encourage clients to listen to the therapist and understand their material instead of advocating for therapists to listen to their clients to understand their struggles (Graybar & Leonard, 2005).

Even within the field of psychology and psychological treatments, it is possible to identify strategies that have been endorsed but are no longer used. These strategies have been refuted (for example, past-lives regression therapy and autism patterning). As someone who has conducted research for more than thirty years and published research studies in more than thirty journals, I am not convinced of the overarching value of research to support an avenue of treatment. Instead, I am more convinced in the importance of clinical experience and the value of thoughtful reasoning. I hope the reader will explore the remainder of this text with an open mind and curiosity, perhaps gaining new insights from ancient ideas.

FOUR

Systematic Questioning

If You Do Not Know, Just Ask

FOUR CORE STRATEGIES underlie the psychotherapeutic use of the Socratic method: systematic questioning, inductive reasoning, universal definitions, and a sincere disavowal of knowledge, with questioning comprising the central tool. Voltaire aptly captures the Socratic method: "Judge a man by his questions rather than his answers." As a psychotherapist, I believe that the questions I ask are more helpful than any answer I could provide.

A Socratic dialogue is a question-heavy discussion intended to test the evidence supporting one's expressed views (Rud, 1994). Questions are the primary tool in Socratic-method-inspired psychotherapy sessions; a skilled therapist might ask fifty or even a hundred questions in a single session. However, a therapy session must always remain a conversation informed by professional curiosity and empathy; contrary to popular opinion, the Socratic method is not synonymous with interrogation.

In this chapter, we will explore the types of questions the use of the Socratic method involves. We will especially consider the subtleties of these types of questions, subtleties that highlight their collaborative and exploratory nature. When a therapist relies more on questions than on direct statements, clients are encouraged to think through their problems on their own (Tomm, 1988). The field can move beyond seeing questions as tools to gather information and accept that questions can serve as key interventions (Freedman & Combs, 1993).

To be useful, a Socratic dialogue requires three elements from the client: an open sharing of thoughts and beliefs, an honest admission of what the client does not really know, and a determination to continue even when it gets challenging (Seeskin, 1987). During sessions, clients are encouraged to say only what they believe, never simply to agree with the therapist in an attempt to remain polite or compliant. The basic rule, "Say only what you believe," is central if the Socratic discussion is to evolve out of the client's beliefs instead of devolve into a lecture from the therapist (Seeskin, 1987; Vlastos, 1992). In a Socratic dialogue, the person must only state what he or she believes to be true, even if it means he or she will "lose" the debate (Vlastos, 1983).

The effective use of Socratic questions requires more than an honest and cooperative client. It also relies on a sound therapeutic relationship based on trust, tolerance, and empathy. Good questions are grounded in empathy, and good questions promote empathy. When the therapist strives to understand the client's unique phenomenological experience, the therapist can work from inside the private distortions and personal limitations that may hinder the client's life. Suddenly, most problems and their affiliated emotions make sense when viewed through the client's own distorted cognitive filters. Therefore, therapists should avoid assuming they understand the client's experience and should not imply they already know what the client needs. For example, a Socratic therapist would never say, "I know how you feel," because of the risk that their interpretation could be incorrect or incomplete. Instead, the therapist strives to ask questions genuinely aimed to gather information.

The therapeutic use of systematic questioning is a unique skill. In a courtroom examination of a witness, lawyers are taught to avoid asking any question unless they have a clear idea of how the person will answer. This is phrased as "Know the answers to the questions you ask" and "Do not ask a question unless you have a reasonable right to believe that the answer will be what you expect it to be" (Lake, 1957). However, in a psychotherapy session, leading the client like this can damage rapport. Instead we say, "Do not ask it as a question if you think you already know the answer." If questions are too focused and point only toward one correct answer, it becomes a game of "Guess what I'm thinking?" and not a collaboration. Good Socratic questions remain neutral and do not signal the "correct" answer (Neenan, 2009).

A therapist should be genuinely curious about the answer the client will provide (Padesky, 1993). It is wise to avoid the "mutant form" of the Socratic method, whereby the professor asks a question for which he or she knows the answer and the students do not know (Vitiello, 2005). This style of Socratic questioning tends to intimidate, humiliate, and entrap students (Areeda, 1996). The conversation only moves forward after both parties agree and have accepted what was said (Seeskin, 1987).

Therapists can use a series of questions to guide the client through the steps of problem solving (Kennerly, 2007). Questions help the therapist understand how things look from the client's perspective. Many psychological problems are related to extreme beliefs that clients have about negative events in their lives (Ellis & Dryden, 1987). The therapist must suspend judgment, assumptions, and biases to understand the situation from the client's subjective world (Graybar & Leonard, 2005).

Throughout therapy, avoid imposing beliefs on a client or disrupting rapport. The therapist does not choose sides in an argument but encourages the patient to rely on critical thinking to examine the validity of an argument (VanRossem, 2014).

It is important for therapists to avoid assuming they might know a client's view. Racial, cultural, and gender differences alter the subjective impact of life events, and personal experiences can greatly influence the power of major and minor events and how they are interpreted by each client. For example, many situations can be more powerfully emotional whenever a client has been abused, neglected, or discriminated against.

Although there are many reasons to value the therapeutic style endorsed by person-centered therapy and motivational interviewing, many clients may need more of a gentle push to get them moving forward. In some ways, relying on therapist paraphrasing, summarizing, and reflection might begin to feel like sitting in a rowboat with one oar: essentially going in circles. A Socratic style augments that approach by using questions to move the dialogue forward. The client's answers steer the discussion, but the therapist's questions propel it (a notion that becomes essential when discussing virtue, spiritual beliefs, and major life decisions). Throughout the dialogue, there are typically no right or wrong answers, but sometimes the discussion can identify beliefs that cannot be supported. Questions help clients consider, explore, and understand their own answers (Freedman & Combs, 1993). The

Socratic dialogue uncovers statements the client believes, but it also requires them to abandon their erroneous beliefs (Seeskin, 1987).

The Format of Useful Questions

A range of questions can guide the process of therapy (James & Morse, 2007; James, Morse, & Howarth, 2010). The type, focus, and format of the question can strongly influence the answer received (Cecchin, 1992). Some questions focus on an individual's memory of personal details, the interpretation of different events, or an analysis of general problems.

The manner in which a question is phrased can greatly influence the answer (Seiple, 1985). Socratic questions can focus the client's attention on specific aspects of a complex situation (Padesky, 1993). In most cases, the best questions are phrased openly, allowing a wide latitude in acceptable answers. For example, asking the client "Can you tell me more about that?" gently invites the client to extend the explanation of specific events. However, sometimes open-ended questions may be overly broad and difficult for clients to answer. For example, during an early session with a distressed couple, the therapist asked a general question: "How do you see your relationship?" This failed to produce a useful response. The therapist tried again, now offering three options: "When you look at your relationship, do you see each other more as roommates, teammates, or soul mates?"

Many times during sessions, the therapist may have a useful idea for managing a difficult situation. If the therapist asks "Would it help to talk directly to your boss?" this is not a sincere question. Instead, it simply asks for the client's public endorsement of the therapist's idea. A more collaborative but genuine approach might frame the issue: "How do you think it would go if you tried talking directly to your boss?" Although similar, this question doesn't ask whether it would be helpful to talk with the boss but instead asks for the client's expectation. At an even more open level, the therapist could ask: "What could you do to deal with this situation?" If this question is too open-ended, the therapist can follow with a sincere dichotomous approach: "If you talked to your boss directly, do you think it could resolve this situation? Or would it make the situation even messier?"

SYSTEMATIC QUESTIONING

Questions can be phrased using an either/or format or a multiple-choice format. In either case, the therapist should offer two or more equally valid options. A bifurcated format provides two options that remain distinct, sometimes in the form of a proposition and its negation (Santas, 1979). Instead of an educational format using a highly artificial x versus not-x, therapy requires a conversation. Consider "Would this help or hurt the situation?" or "Is this a good idea, or does it seem way off base?" Such simple, two-option questions presuppose that one of the options is true (Santas, 1979). For example, a young adult female client was having a continuous string of minor mishaps with her roommate. A more general approach can be a good way to begin: "What can you do to try to resolve the situation with your roommate?" However, open-ended questions often trigger a simplistic reaction from clients, who may say, "I don't know." An ill-prepared therapist may then resort to a more directive response and begin offering potential solutions. A simple yes/no question is typically leading, and the client may see it as a suggestion or direction disguised as a question. Socrates often used a leading question whereby the question implies there is a correct answer and the phrasing of the question steers the respondent toward a specific response (Allen, 1984).

Typically, a leading question is designed to elicit the person's automatic agreement, even to the extreme ("How could it be otherwise?!") (Nelson, 1949). For example: "Do you think it would help to talk to your roommate about your frustration?" The therapist is essentially stating, "I think you should talk to your roommate about your feelings. Do you agree?" A more balanced question might offer two options that appear equally valid and realistic. For example, the therapist could ask: "Do you think that if you tried talking to your roommate about your feelings, it could bring it out in the open so you could work on it, or do you think it would make things totally awkward and even worse than they are now?" Useful Socratic questions focus on abstract interrogatives that assert nothing and make no direct or implicit demands on the person (Harrah, 1982).

Factual questions may be useful in a diagnostic assessment or a class exam. However, most therapeutic questions do not ask for specific facts that could be right or wrong. Useful questions may ask about the client's subjective opinions, memories, creative ideas, and personal values. Exploratory questions are also useful in college teaching to stimulate thoughtful classroom discussions—the same is true for therapy sessions. When using the

SYSTEMATIC QUESTIONING

Socratic method, there should not be a single correct answer to any question posed by the therapist (Vitousek, Watson, & Wilson, 1998).

Likewise, adults are more likely to enjoy a lively dialogue and value an intellectual exchange if it moves away from a mini-lecture by an expert (Furedy & Scher, 1985). As a therapist, it is usually helpful to ask questions but not to answer questions from the client because answering the question would elevate the therapist into the role of teacher and encourage dependency in the client (Dillon, 1990).

Throughout the dialogue, be sincere (Irwin, 1995). Useful questions aim for a sincere search for information. Thus, a simple question such as "What was that like for you?" can be posed sincerely because the question asks for the client's subjective experience. There can be no incorrect answer. Likewise, asking a client, "What thoughts were going through your head at that moment?" can be useful because the question aims to increase awareness of thought processes and the client's internal monologue.

Here are other potential questions:

"What would you prefer to do?" (The question initiates a focus on self-motivation and personal responsibility for change.)

"If a similar situation arises again next week, how would you like to react?" (The question promotes inductive reasoning and learning from personal experiences.)

"What can you do to help you prepare for these events?" (Here, anticipation and preparation are implied as useful coping skills.)

"What is another way of looking at this situation?" (In many situations, this broad question helps unearth the client's attachment to one view and may help the client become a bit more open to alternative interpretations and different perspectives [Beck & Emery, 1985].)

"How do you think (Martin Luther King Jr., Arnold Schwarzenegger, Barack Obama, Queen Elizabeth, Clint Eastwood, Pope Francis, Mother Teresa, the Dalai Lama) might deal with this situation?" (The question helps the client begin shifting their perspective of the situation, thereby stimulating an awareness of different emotional and behavioral reactions. The comparison person should be someone well known, relevant to the current problem situation, and aligned with the client's personal values.)

"How might you handle it if this was not a problem with your boss but instead was a disagreement with your girlfriend or your football coach?" (Here we see a more localized way of shifting the perspective, changing the other person involved in the conflict instead of focusing on the client's own reaction.)

Socratic questions aim to bring insights and ideas that have been forgotten or never integrated into conscious awareness (Kennerly, 2007). A systematic series of questions can generate an array of alternative coping strategies, offering the client a range of acceptable choices. In many situations, the client may provide answers that are as good if not better than any the therapist may have had in mind (figure 4.1). The therapist's series of questions keeps the dialogue moving forward while nonetheless remaining careful to allow the client the agency to steer the answers down a chosen path.

Clients may attempt to solicit advice and guidance from the therapist when struggling with stressors like interpersonal conflict at work or home. The therapist can ask a range of questions to help clients derive their own answers:

"How did you deal with this situation?" (This is a simple question that gathers additional information about the events, subtly shining the spotlight on the client's coping responses.)

"How can you be sure she intended to insult you when she said that?" (Occasionally, questions are used to examine the accuracy of a client's interpretations.)

"Is there a chance she may have meant to imply something different?" (Questions can be used to help clients see there are other views of the same events. For example, one client had a serious leak beneath her kitchen sink. For various reasons, it took ten days before she could arrange for repairs. When the plumber arrived, he asked her, "How can you live like this?" The client appeared calm but later described how upset and hurt she felt, assuming he had criticized her poor housekeeping and messy home. In reality, the plumber was asking about how she managed to live for ten days without being able to use her kitchen sink.)

"What else could you do to manage this tough situation?" (Now, the therapist opens the issue of alternative strategies that might be available.)

"I don't want to minimize the problem here, but maybe you can help me understand it better—so what if it happens? Will life really become that bad?"

(This question confronts the client's perceived magnitude of impact and lets them evaluate the appropriate magnitude of emotional reaction. However, it must be posed gently so the tone does not reject the client's view.)

"Does this attitude help you move forward with energy and enthusiasm, or does it drag you down to where you want to give up?" (Again, the question is phrased using an either/or format, even though the two options become a bit convoluted. This question examines the functional utility of a negative attitude. The question moves away from an examination of accuracy and instead focuses on the benefit or harm of different attitudes and expectations.)

"Honestly, this seems to be a challenging situation. How would you *like* to deal with this situation?" (Some questions can instill an attitude of hope in the client [Tomm, 1987]. Simply phrasing the question in terms of the client's choice of behavior implies the client has control over their own behavior as well as the outcome.)

"If you could do anything different at that moment, how would you have liked to handle it?" (Here, the goal is to push the client toward optimal behavior.)

"Have you ever encountered a problem like this before in which you handled it pretty well? What did you do at that time?" (Such questions can help clients recall past coping efforts and revive their confidence in their current abilities.)

"Would it be possible to try something similar now?" (This opens up the topic of creativity and new approaches.)

"Have you ever seen one of your friends in a similarly tough situation? How did they deal with it?" "How do you think (your best friend, your mother, Daniel Craig, Meryl Streep, Jack Nicholson) might deal with it?" "If this was a mechanical problem with your car, how would you deal with it?" (This last question stimulates a completely different perspective, one aligned with this particular client's background as an auto mechanic.)

Questions can also shift a client's time perspective. For example, an adult female client attending individual therapy sessions often asked to discuss her poor relationship with her live-in boyfriend. During one session, she complained about his apparent infidelity. Recently, the client had been diagnosed with a sexually transmitted disease even though for the past eight years she had not had sex with anyone except her boyfriend. When she confronted him, he admitted to a moment of passion with a female coworker

SYSTEMATIC QUESTIONING

while on a business trip, and he promised it would never happen again. As her therapist, I asked her a series of questions to help her explore her plans and possibilities:

"What will things be like in one year, if you stick it out and stay with him?" She said she was hopeful that things could return to normal. "What will things be like for you if you felt fed up and decided to end the relationship now?" She claimed it would be difficult, emotionally and financially, to break up with her boyfriend now. "During our time spent in therapy, how strong would you rate your investment in your relationship, based on the energy you spend working on things each week?" She replied 95 percent. "During the past eight months, how would you rate your boyfriend's investment in the relationship?" She believed that his investment was a mere 25 percent. Although these responses were limited to subjective speculations, she began to appreciate the severity of her relationship problems. These questions were not designed to damage her relationship but to protect her by enhancing her self-awareness of the relationship problems she must confront, not ignore.

Questions can encourage a change of behavior. For example, an older adult female client was feeling rejected and discarded by her children. Some unspoken discord had also developed with her sister. Their relationship now felt cold, telephone calls had become infrequent and brief, and home visits were rare. A segment of her therapy explored the situation through a series of questions (the client's replies are omitted to protect confidentiality and focus on the use of a series of questions).

"So how do you want to move forward from here?"

"What might you be willing to try to rekindle a relationship with her?"

"If you do nothing and slowly withdraw, are you okay losing your relationship with her?"

"If you go for two months and do not call her or visit her, how would you react if the phone rings, and your niece asks, 'So will you be coming tomorrow?' And you ask, 'Coming where?' To your shock, she then replies, 'To mom's funeral; she passed four days ago.'"

The client became tearful and her voice cracked as she said, "I don't like this line of discussion." As therapist, my intent was to help her see the bigger picture so she could become the bigger person. She had a choice. She could choose to hold onto her feelings of anger and resentment and let her bond with her sister slowly wither. Or she could choose to move beyond their recent disagreements and slowly reconnect.

Content of Questions

A wide variety of questions can facilitate personal problem solving by the client. Thus, problem-solving therapy is a useful framework for the content of Socratic questions. However, the content and form of the questions must be structured in a way that facilitates independence in the client. Otherwise, there is a risk that the focus on problem solving could degenerate into a dogmatic lecture led by a therapist as expert; in such a scenario, the collaborative nature would be lost. The Socratic method examines and cross-examines the client's statements; it doesn't provide a platform for a lecture but instead helps people find their own useful direction (Nelson, 1949). The frequent use of questions invites the client to collaborate and engage in the discussion (Tomm, 1988).

Socratic questions can apply a problem-solving model to a cooperative process (Milliren, Milliren, & Eckstein, 2007). When exploring the problem-solving process in a session, the stages of problem solving can structure the flow of the process (Bell & D'Zurilla, 2009). These stages include a general orientation to life problems, problem definition, the generation of alternatives, decision making, and implementation (Nezu & Nezu, 2001). Problem-solving therapy sessions are usually structured didactically, combined with handouts, the provision of relevant examples, behavioral rehearsal, and homework assignments (Nezu & Nezu, 2001). In some reports, problem-solving therapy is conducted via a handful of sessions (Eskin, Ertekin, & Demir, 2008) or brief sessions of structured group therapy lasting thirty minutes each (Grey, 2007). One study examined the effectiveness of problem-solving therapy provided as a thirty-five-minute narrated PowerPoint lecture given to a sample of college students (Fitzpatrick, Witte, & Schmidt, 2005). Although small reductions were observed, results suggested the effects might be modest and temporary. In the Socratic approach, by contrast, such didactic lectures are replaced with a collaborative questioning style (Milliren, Milliren, & Eckstein, 2007). Each of the stages of problem solving will be enabled and augmented by a heavy focus on the questions that can guide the dialogue.

Rational problem solving relies on a clear articulation of the problem to be solved (Maxwell, 1984). Questions can clarify the client's understanding of the situation. They can also help clients define the problem in clear terms and with attainable goals (Tomm, 1987). Some questions can help clients examine the gap between the current situation and their ideal (Milliren, Milliren, & Eckstein, 2007). Useful questions include:

"What do you see as the problem here?" (Note the generic use of "problem" to capture the situations to be explored by clients.)

"What makes this situation such a big deal?" (Here, the therapist is asking the client to put the events in perspective, helping to determine whether the problem is trivial and could be managed by ignoring it with patience and tolerance or if the situation requires a more active shift of interpersonal behavior. Some questions encourage a shift in perspective by the client [Tomm, 1988].)

"What do you think might be causing this problem to continue for so long?" (Although most clients are poor at identifying possible causes, this question can still help them confront attributions of blame. Ideally, clients can see that the cause does not reside entirely within the other person but that the client plays a role in the onset or perpetuation of the conflict.)

"How would you like things to change?" (Note this question is wide open and that clients can give almost any answer, including fantasizing about unrealistic outcomes. The intent is to cultivate positive expectations and a view toward a better future. The therapist may need to monitor the reality of the client's goals to ensure they aim toward an outcome that is likely over the next few weeks.)

"How do you typically react when this situation occurs?" (Note this question aims to help clients see their restricted range and limited utility of past coping efforts. Many clients continue to react in the same way out of habit, even though it has not effectively managed a difficult or recurrent interpersonal problem.)

After the problem has been defined in a clear and realistic manner, the discussion moves on to coping. Rational problem solving requires possible solutions that are created imaginatively but evaluated critically (Maxwell, 1984).

When confronting problems, the therapist should focus on both the ideal solution as well as on the realistic changes that are possible, desirable, and valuable to the person (Maxwell, 1984). Questions can help clients generate alternative strategies for dealing with a difficult or recurrent problem. The goal is to help clients approach the situation clearly, rationally, and creatively. With some clients, the discussion may fruitfully jump directly into generating alternatives without having first explored the problem in detail. When exploring new and adaptive coping strategies, useful questions include:

"What have you already tried to deal with this situation?" (This question is important for understanding the client's pattern of social coping, and it helps ensure that the plan devised involves new and different coping options.)

"How well did it go? Is the same plan worth trying again, or should we be looking for a new strategy?" (The first question is focused on evaluating and is used to help clients accept responsibility for evaluating their own behavior. The second question uses a bifurcated approach. When phrased supportively, clients are less likely to become defensive and argue the merits of their past coping efforts.)

"Has there ever been a time when you could handle this sort of situation easily, or has this always been difficult?" (Again, this question provides two valid options, reducing the risk of deliberately steering the client down the therapist's predetermined path. Effective questions are genuine inquiries and do not guide the client toward a predetermined answer [James, Morse, & Howarth, 2010].)

"I know there are reasons why you would *not* want to do this, but what would happen if you asked your buddy if you could stay at his apartment for a few weeks?" "In a similar way, have you considered asking your brother if you could stay with him for a bit?" (Although these questions present a viable option to the client, these options are framed deliberately pessimistically. The downcast view provides the client an easy way to decline the proposed plan while nonetheless helping the client move beyond the alternatives that have already been proposed. Furthermore, it gives the client time, even if only the week between sessions, to allow these new options to sink in. There is a good chance that during the next session, the client will begin with a statement such as "I thought about what you said last week, and I talked to a different friend about using his spare bedroom." Thus, the options proposed by the therapist are chosen because of their flaws but also because they break the client out of his or her limited perspective about what options are available.)

"What could you do that might make the situation go a little bit better?" (Again, there are two subtle components to this question. The word "do" emphasizes personal control and behavior change. The phrase "a little bit better" encourages positive expectations but modest gains. Thus, the question helps clients focus on a positive future that can be attained through their own actions.)

After clarifying the problem and identifying a range of possible solutions, questions can help clients decide on the optimal plan for action. Useful questions include:

"So now that we see there are a few possibilities, what looks like the best plan?" (This is a good initial question, laying the foundation for what follows and establishing the client as the person in charge of all decisions. The therapist conveys a supportive attitude but gives the client the control and responsibility for all efforts at behavior change.)

"From the range of options we have discussed, does anything seem like it might work, or do we need to continue developing more options?" (Again, this question could have stopped with a more leading framework and simply asked the client to select the best plan from those already developed. However, by providing two options to the question, clients are given the control to move forward or move backward across the problem-solving stages.)

"I know each of these options would require some effort on your part, but which plan seems like the best fit for you?" (Here, the emphasis is on personalization. The therapist may have selected a different plan, but everyone has different strengths and weaknesses, and clients should adapt the plan to suit their styles and the idiosyncrasies of the interpersonal situation confronted.)

"Now if we put this plan into effect, how likely is it to really be effective?" (This question contains several subtle points. First, the use of "we" implies collaboration and joint investment in the behavior change. Second, the word "really" conveys a practical view that moves beyond abstract speculation and Monday-morning-quarterback chatter. The intent is to help clients take ownership of the plan and become invested in its success.)

"Is there anything you can think of that might backfire? What could we do to make it less likely to backfire?" (Questions such as this can help clients anticipate potential consequences and explore different possible outcomes [Tomm, 1987].)

SYSTEMATIC QUESTIONING

"If we can get detailed for a minute, how would this play out in the moment? And how might things play out over the next few weeks?" (These questions further help the client anticipate upcoming events and prepare for possible problems.)

"I know we have focused on a plan that would be helpful from your view, but how do you think your boss/neighbor/wife will react if you behave in this new way?" (This question becomes a bit long and convoluted. However, the intent is to allow a buffer from an intense interrogation and, more importantly, to help clients step back from their own subjective appraisal of interpersonal events. Instead, clients will benefit when they can develop empathy and insight into the experience of those people involved in daily interactions with them.)

After proceeding through the earlier steps, many clients can move forward with their plan for more effective behavior. However, there remains a risk that the new plan will lie dormant and that the client will take no action. To ensure that clients begin their efforts to improve the situation, problem solving includes a final step for implementation and evaluation. A very broad and expansive goal at this stage means helping clients learn to anticipate and prepare for difficult situations, confronting their expectations and making early preparations in attitude or deliberate practice. At this point, questions can guide clients to anticipate the details of the plan, including when and where they will confront the situation and what they might need to get ready for the new action, so the client can have time during calm moments removed from the conflict situation to anticipate potential problems and make plans to overcome some of the more common obstacles. Useful questions for this stage include:

"So now we have something of a plan. When are you going to try it?" (This helps situate the solution that the therapist and patient have arrived at in a defined timeframe.)

"Instead of waiting for the next time the problem happens and responding, I have found it works much better to plan out how you would like to address the situation and put that plan into effect at a time that suits you. Does that make sense? When might you be willing to take the lead and confront it head on? (Here, the therapist is gently pushing the client forward while nonetheless encouraging the client to steer the direction.)

"As we sit here now, how well do you think it will go?" (This question has two subtle components. First, "as we sit here" conveys an attitude of practicality and asks for a realistic view. Second, "think it will go" guides the client to evaluate options and their potential consequences.)

"Is there anything we can do now to help you prepare for this situation?" (This question sets the expectation that the plan will indeed be implemented; it can also remind clients of the aphorism "Proper Planning Prevents Poor Performance.")

Finally, after the client has confronted the situation, subsequent therapy sessions can be used to review the events and evaluate the outcome. This is a key step, one often neglected by clients. After they have taken new action, they can learn a tremendous amount about their own coping style and from the reactions of friends and family members. In the event that things went poorly, the client may be able to identify what could be improved so the plan could be refined. Even if the outcome was positive, there remains a high likelihood that similar problems will recur. Thus, clients can review the event-coping efforts and identify steps that can be used in further confrontations. Useful questions for this stage include:

"How did it go?" (This simple question encourages the client to take responsibility for the evaluation of the outcome.)

"Are there certain things you felt that went quite well?" (Here, the therapist wants to ensure the client focuses on the positive events that occurred.)

"Are there some aspects of the encounter that did not quite go as planned?" (The therapist now opens up the evaluation to include more of a critical review.)

"If you have to confront a similar situation in a few weeks, how will you respond?" (Finally, the therapist shifts the focus from the past to the future, aiming to identify new actions to implement when the problem situation recurs.)

In sum, the stages of problem solving can guide the therapeutic dialogue. Although a structured format is useful for the inexperienced therapist, a cookbook model is not optimal for psychotherapy sessions (Hegel, Barrett, & Oxman, 2000). A wide range of questions can facilitate a client's ability to shift his or her expectations and interpersonal behavior. Although I have provided many sample questions in this chapter, these examples are not intended to be appropriated wholesale by other practitioners. What is more important than the specific questions are the brief explanations that support the rationales behind each question. The use of systematic questioning may not align with the use of published treatment manuals; there are no fixed, step-by-step, codified, memorizable procedures for conducting a Socratic dialogue. Instead, questions must flow naturally and spontaneously (Brickhouse & Smith, 1994).

Questions may have different meanings in different contexts (Santas, 1979); the best questions are customized to each client and his or her specific situation. For the discussion to be effective, it should rely on a spontaneous flow and interactive exchange between a client involved in the problem-solving process and a therapist curious about new and customized strategies for positive change. When therapists bring creative energy to the discussion, the client will become actively involved and personally invested in the outcome.

Process of Systematic Questioning

Systematic questioning works well when conducted in brief bursts, so as not to overwhelm the client with an interrogation. Many questions promote a shift in the client's perspective about their struggles (Siemonsma et al., 2013), in the effort to move toward a softer interpretation or more hopeful expectations for the future. The Socratic method is closely aligned with other types of psychotherapy that aim to reduce a client's tendencies for extreme overstatements and pessimistic expectations. Socratic questions often aim at exposing a person's illogical beliefs (Guthrie, 1971).

There are important differences between knowledge and belief. The therapist can use questions to help clients develop rational beliefs, explore their underlying assumptions, examine the evidence supporting their views, and refute erroneous beliefs when there is no evidence for them or they are logically inconsistent with other, more strongly held views. It is important to bypass the confirmation bias and help clients search for information that might contradict their beliefs (Kennerly, 2007). The Socratic method examines a person's knowledge, and when found deficient, it helps the person begin the search for more valid beliefs (Benson, 2011). Thus, questions challenge and potentially reject false beliefs (Caminada, 2008). Socrates initiated his celebrated dialogues prepared to learn whether his interlocutor's beliefs could be supported and confirmed (Benson, 2011). However, it must be admitted that consistency across beliefs is not adequate by itself to support someone's views (Goldman, 1986); many people with psychotic delusions develop an entire network of mutually reinforcing interlocking beliefs. Thus, when inconsistencies are noted across a person's beliefs, they should be confronted, explored, and changed.

Throughout the dialogue, the client is compelled to draw certain conclusions that follow from his or her own prior admissions (Navia, 1985). Because the process is designed to test a person's beliefs, it produces wisdom in the form of awareness of the limits of one's knowledge and by removing unsupported beliefs (King, 2008). The process of a Socratic dialogue involves exploring the client's beliefs and testing the client's ability to defend these views. Thus, simply eliciting a client's beliefs, opinions, and personal values is merely the beginning of the exploration. The dialogue then sets out to test these statements, working on the assumption that false beliefs cannot survive intense logical scrutiny (Nehamas, 1994).

The Socratic method uses a systematic series of questions to evaluate the consistency of a person's beliefs (Melling, 1987). The therapist does not argue with clients about the reality of their beliefs, but together they examine different beliefs to see which can withstand logical scrutiny (Taylor, 1956). The discussion can examine evidence available to support or refute a certain belief, or the dialogue can identify the advantages and disadvantages of retaining certain beliefs (Overholser, 2017). Socrates used questions to clear errors of thinking endorsed by the person (Livingstone, 1938). Systematic questioning examines a proposition to see where it goes and to determine whether it contradicts other beliefs of the individual (Melling, 1987).

A rational dialogue can shift the person away from social consensus or conventional acceptance of beliefs to focus on the rational basis for acceptability (Klein, 1986). The validity of a belief does not reside in how the person feels about the matter but whether the belief can withstand the scrutiny of the dialectic (Nehamas, 1985). As captured in the early dialogues, Socrates often progressed through three steps in the elenchus (Irwin, 1974). In therapeutic terms, first, the therapist should encourage the client to express his or her own beliefs. Second, the therapist confronts the client's beliefs and helps the client reject those that cannot be supported logically. Third, the therapist and client search for new and valid knowledge. Thus, although the elenchus relies on refuting a client's beliefs, the process is not entirely destructive. The elenchus functions like a physician who cuts out dead tissue in order to heal the body (Seeskin, 1987). The intent is to help the person discard his or her previous ways of thinking and view the situation from a new perspective (Seeskin, 1987). Questions can help clients step out of their personal experience and view the events from the vantage of an external observer (Tomm, 1987).

The Socratic method confronts and challenges unsupported beliefs. Clients can be asked to pose the simple question: "What justification do I have to support this belief?" (Chisholm, 1979). Simply asking "Why is that so?" can reveal the person's underlying implicit assumptions, which having been made explicit can now be confronted directly (Ennis, 1982). Once uncovered, the underlying propositions also can be explored and challenged (Ennis, 1982). However, as a more basic recommendation, "Why?" questions are typically avoided because they can put the client on the defensive (Milliren, Milliren, & Eckstein, 2007). Also, "Why?" questions allow the person to respond with any opinion they might hold (Dillon, 1990). Finally, such questions might imply the client is to be blamed ("Why the hell did you do that?").

Although Chisholm (1979) rejects some questions as being outside the scope of the Socratic method, it nonetheless seems useful to ask clients, "How did you reach the point where you first started to believe this idea? What additional evidence could you find to support your belief? How would you go about persuading a reasonable person that your belief is true?" Socrates would engage the person in dialogue, using short question-and-answer exchanges to test the coherence of a person's set of beliefs (McPherran, 2011). When the person's belief was found to be incompatible with other held beliefs, it became difficult to retain the original belief (Vlastos, 1983).

Throughout therapy sessions, clients are encouraged to make their own decisions. The therapist avoids the role of expert decision maker who doles out advice or instructions to the passive client. However, it becomes a process of thoughtful exploration to guide the client toward a rational choice. For example, returning to the vignette I described earlier in this chapter, an adult female client was upset when she learned that her boyfriend had cheated on her. Even worse, because of the infidelity, the client was exposed to a sexually transmitted disease. She brought this to therapy, asking for help with an important decision: What should she do about this mess? The therapist had his own personal opinions and gut reactions to these events but realized that his own immediate and quite strongly felt reactions were irrelevant. Instead, the therapeutic goal included supporting the client and encouraging a rational approach focused on the optimal decision for the client's long-term functioning. When the therapist asked the client what she planned to do about this romantic relationship, she stated: "I'm not sure. I'm not ready to give up on him or our relationship. I want to forgive him, but I'm really upset about this whole mess." The therapist asked: "Well, let's jump ahead six months or so. What will life be like if you forgive him and forget about these events?" The client replied: "I think I can forgive him, but I'm not sure I could forget what happened."

THERAPIST: "Do you think you could love him and trust him?"
CLIENT: "I can love him. I like who he is, but I doubt I could trust him. Trust is so important, but I don't know if I could ever really trust him again."
THERAPIST: "Let's look down the other path. What might life be like in six months if you decide to end the relationship and move on with your life?"
CLIENT: "I don't know. I guess I would be alone for awhile, and I would feel sad and lonely, but maybe I would start to get over it."
THERAPIST: "In the past, before you got involved with this guy, how easy or hard was it for you to meet people and start up a new romantic relationship?"
CLIENT: "I guess it was not too hard."
THERAPIST: "So what is your gut reaction? Do you feel that life would be better if you moved down the first pathway or the second path?"

At the end of the session, the therapist asked the client to try a writing project between sessions. The client was asked to write a letter to herself, speaking now to her future self six months from today. As this example captures, decision making is a process, not a quest for the right answer. Like a sheep dog barking to keep the herd on a safe path, the therapist uses questions to keep the client on task and not stray too far onto side topics or irrelevant details (figure 4.1). Likewise, therapists may act like guardrails, keeping the discussion on course (Legomsky-Abel, 1989).

Good Socratic questions are constructive, promoting insight and adaptive actions (Neenan, 2009). Questions are rarely phrased with "Why?" as their focus. Socratic questions do not provide answers but help the client

SYSTEMATIC QUESTIONING

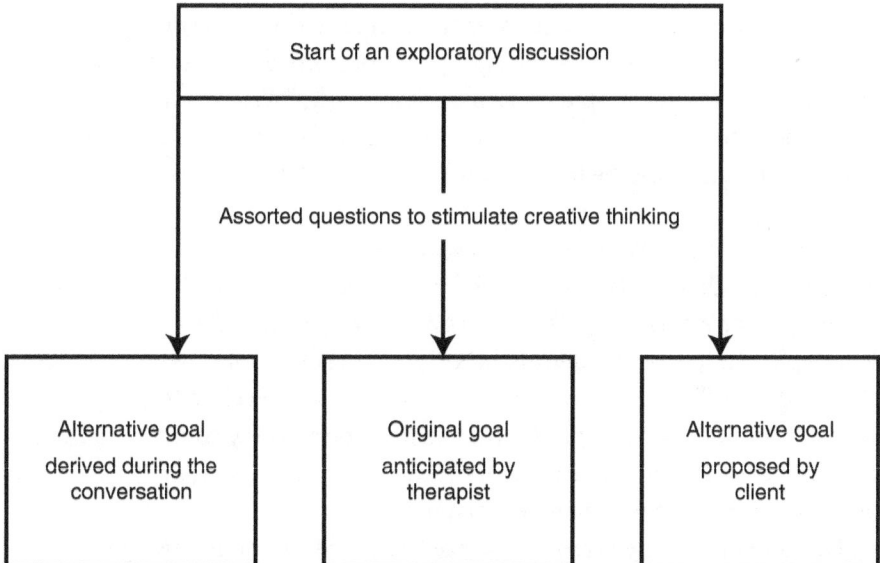

Figure 4.1 A series of questions.

see the situation from a different perspective. Additional information can surround the question, providing context or offering a summary that explains the question's rationale (James et al., 2010). The therapist can "package" questions to avoid the feel of an interrogation (e.g., "Let me ask you an odd question"; "If it's okay, let me change topics for a minute"; "I am not suggesting you try this, but what might happen if . . ."). The questioning style can include several statements to surround the question, or the question can even be presented as a statement ("I am confused—help me better understand what you were going through at that moment").

Conclusions

Good Socratic questions encourage the client to explore the topic in a conversational exchange of ideas (Neenan, 2009) without it ever feeling like an interrogation. A series of questions can gently move the discussion forward. Questions help clients appreciate alternatives and possibilities (Freedman & Combs, 1993). Thus, a simple question like "What can you do to make the situation better?" implies that the therapist believes things can improve and that the client has some control over the events or their interpretation. However, the client may answer by saying, "I don't know." When clients claim ignorance, it can be simple to step back and ask, "Well, do you think anything could be done to make this situation better?" Most clients will respond in the affirmative and be more likely to provide ideas to support their basic claim.

Therapists can develop their skill with the use of questions. Questions can aim to evaluate a mixture of issues (Elder & Paul, 2007), including the clarity of a person's reasoning ("Can you give me an example?"), precision ("Can you explain a few of the details here?"), accuracy ("How well do you trust this evidence?"), relevance ("How does this situation relate to the problem we were discussing?"), depth ("This seems to be a pretty complicated situation; have we examined all factors that might be important here?"), and breadth ("What aspects have we missed?").

The goal of therapy is to internalize the process of questioning so clients can develop a strategy for examining their own life, goals, and values. Shaping develops a process of asking a series of questions to explore topics in a thoughtful and detailed review (Calero-Elvira et al., 2013). Collaborative empiricism helps clients become their own cognitive therapists (Kazantzis et al., 2013). The Socratic method cultivates skills in critical thinking (Leigh, 2007; Zare & Munkundan, 2015). Questions can highlight a client's views in clear, precise, and accurate language (Zare & Munkundan, 2015). Clients can learn to ask themselves a series of questions to guide rational behavior (Paul & Elder, 2007). Thus, people can learn to stop and ask themselves: Is there another plausible explanation I should consider? If I act in this manner, what is likely to happen as a result?

A detailed understanding of questions is related to higher skill as a therapist (James & Morse, 2007). In a study of fifty-five depressed adults receiving sixteen weeks of cognitive therapy, the better the therapist who relied on Socratic questions, the better the results (Braun, Strunk, Sasso, & Cooper, 2015). Unfortunately, some evidence exists that Socratic questions might not be seen as supportive within a simulated therapy context (Bishop & Fish, 1999).

FIVE

Inductive Reasoning

Learning from Personal Experiences

PSYCHOTHERAPY SESSIONS CAN benefit from a logical approach that guides the discussion. At a basic level, it is essential to distinguish between knowledge and opinion (Patterson, 1965). Too many aspects that influence a client's emotions are guided by opinions that cannot be substantiated in a logical or empirical manner. Clients can learn to rely on logic and hypothesis testing rather than on opinion, and they can begin to base their decisions on knowledge more than on opinion. Inductive reasoning moves from specific cases to reach a tentative but more general conclusion (Crossley & Wilson, 1979).

The strength of the Socratic approach lies in the clear thinking displayed by Socrates and in the method's program of avoiding self-contradicting beliefs (Bartlett, 1996). Inductive reasoning includes three general strategies: enumeration, elimination, and analogical reasoning. Each of these can be applied to clinical situations when guiding a collaborative type of psychotherapy.

Psychotherapy Can Help Guide Hypothesis Testing

Therapists can help clients convert their beliefs into testable hypotheses (Beck et al., 1979). It can be wise to trust beliefs only after they have survived a thoughtful and critical examination (McPherran, 1996). The Socratic dialogue is not simply interested in removing incorrect beliefs or cultivating more adaptive views but tries to help the individual develop useful strategies for examining knowledge and beliefs (Seeskin, 1987).

The Socratic dialogue moves from an initial hypothesis, and in attempting to refute and contradict it, searches through various modifications, eventually aiming for beliefs that can withstand close scrutiny (Robinson, 1941). A Socratic dialogue often helps guide a person to turn implicit ideas into explicit statements (Marinoff, 1999). The Socratic method helps clients examine their own beliefs. It can be useful to ask clients: "What is the evidence for or against this idea?" (Beck & Emery, 1985). In the Socratic method, a client's beliefs can be examined by confronting contradictory evidence or other beliefs that conflict within the person's belief system. The method of hypothesis testing involves proposing an idea, examining its coherence with other beliefs, and examining whether any illogical or absurd consequences might follow from the starting premise (White, 1976). If nothing absurd is uncovered, then it may be possible to move forward with a higher hypothesis.

Helping Clients Form New Generalizations

Inductive reasoning aims to help clients reach a general conclusion based on specific pieces of evidence. This in turn helps clients begin to move beyond a tendency to focus on the isolated events that happen across each week. Too often, psychotherapy sessions become a review of recent events, especially in those situations when sessions are conducted less frequently than once per week. When sessions occur on a less regular basis, too much time is spent on getting the therapist "caught up" on interpersonal events. In most cases, a simple review of recent news is not the optimal use of therapy time.

Inductive reasoning helps guide the search for patterns across events in the client's life. Across sessions, the therapist typically learns about the client's life, social network, and recurrent problems. Therapist and client together can review various events to search for a better understanding of the client's life struggles and coping strategies. Over a series of sessions, the gradual accumulation of evidence can help in the identification of recurrent themes. Individual events are gathered to form a generalized view (Goldman, 1986).

INDUCTIVE REASONING

The Socratic method does not rely on deductive reasoning, whereby an expert therapist explains ideas and strategies to the client. Instead, a Socratic approach relies on inductive reasoning. This is a slower process in which questions are used to help the client gather additional information and explore alternative views. A Socratic approach does not imply that the client's perspective is wrong and should be replaced by the therapist's more accurate and objective views. Instead, the therapist works under the assumption that there might be alternative views and that it can be helpful to seek and explore possible different views of a difficult situation. Some of the new perspectives could be helpful to the client—helpful by reducing the intensity of the client's emotional reactions, helpful in generating new options for functional behavior, or helpful in stimulating additional ideas for creative problem solving.

Many therapy sessions begin with a review of recent events that occurred in the client's life. Inductive reasoning can help shift the discussion onto broader issues. Clients can learn to focus on themes and patterns that can be observed across events. The goal is to help clients begin to learn from their own experiences. A guided review of events may highlight lessons learned across events in the client's life ("How did you deal with this conflict when it happened two weeks ago?") as well as lessons learned across psychotherapy sessions ("Do you remember two weeks ago when you told me how you were able to talk to your neighbor in a calm and assertive manner?").

Inductive generalizations are limited because they assume that all unexamined cases will be similar to those examples that have been observed (Capaldi, 1969). For example, a middle-aged male client complained that he would never find love because "it never works out anyway." As the session continued, he explained that his own ex-wife had been verbally abusive throughout their marriage, his most recent girlfriend had been using him for financial assistance in paying her rent, and his best friend was trapped in a troubled marriage where he and his wife argued frequently about everyday responsibilities. When these events were reviewed in combination, it supported his general belief that true love was impossible. However, as the discussion continued, he was helped to see that he was relying on a very limited sample upon which to base such an important generalization. Over time, he began to notice friends, relatives, and coworkers who were involved in mature and satisfying relationships, and he was able to reduce his attachment to his nihilistic beliefs and overgeneralized views of romance.

During therapeutic conversations, the therapist can help clients seek generalizations, as clients aim to infer a general pattern across people and events. Inductive reasoning via generalization is useful because clients often form generalizations that may be incorrect or possibly destructive. For example, whenever a client uses a word such as "always" or "never," it can serve as a hint to the therapist that the client has formed a generalized view, one likely to be incorrect. An erroneous overgeneralization can sometimes be refuted by locating a single example that deviates from the pattern (Guthrie, 1971).

The process of inductive generalizations plays a central role in the search for universal definitions (Armstrong, 1989). The method of collection and division involves gathering a wide range of examples and then dividing them into subgroups (White, 1976). Similar events, objects, or ideas that belong together are collected in the hopes of finding the central essence that underlies all examples (Sallis, 1986). Then, division aims to eliminate any items that had been misclassified in the earlier attempt to collect them into a unified group. The process sometimes results in dividing the assembled group into distinct parts or subcategories (Sallis, 1986).

A more detailed example may be helpful. An adult female with tendencies toward chronic depression had been feeling sad, lonely, and neglected by others. She commented that "no one cares" about her because no one had acknowledged her birthday. Questions were used to explore the extent of her supporting evidence: "Who was aware it was your birthday?" "How can people show they care about a friend's birthday?" "Okay, so no one at work gave you a birthday card or a cake or a present; are there other ways a person might show they care?" "Yes, people will often write a letter, call, or visit. Have you ever cared about someone but not really done any of these activities?" The client had overgeneralized her feelings of neglect across a few recent events, culminating in a global view that no one ever, at any time, showed concern for her well-being. Eventually, the client was able to see that remembering or missing someone's birthday was not a good sign of the quality or importance of the relationship.

In order to cultivate rational views, clients must be willing to express their assumptions, evaluate the foundations of those assumptions, and improve the logical basis for their thinking (Maxwell, 1984). For example, a depressed male client was struggling with assorted stressors. "I am a failure, a complete and total failure." When asked why he would make such a claim, he offered the following emotional declaration: "Look at me, look at my life. What a shambles. I'm struggling at work, I'm getting a divorce I didn't want, and I have no friends. I'm a failure." Clearly, accepting the belief that a person is a failure will result in despair, hopelessness, and possibly trigger a suicidal crisis. The therapist asked a series of questions in the hopes of chopping this view of failure into more manageable components and confronting each problem as a semi-independent entity. Over the course of the discussion, the client was able to see that his current job was not a good fit for his skills and strengths. A few weeks later, he was laid off and again became quite despondent. In therapy, he was able to fight off his despair and hopelessness and began a search for a new job, aiming for a different type of work. He had been working in commercial advertising but was able to see he'd had ongoing struggles on the job. As he gained more insight into his own strengths and natural talents, he expanded his search to include jobs in sales. He landed a new job and quickly found the position much better suited to his personality and work habits. He settled into a new career path, working at a job that was a better fit for his strengths. Soon, he was able to shift his energies onto a similar view for finding a new romance as well as for renewing old and cultivating new friendships.

The Socratic dialogue aims to uncover inconsistencies across beliefs held by the person (Lesher, 2002). The Socratic dialogue, or the elenchus, tests the consistency across an individual's beliefs (Irwin, 1977). A search for consistency is a simple test of a person's beliefs (Allen, 1991). When people become aware of logical inconsistencies across a set of beliefs, they are typically motivated to resolve the discrepancy and change their beliefs (Rosen & Wyer, 1972). The process relies on a decision as to how much evidence is sufficient to support the generalization without reaching a hasty conclusion (Crossley & Wilson, 1979).

Helping Clients Clarify Their Causal Attributions

Inductive reasoning can be used to identify possible causal pathways. Induction by elimination is the phrase used to describe efforts to identify a range of possible causes and then to eliminate each possibility systematically until only one cause remains as the viable explanation for an event. Along the way, the client develops a rational view of life events and common problems.

The basic notions underlying a search for causes can be traced back through many years of writing in philosophy and logic, especially in the writings of Plato, Aristotle, and John Stuart Mill. To qualify as a possible cause, both the specific effect and its presumed cause must be present when the problem occurs, and there must be temporal precedence; that is, the cause always precedes the effect. One problem with inductive causal reasoning lies in the assumption that when two events tend to occur together, this pattern will continue, so that when one occurs, the other will be present as well (Capaldi, 1969).

Whenever relying on inductive reasoning, it is useful to ask: (1) Is there sufficient evidence to support the claim? (2) Is the evidence relevant to the conclusion being proposed? (3) Has the evidence been selected in an unbiased manner? (Crossley & Wilson, 1979). However, it is important for the therapist to remain modest and supportive, avoiding strong speculations about cause-effect relationships. Furthermore, it can be useful to view all beliefs as interpretations, that is, as hypotheses that can be tested empirically. Thus, collaborative empiricism helps the client formulate a hypothesis, clarify the terms, and, as best as possible, test the hypothesis. Often, this process may focus on correcting a client's faulty assumptions about causality. For example, a client expressed the view that she was to blame for her parents' divorce twenty-five years earlier. She had misbehaved at school and been suspended. That evening, from her bedroom, she overheard a major argument between her parents. The next day, her father moved out of the family home and distanced himself from the family. For twenty-five years, the client had assumed that the argument had centered around her troubles at school. It was only now, as an adult, having a conversation with her mother, that she learned her father had been having an affair. On the same day of the client's school troubles, her mother had confronted the father about the affair and told him to get out. The client was now able to see the twenty-five years of darkness that had been created by this misconception about the cause of her parents' divorce.

The process of hypothesis testing can be structured through a series of questions in session. During the conversation, questions can aim to gather information about the sequence of events, searching for possible causes that temporally preceded the effect. This process may apply when clients report problems with negative moods, frequent headaches, or persistent disturbances

INDUCTIVE REASONING

Behavior to track: _____

	Sunday	Monday	Tuesday	Wednesday	Thursday	Friday	Saturday
Early morning							
Late morning							
Noon							
Early afternoon							
Late afternoon							
Early evening							
Late evening							
Bedtime							

Figure 5.1

of sleep. Clients may be asked to complete a simple self-monitoring form in order to track the event between sessions and to notice any fluctuations in their mood, headaches, or sleep (figure 5.1). Then, when potential causes are included in the self-monitoring, clients may begin asking whether their problem (for example, insomnia) might be related to the presence of one or more causal factors (worrying, caffeine, spicy diet, daytime naps). Finally, to verify the accuracy of the new perspective, clients may be helped to alter one condition at a time and notice what effect that has. It can be fairly easy to avoid daytime naps or refrain from spicy foods for a week in order to examine how that affects the client's insomnia.

Inductive reasoning underlies the tendency to project past failures onto future outcomes (Capaldi, 1969). For example, a client with chronic depression and tendencies of self-blame began a session on a critical note:

> CLIENT: "I still feel upset. Late Monday evening, I was driving home alone during that big storm, and I had a flat tire in a really bad neighborhood."
> THERAPIST: "And you're still upset over this? Did anything else happen?"
> CLIENT: "No. Just the flat tire, but I should have known it would happen. I should have known to avoid that part of town."

INDUCTIVE REASONING

THERAPIST: "How could you know it would happen?" (It is often useful to confront a false belief in knowledge.)

CLIENT: "I knew those tires were old. I had planned on getting new ones. I just never got around to it."

THERAPIST: "But how could you know that you'd get a flat tire?"

CLIENT: "I knew the tire needed to be replaced."

THERAPIST: "If you look to the future now, can you see any car problems happening in the next few weeks?" (Turning from hindsight to foresight can confront the mistaken belief in accurate predictions.)

CLIENT: "Well, no . . ."

THERAPIST: "Does it seem like you are being hard on yourself?" (I am now omitting the client's replies to simplify the text and highlight the therapist's use of questions.)

THERAPIST: "From what you have told me, I can't see how you could have known this was going to happen. Do you place this kind of responsibility on yourself in other situations?"

THERAPIST: "Does this seem like something you do on your job too?"

THERAPIST: "How about at home, when you examine how you are raising your kids?"

THERAPIST: "Are you expecting more than 100 percent from yourself?"

THERAPIST: "How would things go if you lowered the bar to 80 percent or so?" (This question plants the seed for a more moderate view of the client's goals and evaluations.)

THERAPIST: "Do you hold such high standards for others, like your coworkers or your children?"

THERAPIST: "Why should you be treated differently than other people?" (Although "why" questions are generally avoided, the hope is that the client will be unable to answer this question. Instead, it pries open the ability to confront justice in terms of fair treatment of everyone, including oneself.)

As a therapist, I was not concerned about this specific instance. Instead, I wanted to be clear that I was aiming for the bigger issue, the tendency for self-blame and the impossibility of predicting future events. This client had a tendency common among depressed clients, which is to blame herself for problems that happened, often holding herself to unrealistically high standards. These tendencies become most clearly visible when a client encounters stress, conflict, or problems, even those that may appear relatively minor, like getting a flat tire. Clients can appreciate the differences between hindsight and foresight. If you look to the past, it can become easy to see how things turned out. However, if you look to the future, prediction is difficult.

Causal reasoning becomes especially useful whenever clients are bothered by excessive tendencies for self-blame. For example, an adult male client with tendencies toward chronic depression and self-blame remained quite upset about his divorce five years earlier. In his words, their marriage ended because "it was all my fault." Through a lengthy discussion, a variety of possible factors were identified that might influence the course of a marriage. In one session, therapist and client devised a simple pie chart to help identify the strength of assorted factors, using the size of each slice to represent the power of each factor. When completing the chart, the client was able to see that his marriage had ended because of multiple forces all combining to disrupt their relationship. Causality usually involves a series of factors in a chain (Swain, 1981). Possible causal factors included his ex-wife's behavior, the pervasive financial stress on the family, complications arising from raising two troubled teens, and a weakened bond with his wife. Although it was not possible to identify one causal factor and unrealistic to examine the exact potency of each possible cause, this project was greatly helpful in guiding the client toward a more nuanced view of the end of his marriage, with responsibility distributed across different people and various events. Possible causes are best explored together. The therapist does not simply refute the client's views of causal attributions. Instead, the therapist may ask the client to defend his or her preexisting view.

A series of questions can be used to identify causal factors, explore possible cause-effect connections (Graesser & Murachver, 1985), and examine the evidence used to support various beliefs. Common questions include: "What would convince you that your view is not 100 percent correct?" "Could anything shake these beliefs?" "Maybe in a less demanding way, what evidence could you find that might get you to start reevaluating your belief here?" "Would it rely more on personal experience or advice from friends?" "Could your beliefs withstand the scrutiny of a courtroom cross-examination?"

INDUCTIVE REASONING

Helping Clients Learn from New Analogies

Inductive reasoning can be guided by analogies. When using analogies in therapy, the goal is to help clients think about their situation from a new perspective. The analogy should help stimulate a new view of the problem or possible coping options. Furthermore, it seems useful to "paint a picture" in the client's mind that helps reconceptualize the pain and struggles (Gallagher, McCauley, & Moseley, 2013). The visual nature of the analogy provides an image that can be retained longer than a simple exchange of words.

Analogies can help clients transfer ideas from familiar to novel situations. An analogy is not used to prove anything but to aid in seeing the situation from a new perspective (Allen, 1970). The analogy helps clarify two concepts that share similarities by mapping the components from one onto the other (Holland, Holyoak, Nisbett, & Thagard, 1986). For example, one client was struggling with ways of managing his unruly son. Because the client was a master mechanic, the therapist first tried using mechanical repairs as an analogy, asking a series of questions: "How would you approach this in a mechanical diagnostic evaluation?" "Based on your assessment, what is working and what is not working?" "When working as a mechanic, you would examine the electrical system, the exhaust system, the fuel system, and so on. What systems might be involved in a fully functional household?"

Because this analogy fell flat, the therapist shifted to a different one. The client was an avid dog lover, so the therapist explained that his dog needed a haircut, but whenever the dog saw scissors, he would run away. The therapist explained how he used a slow process, giving the dog a treat for each short segment of trimming, making it a more pleasant experience for both dog and owner. The therapist then asked the client to translate these procedures into the parenting of an unruly child.

A Socratic dialogue is designed to help a person find what they have been seeking. In an analogous manner, when someone visits the lost-and-found, the manager does not let the customer browse the contents to find whatever might catch his or her eye but instead asks the individual to describe what is being sought (White, 1994). When using analogies, it helps to find similarities across diverse events and transfer the knowledge from the old to the new situation. Some common analogies can be brought to session by the therapist and shared with the client. Thus, most people can relate to the notion of cleaning dirt from an open wound. Even though the process may be painful, the cleaning helps ensure proper healing. In a similar manner, psychotherapy provides a sterile environment in which to clean the client's deep emotional wounds. Even when it gets painful, the process is designed to facilitate proper healing.

In therapy, analogies can help identify the essence of a construct by seeking the common element across two situations. Then, ideas for managing one situation may be extrapolated to the current problem area. For example, a lonely male client remained focused on a romantic relationship that had ended twelve months earlier. It was explained that in some ways, 90 percent of his emotional energy was still being invested in a dead relationship. Such a pattern could be viewed as similar to investing in a company that had gone bankrupt and had now been out of business for the past year. The business was not going to revive, and, even worse, now there is no money to invest in a new business. The client began to see the downside of pining away for the lost love instead of moving forward to invest in new relationships.

Often, the therapist proposes an analogy to stimulate a new perspective on a difficult situation (Mathieson et al., 2016). However, in some sessions, clients present their own metaphor, using it to articulate their downcast view of their life situation. The therapist can build on the client's metaphors and analogies in an attempt to redirect the imagery. For example, an adult female client was encountering problems with several family members, her romantic partner, and a need to move into a new apartment. She described her life as similar to the Mad Mouse ride at a local amusement park. The therapist was familiar with this ride and listened to the client's description of anxiety and agitation. Then, the therapist replied: "Yes, the Mad Mouse is an exciting ride, and frankly it can be a bit terrifying when it reaches a corner, three stories up, and pivots a fast, sharp turn. However, if we had the option to remove the car and place it in your living room, it would immediately become completely safe. There would be no risk, no fear, no movement, no excitement. It would be incredibly boring. Unfortunately, being involved with other people does involve risks, and sometimes those relationships encounter conflict or disagreements. However, I hope the fun and excitement is worth the risk."

Many clients struggle with the end of a romantic relationship and may try to maintain the relationship even after the romance has faded. It can be useful to use a metaphor of rebuilding. The past romance had created a vision of a lovely future together. Now that the relationship has ended, this vision has crumbled, in a manner analogous to a wonderful castle that has decayed into ruins. The old remnants block the path and do nothing but trigger memories of brighter past days. Unfortunately, these remains also cut off a view of the scenery and must be cleared before any new construction can be built. If it is not possible to repair the relationship, then these old remnants should be removed. This can be a slow and difficult process, but with time, the path to a new and bright future will become visible.

A variety of analogies can be useful in psychotherapy sessions. A simple analogy describes the pain of a skinned knee, especially when dirt and gravel get trapped under the skin. A simple bandage may appear helpful, but the wound may not fully heal. Several weeks later, the person may complain of soreness and pus. Despite the pain involved, eventually the person may need to clean it out in a sterile environment. In the long run, the process will promote true healing, even if it leaves a small scar as a reminder.

When using analogical reasoning, a series of observed similarities across two situations are used to support additional similarities that have not yet been observed (Crossley & Wilson, 1979). The therapist can use each client's personal life experiences to find a useful analogous process and then to transfer established coping skills to a persistent problem or event. For example, a young adult female client had been in an auto accident and damaged her spinal cord. She was now chronically upset over her paraplegia and her difficulties fulfilling her typical weekly responsibilities. One day, during her physical therapy session, she was required to participate in wheelchair volleyball, using a beach ball and a low net. She had been reluctant to join the game but soon was surprised at how much fun she was having. Later that same day, in her therapy session, she was helped to see that volleyball could still be fun, even if it would never be quite the same as before her injury. She had been upset over the expected loss of a sex life, and now, using the analogy, she was asked to explore similarities with her experience playing volleyball. Surprisingly, she could easily see some similarities; in both cases, it will never be the same, but it can still be quite enjoyable. A lot of the enjoyment depends on the person's attitude. These different activities might be topographically different, but in some ways they are procedurally similar.

Clients can learn from a combination of direct experience and rational reflection. For example, a middle-aged client reported chronic problems arising from two dominant areas: recurrent marital discord and recent occupational stress as a long-haul trucker. During one session, he described a problem at work where his truck lights indicated mechanical problems. He believed the problem was in the wiring for the indicator light, thereby producing a false alarm. However, his supervisor insisted a mechanic should examine the entire electrical system.

The mechanical inspection caused a five-hour delay, and his customer was quite angry when he finally arrived. It was clear that a minor problem at work had caused a lengthy delay and much aggravation. As he described these events in session, he became visibly agitated, yet he managed to control his emotions, dealt with the delay, and remained calm when confronted at the delivery site. He was asked: "What did you do that helped you to remain calm?" "How is this situation, waiting for the mechanic, different from when you have to wait for your wife to get ready to go out for a movie?" "What can we learn from this situation at work to help you manage times of frustration at home?"

Questions can be used to examine the client's understanding and search for novel ideas. For example, an adult female client struggled with chronic feelings of depression that she had labeled as "dread." These feelings dated back thirty years and impaired her ability to enjoy life and be true to herself. In session, a series of questions helped explore these notions and look for new ideas.

THERAPIST: "How have you been this week?"

CLIENT: "Well, it's been a mix of ups and downs."

THERAPIST: "How would you describe your mood lately?"

CLIENT: "Too much of the time I have been feeling depressed, or that sense of dread."

THERAPIST: "Aside from the dread, how often have you felt okay?"

CLIENT: "Not very often. I cannot remember the last time I felt exhilarated."

THERAPIST: "Let's look for times when you felt okay, not exhilarated. I usually think of exhilaration as moments of really strong enjoyment, brief moments, nothing that lasts very long."

CLIENT: "I guess I feel okay sometimes."

THERAPIST: "Over the years, I have learned the word 'contentment' captures a lot of feelings that are good enough. How much of the time have you felt content during this past week?"

CLIENT: "Hmm, I guess fairly often. Maybe 40 percent."

THERAPIST: "If we created one of those new health monitors everyone seems to be wearing, and you had a simple wristband that tracked your mood, what would we learn about your feelings of contentment?"

CLIENT: "I guess it would show a range of moods, some good, some not so good."

THERAPIST: "When we finish today, if I ask you to increase your feelings of contentment from 40 percent and bring it up to 60 percent, what would you do to try to increase these pleasant feelings?"

CLIENT: "I don't know. I guess I'd try to keep busy."

THERAPIST: "How does keeping busy help increase your contentment?"

CLIENT: "When I am busy, I have less time to worry. I can usually focus on what I am doing and not get so bothered by 'what ifs.'"

THERAPIST: "If you want to sit and relax on a quiet day and enjoy the spring weather, what can you do to increase contentment during times that you are not really keeping busy?"

CLIENT: "I guess I could try to just relax, not worry so much. Too much of the time I end up worrying about problems that never end up happening."

THERAPIST: "What do you think—how much of contentment comes from external activities like keeping busy, and how much of contentment comes from internal attitudes?"

CLIENT: "I guess attitudes are more important. I tend to worry. I think I have some negative attitudes that drag me down, put me in a bad mood."

THERAPIST: "So what kind of attitude do we want to cultivate to help you feel content more of the time?"

CLIENT: "Maybe I could spend more time appreciating the good things I have in my life."

THERAPIST: "Okay. Currently, how often do you reflect on the good things in your life?"

CLIENT: "Not very often."

THERAPIST: "40 percent of the time?"

CLIENT: "Well, I might say even less often."

THERAPIST: "What would you consider some of the good things you have in your life?"

CLIENT: "Hmm, well clearly my husband and my kids, and my grandkids too."

THERAPIST: "Anything else?"

CLIENT: "Sure. We are all healthy. We own our home. We have a group of friends."

THERAPIST: "So if we help you stop, relax, and feel content, you can focus on your family, your health, your marriage, your children, your friends..."

As seen in this example, the therapist can use a series of questions to help clients explore the validity and utility of their own beliefs. There are many situations in which the accuracy of a client's beliefs may appear adequate but where his or her personal utility has become the major problem. Thus, a tendency to worry about the safety or health of loved ones cannot always be challenged for its accuracy; many people do suffer from the most recent virus or a current crime spree. However, there is often little benefit gained by devoting extended amounts of time to worrying about future possible problems or in ruminating about past problems. A simple pragmatic approach asks clients to evaluate whether certain beliefs are helpful or hurtful to their mood and their actions.

Conclusions

When exploring areas that rely on opinion, evidence may be inadequate to change a person's opinion, and persuasion may be too powerful (Bostock, 1986). Thus, logic becomes the main tool for rational dialogue and a mature exploration of ideas. The Socratic method is guided by the belief that true ideas, especially those pertaining to virtues and morality, can be established through logical reasoning (Allan, 1940).

According to the Socratic method, a therapist can use inductive reasoning to help clients develop a more rational approach to various situations, distance themselves from their emotional reactions, and become more objective in their interpretations and assumptions about various life events. The goal is to notice patterns, identify recurrent themes, and change any maladaptive views. Over time, clients can learn from their own life experiences and begin to develop more adaptive beliefs and behaviors.

SIX

Universal Definitions
What Do You Mean by That?

THROUGHOUT THE DIALOGUES of Plato, Socrates would ask for a definition and then examine it in a detailed and critical manner (Santas, 1979). When the definition proved unsatisfactory, Socrates used principles of inductive reasoning to examine various examples, searching for the common essence that could serve as a better definition (Tredennick, 1969). Socrates attempted to define various terms across the dialogues, including courage (discussed in *Laches* and in *Protagoras*), friendship (*Lysis*), justice (*Republic*), moderation (*Charmides*), and piety (*Euthyphro*). The search for definitions was frequently used to explore a person's understanding of the various types of virtue.

Socrates often maintained a persistent focus on a search for a valid definition. Socrates was not interested in clarifying the shared meaning or in understanding the person's individualized use of a term; he was instead curious about the nature or essence of the topic being discussed (Crombie, 1962). As a conversation continued, his interlocutor's initial definition was often rejected because Socrates could identify an example that conflicted with it (Santas, 1979). In addition, the definition was rejected because it conflicted with other beliefs held by the person (Santas, 1979). Thus, the search for a definition of universal appeal often ended in failure, or *aporia*. A final and acceptable definition was not necessary for the dialogue to be successful; the very process of exploring terms and their usage is illuminating (Haden, 1984). Nonetheless, it is best to view the search for definition as a valuable process that can guide psychotherapy and stimulate new and

UNIVERSAL DEFINITIONS

adaptive life views. There is no inherent need to arrive at an acceptable and final definition. The process itself can help therapist and client confront important issues and challenge long-held beliefs. Especially when the conversation becomes focused on moral issues, the therapeutic process becomes analogous to discovering new geographic territories that will always need further exploration (McLaren, 1989).

Ambiguity in terms is a sure cause of confusion in most discussions. Thus, client and therapist are encouraged to be specific and clear in the terms they use. In sessions I am often reminded of an amusing exchange during the Mad Hatter's tea party, in *Alice in Wonderland*:

> "Do you mean that you think you can find out the answer to it?" said the March Hare.
>
> "Exactly so," said Alice.
>
> "Then you should say what you mean," the March Hare went on.
>
> "I do," Alice hastily replied; "at least—at least I mean what I say—that's the same thing, you know."
>
> "Not the same thing a bit!" said the Hatter. "You might just as well say that 'I see what I eat' is the same thing as 'I eat what I see'!"
>
> "You might just as well say," added the March Hare, "that 'I like what I get' is the same thing as 'I get what I like'!"
>
> "You might just as well say," added the Dormouse, who seemed to be talking in his sleep, "that 'I breathe when I sleep' is the same thing as 'I sleep when I breathe'!"

A search for definitions can play a useful role in psychotherapy conducted according to the Socratic method. Most people rely on key terms without ever providing (or having) a clear or useful definition. Ambiguity in terminology can complicate the communication between therapist and client. At an even more basic level, unclear definitions can make it difficult for clients to hold accurate or useful views. A simple request for a definition can be helpful for the client and for the process of therapy. Thus, as in the Socratic dialogues, the therapist will search for a clear understanding of the client's subjective interpretation of different terms while also exploring the various ramifications of the client's definitions.

It is common for a therapist to shift from a focus on particulars and begin to search for more universal meanings and for the potential limitations of various terms. For example, "love," a term considered important to many people, can be examined for its definition and its logical extensions. In many discussions of love, clients will use a variety of adjectives to qualify their evaluations and interpretations. Thus, clients often mention their desire for "a good relationship" or "a successful marriage." If a therapist allows these terms to be expressed during a therapy session without pausing to explore their definitions, it seems fair for clients to assume that the therapist has followed their reasoning and agreed with the implicit logic in the statements. Hence, it becomes important for the therapist to stop and politely ask a client, for example, "What do you mean by 'a successful marriage'?" During a conversation, a casual question can be used to seek the denotation for a term: "What does that mean?" However, Socrates was more interested in the connotations of a term, as identified through the question "What do *you* mean?" (Calogero, 1957).

The Priority of Definitions

A search for meaningful definitions may be necessary before two people can hold a conversation with shared value and equal understanding. This idea is often described as "the priority of definitions." Thus, at times, Socrates focused on constructing useful definitions before any further dialogue could continue (Benson, 1990a). In a Socratic conversation, the intent is progressively to move through a series of weak initial definitions until a more adequate definition is reached (Chessick, 1982). Thus, a person cannot act with courage or justice unless there is a firm understanding of what such a virtue involves (Guthrie, 1975b).

Whether or not a person is aware of implicit definitions, it is clear that definitions often guide a person's thoughts and restrict an individual's views. A person needs to have a definition in mind in order to determine if any specific example belongs inside or outside the proposed definition (Seeskin, 1987). Simply asking for an example can be a useful tool in many discussions (Paul & Elder, 2008). However, a true definition must involve more than just a series of examples (Santas, 1974).

Universal definitions are used to help clients shift their focus from daily struggles to major life issues. Too often, clients become focused on recent events, interpersonal conflict, and negative emotional reactions. A therapist may find him- or herself caught up in trying to help manage a different crisis each week. Effective therapy relies instead on a broad and comprehensive treatment plan that addresses major life issues. A discussion in session can be used to confront topics such as "a good job" or "a satisfying relationship," which can be explored, defined, clarified, and modified as needed.

Instead of a true definition, clients sometimes provide a few examples that demonstrate their conception of the term. In the historical dialogues captured by Plato, Socrates would persistently guide the person to move beyond a string of examples, searching for the core essence that underlies the term, an essence that can be comprehended by the mind, not perceived by the senses (Dorter, 1994). An important term cannot be discussed in meaningful detail by using instances without a clear definition (Crombie, 1964). To be useful, a definition must not vary across particulars or circumstances (Grube, 1966). The aim is to culminate in a definition that has universal appeal and that does not vary over time, place, person, or situation. The search for definition needs to focus not on subjective opinions, transitory events, or temporary sensations but on lasting ideas that remain true for all people across all times (Copleston, 1946/1993). This universal nature is especially important when the discussion confronts the use of moral terms. Apparently, Plato had become troubled by the use of moral terminology that could be shifted to suit a person's current needs (Allan, 1940). In ancient Athens, people were willing to discuss topics such as virtue even when no one clarified the definition of the central terms (Seeskin, 1987). The situation has not changed much in modern times. Even today, discussions about morality and virtue are frequently guided by the individual's interests and desires at the moment.

The search for definitions helps move the focus of therapy from the specific details of daily life and back to the bigger picture of life goals and personal values. To be acceptable, a definition must capture the term in a broad and general manner and not rely on a string of examples (Santas, 1979). The search for universal definitions becomes a central strategy when therapy examines the virtues as related to daily life. However, definitions can also be relevant when discussing a mixture of other topics.

Definitions can be identified and clarified in a collaborative manner. The goal is to define common words that most people already use, though perhaps with some degree of ambiguity or confusion in the understanding of the concept behind the term. Thus, Socrates is not asking for a dictionary definition but for a clarification of an individual person's use of a common term (Robinson, 1971c). Many common labels become rigidly attached to a limited range of behaviors, such as the definition of "father" and how it defines the role of a father in relationship to his son.

A collaborative dialogue is useful. When a definition is provided by a teacher, even college students are likely to accept the definition in an uncritical manner (Rocklin, 1987). It is useful to explain, explore, and discuss the use of various terms. In the Socratic method, the goal is to explore broad issues and their implications for everyday life. Thus, definitions are not simply focused on semantics. When confronting issues related to evaluations, definitions are not limited to how something is said but how it is seen. It can help clarify the steps involved in cognitive processing as an idea moves from initial observation to the person's interpretation and onto the broader conceptualization. This process can be especially difficult with complex terms that reveal important issues such as what is considered "normal." Clients struggle with issues such as "Is it normal to wash my hands thirty-five times a day?" or "Am I a failure if I drop out of college?" Therapy can explore what "normal" and "failure" mean.

The Necessity of Knowledge

According to the Socratic method, knowledge is essential for any meaningful discussion to take place. Basic knowledge is required before a person can explore the meaning of a definition or determine whether an example satisfies the definition (Benson, 1990b). A series of questions can be used to seek the essence of the term (Robinson, 1971c). However, people often provide a string of examples. Unfortunately, as I have stressed repeatedly in this chapter, it is not effective to define a term through a series of examples (Beversluis, 1987). Examples can be examined to see if there is a common pattern running through all individual cases that may be classified as the essence, or *eidos* (Beversluis, 1974). Nonetheless, the therapist must persistently search for the essence of a term. Specific examples are subject to change and variation, whereas the core essence of a term should remain immutable across time and circumstances (Guthrie, 1975b). For example, beautiful things may vary and decay, but the idea of beauty remains the same across objects and over time (Edman, 1928).

UNIVERSAL DEFINITIONS

The Socratic dialogue includes several steps. First, the therapist (gently) points out inconsistencies across various beliefs held by the client (Mackenzie, 1988). The therapist can test a definition by applying it to a series of examples and identifying any counterexamples or by examining how internally consistent a person's set of beliefs is (Santas, 1969). Second, the client may become distressed or confused after becoming aware of the inconsistencies he or she holds, and the discussion may hit a temporary impasse (Mackenzie, 1988). The state of confusion ideally will stimulate curiosity and an eagerness to learn (Watson, 1985). Third, several new lessons are learned along the way toward revealing any inconsistent beliefs (Mackenzie, 1988). Throughout the dialogues, Socrates aimed at identifying and revealing any logical inconsistencies across different beliefs held by the individual. However, it is also important to bear in mind that a coherent set of beliefs can still be incorrect (Goldman, 1988).

In some situations, a single counterexample can be used to reveal a critical flaw in the person's definition (Whiteley, 2014). Socrates often relied on counterexamples to demonstrate the need to revise the person's original definition (Beversluis, 1974). Thus, a "dog" may be defined as "a furry animal that has been domesticated into a common household pet," and this definition can be supported by examples that include the dachshund, spitz, Great Dane, Labrador, and Pekingese. However, this particular definition of "dog" can be refuted by the presence of a single cat, which is also a furry animal that has been domesticated into a common household pet. Thus, the problem with a definition constructed exclusively by examples can become obvious if even one counterexample exists.

Definitions can be used to clarify terms that clients use to label themselves or their life experiences. Socrates would elicit a starting proposition and move forward, working on the assumption: "what consequences must follow if the initial hypothesis is assumed to be true?" (Taylor, 1953). For example, an adult female client with depression referred to herself as "a failure." When asked why she would make such an extreme statement, she replied: "Just look at me. I'm an adult with no job. I don't even have a car. I had to ride the bus to get here. Only failures ride the bus." The therapist stopped all discussion of other issues to confront this central erroneous definition. The therapist considered the dilemma: If we accept the belief that the client is a loser because she rides the bus, then it seems to imply that everyone who rides the bus must be a loser. The following sequence of

UNIVERSAL DEFINITIONS

questions posed by the therapist can help capture the process used by the Socratic method to confront a definition, explore its limits, and hopefully force a client to reject the original definition as erroneous and damaging. (Most client replies have been omitted to focus on the queries posed by the therapist.)

"Seriously, do you believe that everyone who rides the bus is a failure as a person?"

"What if I told you that just last week, I rode the bus?"

"Do you feel that everyone who drives a car is not a failure?"

"Really, so anyone who drives a car is successful?"

"Have you ever met someone that was deeply troubled but had their own car?"

"What about the news last night about the people who stole an ATM and drove away in a pickup truck? Would they be considered successful simply because they had their own vehicle?"

"What does it mean to be a failure?"

"How about the opposite? What does success mean to you?"

"So success is not just measured in dollars earned, right?"

"So how is success measured?"

"Is there a chance that you might be being a bit hard on yourself?"

"What does it mean to be a success?"

"Do you know many people that meet all of your criteria for being a success?"

"Can you think of anyone who meets those criteria but for some reason you do not consider them a success?"

"How would you evaluate a professional athlete who earns millions each year but spends the off-season at wild parties and indulging in selfish interests, without any effort to give back to the local community?"

"Can you think of someone who does not meet your criteria but for some reason still seems successful in life?"

"How might you evaluate a person who works at the local food pantry, making minimum wage, but playing a central role in caring for others?"

"What can we take away from our discussion?"

The client responded: "I guess based on our conversation today, I feel that labels like success and failure are somewhat dangerous, especially when applied to a person as a whole." When encouraged to continue expanding on the lesson learned here, the client continued: "Maybe money and income

[74]

are not the end-all of success. Maybe it is more important to be a good person, doing good work to be helpful to others in some way." Through this dialogue, the client was able to reach the conclusion that most people hope to contribute to society by finding a job that aligns with their strengths, talents, and personality style. Income is only a small part of a job and does not always reflect the degree of contribution to society made by that particular type of employment.

Obviously, during the therapy session, each of these questions was asked in a slow and supportive manner. The therapist wanted to use each question for multiple purposes: to gain more insight into the client's subjective experience, to help the client appreciate the limits of the definition, and to support the client as a person who may have flaws and limitations, just like every other person in the world. Furthermore, this example, by itself, is quite minor. However, if confronted in a thoughtful and playful manner, it can become a reference point. In later sessions, the therapist can refer back to this discussion, asking the client, "Do you remember two weeks ago when we talked about whether all bus riders are losers? Do you think you might be applying similar harsh standards to yourself again?"

Many psychotherapy sessions help clients sort through various life events. Clients often appreciate time spent reviewing their recent concerns, worries, struggles, and interpersonal conflict. Therapy discussions can center on problem-solving strategies and common advice for approaching difficult situations. However, it is essential for the therapist to avoid the role of a dogmatic wizard who offers advice and solves problems for the client. Instead, therapy is best aimed toward promoting the client's personal strengths and expanding the client's interpersonal resources. These broader strategies can have more lasting benefits for each client.

Because of the current reliance on time-limited psychotherapy provided once per week, most sessions begin with a review of recent events. This focus on current events becomes more pronounced when sessions are even more widely spaced, such as meetings scheduled every two weeks or once per month. In such cases with infrequent therapy sessions, there is little chance of being able to do substantive work on the client's psyche.

Often, clients can be asked to complete a therapeutic activity (sometimes referred to as homework assignments) to bridge the gap between sessions. Some activities can help the client formulate a definition, and then in session, the therapist can use a series of questions to anticipate the logical implications that follow (Seiple, 1985).

A focus on universal definitions can help clients move beyond current events or trivial concerns, which can help keep the therapy's focus on bigger issues related to their problems. The discussion can search for recurrent themes in the client's life, clarify central goals for each client, or correct the improper use of emotionally loaded terms. In the *Theaetetus*, Socrates clarifies how true knowledge is not relative. For example, one person comes in from the cold and puts his hand in a pail of water, and the water feels warm. A second person has just finished warming her hands by the open fire, and when she places her hands in the pail of water, it feels cold. In many ways, a person's view (for example, a subjective rating of warm or cold) is relative to his or her comparison reference point. Thus, if a client spends time with wealthy friends, he or she may feel deprived and impoverished. However, if the same client spends time with an unemployed cousin who is struggling with unpaid bills and mounting debt, he or she may feel well off and financially secure. Similar issues arise with a person's view of career success or romantic relationship. It can be helpful to shift clients away from this type of specific comparison and focus on the broader issues involved in happiness and success in life.

The Content of Universal Definitions

Universal definitions are often used to clarify important terms that appear relevant to the client's therapy. The terms are likely to focus on general topics with broad appeal. The topics are likely to be aligned with the client's struggles or potential improvements, and they are often focused on common, widely used terms that are often misunderstood or used improperly. For example, terms such as "love" can be central to many clients' struggles. Even Plato struggled with the topic of love, as seen in his *Symposium*, an interesting if not confusing dialogue. It is common to hear clients express their concerns that "no one loves me" or "I just want to find the right person and fall in love." However, many people lack an unbiased definition of love. Questions can be used to shift the client's focus from specific examples to a more abstract level (Padesky, 1993). For example, a client made the claim: "If I am not in a relationship, it means no one loves me." The therapist responded with a series of questions, presented in a slow, casual, conversational format: "So does that mean that everyone who is not in a relationship is unloved?" "Does it mean that everyone who is in a relationship is loved?" "What about situations where the relationship has become physically or verbally abusive?" "What about the situation where there may be no abuse but the relationship has cooled and the couple has become cold and stiff toward each other?" When attempting to define love, the therapist was not looking for a detailed answer but instead wanted the client to confront the key issues involved, to elucidate her personal values for a successful intimate relationship. Additional questions can be used to explore and define love: "What makes someone attractive to you?" "What does it mean to be attractive?" "Do these same qualities apply to make you attractive to someone else?" "So attraction relies more on personality than physical appearance?"

Over the past twenty-five years, numerous psychological terms have become common in the lay public. News reports and television talk shows often confront problems such as sleep disorders, eating disorders, and psychosexual problems. Because of the interest from the media, a variety of diagnostic terms are now used by the general public, often incorrectly. For example, it is relatively common for clients to describe strong feelings of anxiety and worry as a panic attack. However, in reality they have occasional periods of anxiety that do not meet diagnostic criteria for panic. In a similar manner, many clients report they suffer from bipolar periods, and they may even use the diagnostic label "bipolar" to capture their periods of mood swings. However, upon closer diagnostic inspection, they may experience periods of moodiness that fail to meet the criteria for bipolar mood swings.

There are a variety of general terms that may be confronted during a psychotherapy session. Definitions can be used to help clarify the evaluative standards being used by the client. Certain terms are strong and carry intense emotional connotations. For example, many clients use common terms such as "horrible," "terrible," "catastrophe," "success," and "failure." These terms can each have destructive powers on the client's moods and expectations. Even the opposite terms ("amazing," "awesome," "incredible," "unbelievable") can be problematic because they are often incorrect, inaccurate, or exaggerated out of proportion to the real events.

To clarify a client's use of key terms, the therapist can ask a series of questions: "What makes something a catastrophe?" "Would a flat tire on your drive home qualify as a catastrophe?" "Would a bad cold that causes you to miss an annual costume party constitute a catastrophe?" "So what type of event might we need to see if we want to use the term 'catastrophe'?"

Over the course of the discussion, clients can begin to appreciate that terms such as "horrible," "terrible," or "catastrophe" are best reserved for major events, like those covered on the national news where people have died. Terms like "catastrophe" should not be used for common and relatively trivial events that create a sense of discomfort or minor inconvenience for the client.

The use of various evaluative labels can become quite complicated when paired with a specific important life domain. For example, many clients are hoping for "a good marriage" or a "good relationship." Alternatively, many clients complain of "a bad marriage" or "a horrible boss." When helping clients expand their interpersonal connections, the discussion can explore notions of what defines "a close friendship" (figure 6.1). Over the course of the discussion, clients may appreciate the stages involved when cultivating new social bonds, gradually helping the relationship move from "stranger" to "acquaintance," which would designate the level of intimacy commonly found with a coworker or neighbor. It then takes more time together to move from "acquaintance" to "friend" and includes sharing time, identifying common interests, and developing a deeper bond. Finally, it often takes years to move from "friend" to "good friend," "best friend," or "confidant." Thus, over

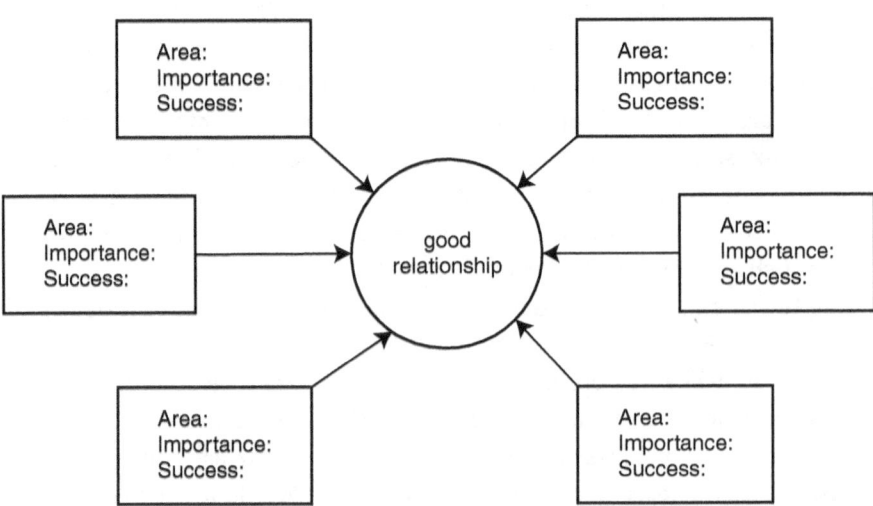

Figure 6.1 Worksheet for clarifying a definition.

the course of sessions, therapy can help clients move from a focus on specific situations to confronting broader concepts, such as the meaning of friendship.

A mixture of evaluative terms seems to underlie negative emotions such as sadness, frustration, or anger. It can be useful to clarify or avoid the use of terms like "unbearable," "impossible," "worthless," "loser," "enemy," or "jerk." These terms are often extreme, inflammatory, and unhelpful. Therapy can help redirect clients toward appropriate terms and useful goals. For example, a female client was recently married but already struggling with interpersonal differences with her husband. In session, she was asked, "Which would you prefer, a good relationship with your husband, but little contact with your friends, or lots of time bonding with your friends, but before long you are divorced?" It was clear she wanted to maintain and improve her marriage, yet she continued to struggle with her implicit definition of an ideal marriage. In session, she was asked, "Okay, maybe we can eventually aim to get both, but for now, for the sake of argument, what can you do to make it happen?" "Would it be possible to be successful in both areas?" "What can you do moving forward from here to protect both your marriage and your most important friendships?" Later sessions continued to explore her view of an ideal marriage, trying to help her develop realistic goals and standards for her relationship.

Another life domain that often gets paired with strong evaluative standards can be found in a person's occupation and income. For many people, "a good job" means making a lot of money, and after a moment, many people will add "without working too hard." However, we can easily see that a corrupt politician or a drug dealer would satisfy these standards. Therefore, the definition must be rebutted and replaced with a better one.

When attempting to confront, challenge, and potentially refute a client's original definition, a series of questions can be used. For example, when clients struggle with a perceived lack of success, it can be useful to ask, "Can you think of someone who has made a lot of money but might not be considered successful?" Ideally, the client will recall a famous celebrity legal case, such as the financial advisor Bernie Madoff, who fleeced investors of millions of dollars. Alternatively, clients may provide the name of a friend or colleague who satisfies the question. Then, the opposite side of the definition can be challenged. The therapist may ask, "Can you think of someone who seems successful even though their finances are quite limited?" Again the client may identify a famous historical figure, such as Mother Teresa, who gave up family wealth in order to help the poorest people of India. The goal is to encourage clients to reevaluate the criteria they use to define important concepts such as success.

Refuting Incorrect Definitions

In some therapy sessions, the dialogue can confront and refute the improper use of terminology. Ideas are tested according to two criteria. First, the definition is examined for its correspondence with available evidence (do the beliefs correspond with personal experience?); second, the definition is examined for its coherence (is the belief aligned with other beliefs held by the individual?) (Capaldi, 1969). In addition, when attempting to seek definitions for the virtues, a definition can be seen as inadequate for several reasons, including that (1) the definition is too broad or too narrow in scope, (2) the definition does not clarify which acts are virtuous and which are not, (3) the definition fails to identify the core quality required for the virtue to be deemed present, or (4) the definition does not adequately explain what quality makes the act qualify as a virtue (Kraut, 1984). Thus, a variety of issues can be examined when testing the utility of a term's definition.

The process relies on a fluid interchange between collection and division (Guthrie, 1971). Collection refers to gathering a variety of examples that both parties agree meet basic criteria for the construct being defined. Then, division is used to examine these instances in order to uncover the common quality present in each.

Some clients struggle with the notion of "normal" and become upset when they deem themselves not to qualify as normal. This may revolve around their physical appearance, emotional reactions, or daily habits (for example, how much time they spend washing their hands). Refutation plays an important role in the Socratic method. The discussion aims to help clients begin to confront the limits of their understanding and find flaws in their reasoning. The Socratic therapist requests a definition from the client but then examines it in detail. When imperfections and contradictions are highlighted, the person is forced to reject the original definition and search for a better way of understanding the term (Reale, 1987). A person should be willing to reject any definition when it contradicts other core beliefs (Seeskin, 1987).

Definitions Related to Evaluative Standards

Therapists should avoid imposing their own definitions on the client. However, the therapist does begin by assuming that there are flaws, limitations, and biases in the client's initial definition. Furthermore, by helping the client see the limits of their definition, the therapist can help the client develop a broader and more balanced perspective on the terms used to evaluate the client's own life. The process often involves showing clients that their definitions conflict with other beliefs they hold more strongly (Taran, 1985). The Socratic method relies on a process of critical evaluation to remove any erroneous beliefs, and then it begins constructing more useful views (Richmond, 1955). For example, a client placed tremendous pressure on herself because of the struggles she experienced as a budding artist. She was experiencing recurrent depression, loss of enjoyment, and social withdrawal. She was struggling with her career path as an artist and with her family's criticisms of her choice of career. She expressed pervasive doubts over her career choice and was becoming skeptical of her artistic ability. She was afraid she was disappointing her parents and that she could not satisfy their expectations for her success.

> THERAPIST: "What does success mean to you?"
> CLIENT: "I don't know. I guess like my friend who already owns several rental properties, or I have another friend who just finished his master's degree at Yale. They seem successful."
> THERAPIST: "So how much of your success is evaluated by comparisons with others?"
> THERAPIST: "How much of success is based on a person's job versus other areas of their life?" (Here, as therapist, I deliberately start shifting the focus from her idiosyncratic views to the more universal qualities that should apply to most, if not all, people.)
> THERAPIST: "If you had to choose, would you rather make art that sells quickly but not be satisfied as a creative artist, or love your art but no one else seems

to notice it?" (This question uses a forced-choice format, hopefully proposing two viable options from the client's perspective.)

Personal examples are acceptable, but the client may be confronted with any logical inconsistency that exists across these statements. The therapist can ask: "Well, based on these examples, does it seem that success may be independent of wealth?" When the client agreed that success and wealth are distinct dimensions, the conversation returned to where it had started: "So, what is the best way for us to view success?" At this point, the client paused and replied, "I don't know." The therapist must be careful to not push too hard or overwhelm the client's belief system.

> THERAPIST: "Would you rather make a lot of money designing the latest fad, like Beanie Babies or Pokémon cards, so you can afford a nice car and a great home, or remain a starving artist who might be wildly creative and years ahead of your time, but your work is only discovered and appreciated after you have died, so you remain poor, living in a rusty trailer home?" (Obviously, this is a long question. However, the client was bright, educated, and fully involved in the discussion. I had to track her ability to follow such a convoluted question, but had I chopped it into segments, it would have lost the contrast that underlies the key decision.)
>
> CLIENT: "These are hard questions. My head chooses the money, but my heart says art."

Because these questions confronted a core area for the client, I asked her to write about her thoughts during the interval between appointments. She was asked to write her views of life success in terms of both career and social aspects. She spontaneously added a third area, the "inner reserves needed to get though hard times." During the next session, we explored her term "inner reserves" and how those reserves can help her with her career and her social functioning. She started to see that her inner reserves could help her improve both her social functioning and occupational success. The notion of inner reserves led to a discussion of persona, which she differentiated into her surface persona and her "true self." In terms of her true self, she was able to describe herself as a good person with a flair for creativity, but she also saw that she tended to be vain and had a strong fear of failure. A Socratic view of inner reserves includes the courage to confront risk, a determination to pursue important goals, and a pathway to become self-reliant (Slote, 2007).

During the same session, the client also identified a good friend who tended to remain calm and tolerant, so the therapist and the client discussed visualizing her friend and using him as a role model for tolerating struggles. Again, these issues were discussed in order to confront her definition of success versus failure. The dialogue continued to explore the frequency and breadth of her view of failure in her life. The therapist asked her to describe a recent event that had ended in her "failure." She described a class project for which she had to design a novel household tool or appliance. She had done quite well in several other similar projects in the past. However, this time, the item she had designed worked, but poorly. She was ashamed of it and her low grade and hid it in her apartment.

THERAPIST: "How would your easy-going friend cope with such a failure?"
CLIENT: "He would just show it to friends and laugh about it."

The dialogue explored her internal reserves, continuing to use the term she had provided in an earlier session. The therapist asked what internal reserves could help her tolerate a minor experience with failure. She was unable to identify anything useful. The therapist explained that internal reserves seem like something inside a person, like an invisible cloud we cannot see or touch.

THERAPIST: "As a minor experiment, would you be willing to try something this week, where you deliberately fail at something?
CLIENT: "What? No!"
THERAPIST: "Well, how would you react now to this recent project that 'failed' if we looked at it differently, as if it had been a planned failure?"
CLIENT: "Well, I guess I could tell people I had planned to mess it up. Then it would not be a problem."
THERAPIST: "Okay, but I'm not sure if people would believe you."

The client realized it would result in the same evaluation. An external evaluation of failure and her internal knowledge of failure were being compounded now by lying to friends. The important thing would instead be her honesty and intentions to improve. Therapy then focused on the inner reserves (again building upon the term proposed by the client) necessary to tolerate failure without embarrassment. In addition, therapy continued to explore her definition of success and how it was potentially derailing her career.

Some discussions will explore the client's idiosyncratic definition of abstract qualities such as love, friendship, or happiness. When clients are struggling to find a romantic partner, they may focus heavily on their view of beauty. It can help to explore notions of "lasting beauty" or "inner beauty," such as those qualities captured in the comedic movie *Shallow Hal*.

According to the Socratic method, the discussion aims to collect examples, search for logical inconsistencies, refute erroneous beliefs, and ultimately search for the central essence that truly defines the term. This can be a slow process, and if it is not pursued in a thorough fashion, the results can be spotty. When first asked to define a term in session, clients often provide a simple but incomplete definition. It is useful to keep the initial question posed in a simple and supportive manner. The therapist can listen to the client and use the client's own words. However, it can be important to stop any forward movement of the dialogue and ask the client, "What did you mean by that?" Thus, the therapist can step out of the flow of the dialogue by asking clients to clarify what they mean when they use a certain term: "Let me stop you for just a second. When you talk about *a good marriage*, what do you have in mind?" In this way, the therapist keeps the discussion focused on the main topic and ensures that both parties understand the central terms and agree to the meanings. For example, in intimate relationships, minor areas of conflict can generate feelings of disrespect. When a wife was asked to provide a definition of respect, her replies were often limited to a string of negative examples of when she felt her husband had acted in a disrespectful manner. As the conversation moved forward, the "disrespected" person was helped to clarify that she desired a good bond with her husband as equal partners in the relationship, aiming not simply at specific actions but seeking respect for her as a person, with a sincere tendency to value her opinion, seek her advice, and see the benefits of her qualities even when they were vastly different from his own. Respect goes beyond patiently listening to her when she complains about her day; it meant asking, understanding, helping, being patient, and sacrificing for the life they now share.

UNIVERSAL DEFINITIONS

Definitions can be used to clarify various behavior labels, such as polite versus timid behavior. When confronting a client's informal definitions, the goal is to help improve communication and clarify idiographic meanings applied to certain terms. Clear and useful definitions can provide a pathway toward strength and virtue (Hawtrey, 1972). When terms related to virtue have been confronted in session, the clients may begin to review events from a different vantage point, and they may begin to reevaluate their own behaviors. The therapist might use counterexamples to evaluate the general definition and test the limits of the original definition. The therapist should look for logical inconsistencies across two beliefs, collect a variety of acceptable examples, and then search through them for common themes and

Table 6.1

Theme	Common Hazardous Words	Adaptive Alternatives
External pressures	Should, ought, must	Can, will, hope to, do, did
Negative expectations	Can't, impossible, hopeless, futile	I will
Excessive demands	Need, demand, deserve	Want, desire, would like
Magnified negative outcomes	Awful, horrible, terrible, catastrophe, miserable, dismal	"not a big deal," "could be worse," "it's not great," unfortunate
Extreme ratings of frequency	Always, never, everything, nothing, everybody, nobody	Often, frequently, sometimes, rarely, some people
Extreme ratings of outcome	Perfect, failure, loser, worthless	Okay, good enough, pretty good
Excessively positive evaluations	Amazing, fantastic, incredible, wonderful, awesome, unbelievable, extraordinary	Pretty good, very nice, interesting, fun, enjoyable
Tendency for absolute certainty	"I know," absolutely, "100 percent," "I am sure," definitely	"I think," "I believe," "in my opinion," "I expect," "I hope"
Signs of hatred	Hate, enemy, evil, can't stand	Dislike, "hope it can change"
Negative global labels	Idiot, moron, imbecile, jerk, asshole, freak, weirdo, stupid	Person, friend, neighbor

recurrent patterns, seeking the core essence that remains present across the range of examples.

Conclusions

Psychotherapy sessions can be used to explore and refute problematic beliefs and can help clients develop new and more accurate definitions for a variety of key terms. Sometimes, the focus on definitions can become a search for potential causes of their struggles and thereby help guide clients' behavior toward more adaptive strategies. The goal is not simply to ensure a proper dictionary of terms but to examine the implications of certain emotionally loaded words. Table 6.1 provides a set of words and phrases to avoid because they could magnify negative emotions or maladaptive behaviors.

Accurate definitions play an important role in the search for knowledge (Santas, 1979) and therefore can be useful in many therapy sessions (Overholser, 1994a). Based on notions expressed by a client, the therapist may push for a useful definition. A dialogue can help clarify whether the client's term is being used accurately and reduce the client's tendency to make statements that overgeneralize beyond the facts. Accurate definitions can help broaden the client's view of life, goals, and evaluative standards.

When exploring definitions, it may not be necessary to reach a final, acceptable definition. Although specific examples are used, a definition needs universal generality and deep understanding. Through the process of exploring words and confronting their proper usage, clients may become better able to appreciate how words influence thoughts, which guide emotions and behaviors.

SEVEN

Socratic Ignorance
Accepting What You Do Not Really Know

SOCRATIC IGNORANCE IS a term derived from the Platonic dialogues, capturing Socrates's belief that he knew nothing; he was nonetheless considered wise because he was the rare person who was aware that he knew nothing. Obviously, for Socrates to become aware of his own ignorance, he needed to have a strong background of knowledge and experience (Austin, 1987). In a similar manner, the quotation attributed to Albert Einstein is useful: "The more I learn, the more I realize how much I don't know." This paradox can be useful to help therapists and clients distance themselves from their beliefs and begin to approach life with curiosity and wonder (Anderson & Goolishian, 1992).

A quotation attributed to Socrates makes the claim that "there is only one good, knowledge, and one evil, ignorance." I hope to clarify and revise this statement to: "The only good is wisdom, and the only evil can be found in ignorance." To justify my rephrasing of Socrates, let me first explain that according to Socrates, knowledge often pertains to specific facts. However, facts can be overturned or refuted by later investigations. In contrast, wisdom refers to a broad and comprehensive view of life and life meaning. Ignorance refers to the consideration of the false beliefs that a person holds as knowledge he or she really lacks. Socrates admitted to his own lack of knowledge about most issues, but he was troubled that *most people retained a false belief in their own knowledge*; that is, most people remain ignorant of their ignorance.

Socrates never claimed to have knowledge or intelligence, merely the insight that comes out of the awareness of one's own ignorance. Socrates explained: "I know that I have no wisdom, great or small" (*Apology* 21). A short bit later, Socrates continued to expand his ideas about ignorance: "I found that the men most in repute were all but the most foolish; and that others less esteemed were really wiser and better" (*Apology* 22).

There is a paradox captured in the Platonic dialogues, and scholars hold different views as to whether Socrates truly believed himself to be ignorant (Hawtrey, 1972) or valued and respected his own beliefs as true (Vlastos, 1985). This dilemma was created by the discrepancy between Socrates's public proclamations of ignorance and the certainty with which he confronted others (Vlastos, 1985). In a similar manner, many mental health professionals may profess knowledge about a wide range of topics. However, when questioned or challenged, they are likely to back down and reveal some gaps in the evidence available to support their beliefs. In most cases, it is best when a therapist accepts a state of ignorance. There should be a willingness to move forward with knowledge even if that knowledge is seen as fallible (Vlastos, 1985). If curious, therapist and client can work together to explore ideas and gather information.

As described by Socrates in the *Apology* (21–22), Socrates's friend Chaerephon asked the Oracle of Delphi, "who is the wisest of all mortals?" The Oracle replied, "no one is wiser than Socrates." Chaerephon was thrilled and hurried back to Athens. Socrates was puzzled by this proclamation because he doubted his own beliefs; he was also aware that the oracle often spoke in riddles (Brickhouse & Smith, 1983). This proclamation initiated Socrates's search for knowledge among the leaders of Athens, in the hopes of refuting the oracle by finding at least one person who possessed more wisdom than Socrates (Brickhouse & Smith, 1983). Socrates asked the generals about courage, but they seemed confused by his questions. Socrates asked the politicians and judges about justice, but they gave inconsistent answers. Socrates asked the poets about love, but they rambled in an almost incoherent manner. The more Socrates investigated the wisdom of others, the more clearly he saw their ignorance. Central to the Socratic method is the tendency to accept your ignorance while endlessly striving to overcome it.

Some people display a self-deceptive illusion that they know what they do not really know for certain (Cushman, 1978). When a person claims to know something, they are excluding the possibility that they may be wrong

(Cross & Woozley, 1978). Socrates engaged poets, politicians, and craftsmen in philosophical discussions, seeking to understand their knowledge and learn from the experts of his time. However, Socrates soon realized that these "experts" had only false beliefs and that they often thought they knew things that in reality they did not fully comprehend (Stalley, 1986). As he continued with his conversations, Socrates began to see the elenchus as a conversational tool that could help remove a person's false knowledge (Stalley, 1986). However, when Socrates explored ideas about the virtues, the conversation often ended in confusion. Socrates explained: "The result of the whole discussion has been that I know nothing at all. For I know not what justice is, and therefore I am not likely to know whether it is or is not a virtue, nor can I say whether the just man is happy or unhappy" (*Republic* 1.355–56). Thus, Socrates's claim to wisdom was limited to his awareness of his own ignorance (King, 2008). Expressions of ignorance are important to clear the path for a search for true beliefs and a better way of living (Copleston, 1946/1993).

It must be emphasized that Socrates was not trying to win an intellectual debate but simply aiming to remove the false conceit of knowledge that is not really present (Edman, 1928). A common goal of a Socratic dialogue lies in helping people accept their ignorance in areas where they thought they knew something (Guthrie, 1971). According to the Socratic view, the ability to admit one's ignorance is the starting point for the journey toward true learning (Navia, 1985). The same attitude applies to a therapist. Whenever a person claims "I know it is true," there is a tendency to believe that nothing can change the individual's mind (Unger, 1975). Theories are best viewed as educated guesses (Popper, 1979). When people remain thoughtful enough to accept that there are things they do not know with certainty, they can be more tolerant of other people (Cropsey, 1995). Certainty often implies simplicity of thought and a rigidity of beliefs and values. An adoption of Socratic ignorance shares similarities with the Zen principle of the beginner's mind, which remains open to new ideas and free from preconceptions or expectations.

Beliefs and Opinions Are Fallible

Most "knowledge" is actually mere belief or opinion. Many ideas we hold are not based on actual knowledge or firsthand experience. Opinions are preferences that may or may not be true (Gambrill, 1993). Furthermore, even when a person's beliefs could be supported, the belief does not qualify as knowledge unless the individual holding that belief can support and defend the view. Informed opinion can be viewed as being halfway between knowledge and ignorance (Prior, 1985). However, even when an opinion may later turn out to be based in correct knowledge, opinion remains different from knowledge (Taran, 1985). To be considered knowledge, the person's beliefs must be seen as more than a true belief reached via a lucky guess (Goldman, 1986) or random coincidence. Even a broken watch is correct twice a day.

When people view information as beliefs, not facts, it becomes easier to admit there is some evidence to support the claim, but the person also remains open to new information that could cause a shift in perspective (Cross & Woozley, 1978). For many topics confronted in therapy sessions, both therapists and clients should remain cautious about what they "know" to be true, as most views are mere opinions that can be overturned later when new evidence is revealed. During the age of Columbus and Copernicus, most people "knew" that the world was flat and "knew" that the sun rotated around the earth.

It can be useful to remember that even science can be wrong and that scientific claims have been overturned many times. Mental health professionals should realize there have been many times when society or academia "knew" something to be true that was later recanted. Keeping this in mind can promote a bit of intellectual modesty. Errors of false knowledge have continued into modern times. For example, there have been findings that show vaccines cause autism in children. However, it was later found that the investigator falsified his own data and manufactured these beliefs, sometimes to endorse ideas that would boost investment in a new medication. Scientists and researchers should accept that their methodology is not infallible. No matter how carefully gathered or copious the evidence, future work could overturn the findings (Odegard, 1982). For example, recently there have been mixed reports about the health benefits of various foods (caffeine, wine, cholesterol). In many cases, an initial report claimed that daily ingestion of some food substance is bad for a person's health. Later, subsequent reports reveal that a food substance is either harmless or is now claimed even to be good for a person's health. Many research findings are later reversed by subsequent research.

Opinions can be accepted in a blind or naïve manner; true knowledge typically requires effort, evidence, and activity (Versenyi, 1963). Beliefs and opinions can later be found to be incorrect. Opinions can be confronted, examined, and overturned (Seeskin, 1987). However, the therapist does not lecture to clients but simply shares different beliefs and opinions about various events. As noted by Socrates (*Apology* 49d–e), "if you have a different view, speak and explain it to me." However, it can be difficult to appreciate both sides of an argument, especially involving controversial topics, whether major (is there life after death?) or minor (is the Loch Ness monster real?).

Did astronauts land on the moon in 1969, or was it staged in a studio? Do vaccines cause autism, or was the data falsified? Are crop circles made by aliens or by pranksters? Is the earth five thousand years old or many millions of years old? Was John F. Kennedy assassinated by a lone rogue sniper, or was there an elaborate conspiracy to eliminate the president? The honest answer to each of these questions is "I do not know." We rely heavily on beliefs, and we often lack true facts. When we can accept the dominant role of beliefs, it becomes easier to appreciate the malleability of most situations. Are people mad at me? Do my coworkers like me, or can they barely tolerate my presence? These diverse situations can be confronted and sometimes effectively changed by challenging the belief system that underlies the person's mood and behavior.

Socrates often engaged in discussions of abstract concepts in his search for clear knowledge of the virtues. Although Socrates possessed his own speculative ideas about virtue, he was sincere about lacking knowledge, clear definitions, or an understanding of the core essence about these important topics (Fine, 1992). Socrates knew he lacked the type of knowledge he was seeking, even though his companions often confidently claimed to hold that very knowledge (Evans, 1990). Thus, Socratic ignorance is best viewed as a sincere disavowal of knowledge or factual certainty, a disavowal that helps promote an openness to learning, exploring, and discovering things about one's self or others.

Obstacles to an Open Mind

Many people display a confirmation bias, defined as the tendency to notice, accept, seek, and remember information that supports their preexisting beliefs while largely ignoring, disregarding, or belittling information that might challenge or refute their views (Evans, 1989; Goldman, 1986). One sees such a biased way of processing information especially around charged topics such as politics, abortion, same-sex marriage, gun control, and recreational drug use. However, the tendency to seek information that conforms to our beliefs extends further than social and political issues. People will seek and remember information that supports their views about, for example, their own self-value, the stress or conflict they experience on the job, and disparities in the workload inside their own family. It can be important to help clients approach each of these situations in a more open-minded manner, so they become willing to gather information in an honest way. This strategy underlies the notion of collaborative empiricism that is central to cognitive therapy (Kazantzis et al., 2013).

Ignorance can include a combination of false beliefs and a misguided faith in those beliefs (Schmid, 1983). Thus, the problem becomes compounded when a person holds mistaken beliefs and fails to accept that these beliefs might be false (Seeskin, 1987). It makes sense that a false trust in one's beliefs will block one's search for new information. People will not search for information they believe they already possess (Versenyi, 1963). When attempting to remove the false conceit that one knows what one does not really know, falling into a state of confusion can be a useful part of the process (Seeskin, 1987). People are only ready to search for new knowledge after their false conceit of knowledge has been removed (Benson, 1990a).

Effective psychotherapy requires a mental health professional who is well trained, competent, and skilled. Professional competence derives from adequate education, supervision, and training. Professional competence as a psychotherapist begins in academia, with a strong foundation in coursework and the theory and research underlying the field of psychology, psychotherapy, and psychiatric diagnosis. The development of one's professional skills continues through ongoing clinical experience. Expertise is usually related to a specific area and built upon years of experience.

Despite the importance of competence and expertise, a Socratic therapist will maintain a strong sense of intellectual modesty. Neither therapist nor client should take a superior role in therapy (Beck & Emery, 1985). Sometimes, clients talk using third-person phrasing, but their comments may actually be directed at the therapist. For example, a client recently claimed:

"No one listens to me. I am not stupid. I have some good ideas." He was quite upset as he described recent conflicts with his wife and his teenage son. However, it was helpful to work on the assumption that the message could apply to his view of his therapist. Thus, the therapist, proceeding slowly, showed respect for the client's input and praised the client when he offered a viable suggestion for managing the conflict at home. The client's negative energy subsided, and they had a productive session.

There is a subtle difference between modesty and humility. Modesty refers to not overrating oneself, out of the awareness that everyone has strengths and weaknesses and that there is no common standard for evaluating the worth of different people; humility is a false underrating of the self (Ben-Ze'ev, 1993). All people should remain modest and cautious about their beliefs unless those beliefs have managed to survive a Socratic elenchus (McPherran, 1996). Intellectual modesty helps a person remain open to new ideas, recognizing that all views are potentially fallible and every perspective is limited in some way (Kaplan, 1979). Modesty is important for protecting the relationship between therapist and client (Woolfolk, 2015).

Skepticism and Uncertainty

It can be useful to retain an attitude of skepticism and uncertainty about one's factual knowledge. Perhaps the term "ignorance" is a bit harsh. The phrase "disavowal of knowledge" may be more useful in most clinical settings (Vlastos, 1985). A Socratic therapist tends to disavow knowledge of most topics. An even more gentle term, "rational uncertainty," is a useful way of viewing Socratic ignorance (Ballard, 1965). A Socratic therapist remains curious and inquisitive while nonetheless being cautious and somewhat skeptical of most views.

Philosophers often try to avoid the notion of certainty. In most circles, certainty implies absolute certainty, the belief that one's knowledge is 100 percent accurate and certifiably true. However, too many situations have been trusted, valued, and respected only to see the evaluation reversed a few years later when the claims have been rejected, disproven, mocked, and ridiculed. Reversals can be found in popular opinion, such as when a particular fashion statement later appears quite humorous or when reporters uncover troubling revelations about beloved celebrities who have been found guilty of major crimes. Equally important reversals have been found in science, such as dietary recommendations that become debunked or the latest medications that are marketed as safe and effective but later provide fertile ground for wrongful-injury lawsuits.

One way Socrates expressed his own ignorance was via skepticism (Hawtrey, 1972). Skepticism can be a valuable tool, especially when people are exposed to a variety of sources that provide conflicting information or mixed reports. It can be best to make most rational decisions in terms of probabilities and practical utilities and examine beliefs based on the validity of sources and probabilities of accuracy (Lehrer, 1971). Therapists should not assume they understand the client beyond a superficial level as an outsider. Therapists should avoid using empty statements and trite platitudes such as "I'm sure everything will be okay," "Hold on, you'll do just fine," or "You have nothing to worry about." Each of these statements presents a view that extends beyond the therapist's ability to appreciate the client's subjective distress. Furthermore, statements such as these disavow the client's experiences and invalidate the client's concerns. In a way, these statements are implying "You are wrong, I am right, I know more than you" or "Your problems seem minor, so get tough and move on." Such implicit attitudes can be damaging in a therapeutic environment. Socratic ignorance helps encourage both a modest view of one's self and a relentless process of inquiry guided by critical evaluation (Evans, 1990).

False knowledge can produce potentially damaging self-fulfilling prophecies. For example, a client was struggling with her teenage daughter, raising the girl as a single parent in a home with limited finances. She became quite upset when her daughter made preliminary plans to move away for college. Instead of worrying about her daughter's adjustment to college, the client worried about her own future, anticipating that she would spend her days alone. In her sadness, the client tended to withdraw from most people and activities, which aggravated her distress. In session, the therapist asked: "How do you know that life will be bad after she moves out?" The client did not have a sudden shift of perspective, but over several discussions, the client was gradually able to see that she did not know for certain and that she could begin making daily changes to become more active with friends and other family members. Here we see how uncertainty is better than holding a false belief and a negative expectation.

Reasons to Become an Ignorant Therapist

"Ignorance" is important whenever a therapist uses a systematic series of questions to push the therapeutic dialogue forward. Socratic questions work best when the therapist approaches the discussion with a genuine sense of curiosity (Kennerly, 2007). To be useful, any profession of ignorance cannot be a sham. To be effective, the therapist's disavowal of knowledge must be genuine, representing a sincere modesty and a genuine interest in the client's life, problems, and subjective experience, even when those might be different from the therapist's own views.

Socrates placed a high value on helping others know what they know and respecting what they do not really know (Santas, 1979). Ignorance was liberating to Socrates, and it can help all people become open to new ideas (Kierkegaard, 1841/1989). However, the individual must struggle through various incorrect beliefs along the path toward learning the meaning of major ideas (Vlastos, 1987).

When Socrates confronted areas that seemed confusing, it helped expose the person's false conceit of knowledge. As captured in the dialogue *Meno* (84), Socrates summarizes the events occurring during the dialogue with the slave boy:

> He did not know at first, and he does not know now. . . . But then he thought that he knew, and answered confidently as if he knew . . . now he has a difficulty, and neither knows nor fancies that he knows. . . . Is he not better off in knowing his ignorance?. . . Have we done him any harm?. . . We have certainly . . . assisted him in some degree to the discovery of the truth; and now he will wish to remedy his ignorance.

It can be helpful to admit that a therapist's theoretical orientation is likely to restrict how a client's problems are viewed and how treatment should be conducted (Joyce-Moniz, 1985). When people feel certain about their beliefs, they become dogmatic and tend to exclude any new information that might conflict with their preestablished beliefs; they therefore become unable to correct errors in their beliefs (Unger, 1975). When therapists can accept their ignorance, their style in therapy sessions may change. Effective therapists must be willing to test the validity and confront the limitations of their own knowledge, beliefs, and principles (Poland, 2008).

With the current emphasis on empirically supported treatments, many novice therapists yield to the urge to serve as an expert. The therapist may feel obligated to solve the client's problems, provide useful advice each week, effectively becoming more like a radio call-in show's host than a therapist. It is important for therapists today to retain an attitude of curiosity when working with clients. Curiosity helps the therapist accept a role as coauthor in constructing a new life story and a better way of interpreting the situation (Cecchin, 1992). The therapist is aided by general principles and useful theories about psychotherapy and the development of adaptive behaviors. These principles and theories can provide the guidance that manuals, being overly restrictive and limited, cannot.

In this age of manual-driven psychotherapy, Socratic ignorance may help reduce the therapist's reliance on psychoeducation or bibliotherapy (that is, lecturing the client on psychological theories and assigning them "helpful" readings). Socratic ignorance shifts the role of the therapist from being an expert who brings a didactic and deductive style to being a collaborator who is eager to explore, learn, and help understand each client as a unique person. A trained mental health professional may have a competent grasp of psychological theories and research studies but may not know how well any of the treatments might work with a specific client. Also, it helps to keep in mind that any theory is not the only theory but merely one, hopefully helpful view of a complex situation.

Rather than spout his own view, Socrates aimed to elicit his interlocutors' opinions (Stokes, 1986). When people expressed their views, Socrates would use questions to encourage them to expound on those views (Stokes, 1986). The use of Socratic questioning aims to remove any false appearance of truth (Meyer, 1980). Thus, questions are used to elicit, clarify, and confront a person's beliefs and values. The use of Socratic questions can sometimes feel like a bucket of cold water thrown on a client's sleeping intellect (Howard, 2011). Done skillfully, a series of questions can help people appreciate what they know, as distinguished from beliefs they do not truly understand (Paul & Elder, 2007).

Intellectual modesty promotes a search for new information and a sincere desire to learn. Unfortunately, when people trust their knowledge, it can create a sense of pride or even arrogance (Drengson, 1981). The fundamental impediment to learning is the assumption that the person already possesses knowledge (Burger, 1981). However, becoming aware of ignorance can help foster a sense of compassion and intellectual modesty (Drengson, 1981).

A therapist should remain sincerely interested in learning about each client's life, recent and past events, and the subjective experience of each client. Socrates explained: "In reality none of these theories come from me; they all come from him who talks with me. I only know just enough to extract them from the wisdom of another, and to receive them in a spirit of fairness" (*Theaetetus* 161). The underlying assumption that client and therapist are starting from a place of ignorance can promote a collaborative approach, one relying on consensual validation to determine acceptable beliefs. People should be willing to take risks, make errors, and admit mistakes (Seeskin, 1987). Therapists may bring knowledge of psychology, but the client remains the expert on their own life experiences, views, opinions, personal values, and beliefs about virtue (Vitousek, Watson, & Wilson, 1998; Anderson & Goolishian, 1992).

Help Clients Accept Their Own Ignorance

A central strategy in the Socratic method involves reducing clients' faith in their beliefs. The Socratic dialogue aims to remove false beliefs and encourage clients to begin reexamining what is truly meaningful in life (Schmid, 1983). Erroneous beliefs can become self-perpetuating because clients' ignorance blocks them from seeking new evidence or testing the validity of their beliefs (Seeskin, 1987). The stronger a belief is held, the more evidence is needed to challenge it (Unger, 1975). It seems counterintuitive, but beliefs tend to become most dogmatic and impervious to counterarguments around issues that are complex, ambiguous, and have no clear answers (Unger, 1975). Thus, topics such as religion and politics can be difficult to confront in an unbiased manner.

Questions are used to see if clients have evidence to justify their beliefs (Swain, 1981). Sometimes, the questions continue until the client is willing to admit ignorance about the belief (Stein, 1991). When challenged, it is not acceptable to support one's beliefs by relying on popular opinion or appeal to authority (Seeskin, 1987).

Attitudes and opinions are best viewed as hypotheses to be tested. Clients often hold erroneous beliefs and misguided expectations. Most forms of cognitive therapy aim to elicit, challenge, and replace erroneous beliefs. Clients can move away from certainty and instead aim for probabilities and degrees of corroboration (Popper, 1979). A crucial element of therapy involves examining the evidence for the client's inferences, assumptions, and conclusions (Beck, Rush, Shaw, & Emery, 1979). Furthermore, it can be useful to evaluate beliefs in terms of both their accuracy and utility.

In a typical session, a Socratic therapist will ask questions that have no correct answer. Instead of seeking factual information, the questions will aim to explore the client's opinions, desires, experiences, and expectations. A therapist can guide the session without having a predetermined destination in mind (Padesky, 1993). The therapeutic dialogue seeks observable evidence and sound logic to support beliefs. The therapist uses a series of questions to search for evidence (figure 7.1). A therapist should not hide behind hypotheticals (Seeskin, 1987). Instead, the discussion should focus on actual situations that have been encountered in the client's life experiences. It usually works best to stay anchored within real examples, especially those situations that may have been encountered by either the client or the therapist. Each person should be willing to examine the probability of various beliefs or hypotheses (Klein, 1981). A belief may be viewed as acceptable even if it has not been confirmed if it has an adequate level of probability and a low probability of counterevidence (Klein, 1981).

Therapy can gently dislodge the client's view, untangling beliefs and fact. The therapist may ask the client: "How strongly do you believe it?" "What would it take to convince you that you might be wrong?" "As we sit here today, do you feel it could be possible to be wrong about this issue?" A temporary goal is to create a sense of confusion in the client, after established beliefs have been challenged. There is a risk of humiliation when a person's beliefs are shown to be mistaken (Seeskin, 1987). However, it should be respected that people may be influenced by goals and values that have not been examined in any type of clear or objective manner (Schmid, 1983). The Socratic dialogue helps guide clients from a state of ignorance, in which they falsely believe they "know" something, toward a more open and inquisitive mind (Robinson, 1971a). The process involves refuting false beliefs, similar to how a physician may perform surgery in order to heal the body (Seeskin, 1987). After becoming frustrated or confused, the client should become motivated to learn new ideas that can be tested and supported. When a dialogue makes a person feel ignorant and confused, the person may begin to abandon false options (Drengson, 1981).

A therapeutic dialogue can help clients to reach the point where they can say: "I have certain beliefs, but there is little I truly know." Clients can thereby discontinue their reliance on unsupported beliefs. A client's beliefs can be challenged by finding examples that fall beyond the scope of the original definition or by showing items that are inaccurately contained within the definition (Robinson, 1971b). Thus, when clients make extreme statements ("*I know* my neighbor is mad at me"; "Why bother applying for jobs; *I know* no one will hire me"), there is a risk of self-fulfilling prophecy; if clients behave as if the belief is true, it will become more likely to be supported because they will not apply for any jobs and therefore not get hired. When clients can inductively examine their own life experiences, it may be possible to identify situations in which their beliefs were refuted or to uncover evidence that may conflict with the current belief. For example, an adult male client claimed, "*I know* my brother would never loan me the money I need"; therefore there is no reason even to ask him. Sometimes, a simple behavioral task can be negotiated to test the accuracy of the prediction. If, in spite of his beliefs, the client is encouraged to ask the brother for money, and if the brother indeed agrees to loan the funds, not only does it refute the specific belief, but it can be used to help dislodge the certainty with which other beliefs are held. It can be useful simply to convey the attitude "you won't know unless you give it a try" (Beck & Emery, 1985). However, for many clients, a bit more gentle pressure may be needed to ensure their compliance with the task.

Beliefs can be tested by working on the assumption that if the initial hypothesis is true, all derivative claims must also be true (Taylor, 1953). Thus, if the belief is accepted as true, where does it take the discussion (Prior, 1991)? The therapist may use questions to push for useful definitions, seek contradictions, or search for a clash between words and actions displayed by the client. Throughout the discussion, it is important to search for alternative explanations and to pay attention to negative examples that do not correspond to a person's preestablished beliefs (Gambrill, 1990). Even when no clear and acceptable answers are obtained, it is still important to ask the key questions (Mitchell, 2006). The goal is to help clients learn the process of questioning their own beliefs.

Conclusions

The acceptance of one's ignorance lies at the heart of the Socratic method (Overholser, 1995a). To be effective, the disavowal of knowledge must be sincere (Lesher, 1987). Intellectual modesty in the therapist is essential for rapport and collaboration with most clients. Socrates avoided speculation and did not pretend to know things he did not (Hackforth, 1933). As a therapist or a client, it can be honest and useful to make an open claim: "I am ignorant; I do not know very much. I have a lot of beliefs and opinions, but my views could change if I get new information." By accepting one's limited and fallible knowledge, the Socratic therapist does not teach or preach to the client. Instead, both therapist and client respect the limits of their knowledge and jointly search for useful information. Throughout each session, the therapist must strive to balance structured plans with spontaneous redirections. Both therapist and client should remain active and collaborative throughout the process of guided discovery and self-motivated change.

Therapy involves a process whereby a thoughtful discussion is used to examine the evidence to support a client's beliefs. A belief is found to be true based on its ability to withstand logical scrutiny via the dialectic; a belief is not true because it adheres to or supports the person's faith or feelings (Nehamas, 1999). The therapist aims to help clients become reasonable people, that is, to have reasons for everything they do. Even with attitudes, it is important to be reasonable, that is, to have reasons for one's beliefs (Unger, 1975). Therapist and client should both be willing to examine the validity of their own beliefs and values (Schmid, 1983). A therapist can help clients articulate their implicit assumptions and evaluate the evidence supporting their beliefs. It can be best to examine beliefs in terms of likelihood, coherence, and degree of justification (Odegard, 1982). Clients can learn to evaluate the quantity, quality, diversity, and coherence of evidence available both for and against their beliefs (figure 7.1). The therapist may use a broad spectrum of questions to explore various pieces of evidence but always allows the client to make the ultimate decision to accept or reject the input. To be trusted, a person's beliefs should be clear, useful, and stable over time (Roochnik, 1990). The therapist can use a series of questions to help clients examine the information that supports or contradicts their personal beliefs (figure 7.1). Furthermore, evidence can come from direct personal

SOCRATIC IGNORANCE

	Supportive evidence	Contradictory evidence
View from personal perspective		
View from a different person, e.g., comedian, superhero		
View from a different time, e.g., jump ahead fifty years		
View from a change of location, e.g., impoverished country		

Figure 7.1

experience, circumstantial pairings, or hearsay (evidence as told by someone else or read in a book, journal, or online news feed) (Gambrill, 1990).

Ignorance steers people toward improper goals and values, making it more likely for someone to engage in harmful activities or pursue worthless goals (Brickhouse & Smith, 1994). Therapy can help enhance the client's critical-thinking skills and rational approach to problems.

EIGHT

Guided Discovery

Searching Together as a Team

CLIENTS ARE MORE likely to value the lessons learned in therapy when they play an active role in the discovery process. Guided discovery is used throughout psychotherapy sessions to emphasize the collaborative and exploratory nature of the learning process. The therapist helps clients confront, search, explore, and change their attitudes and expectations. Guided discovery is compatible with most current forms of psychotherapy and helps extend the widespread utility of the Socratic method.

An exploratory style of the therapy process is directly aligned with cognitive therapy. In his seminal writings, Beck and colleagues (Beck, Rush, Shaw, & Emery, 1979; Beck & Emery, 1985) describe the use of guided discovery and collaborative empiricism. Both of these strategies are closely aligned with the Socratic method (Dahlen, 2007). However, many contemporary therapists have shifted to a more direct and rapid approach to therapy sessions. Most strategies that incorporate psychoeducational elements encourage the therapist to act as an expert teacher who lectures to clients about common forms of mental illness and the treatments that are available. In these structured sessions, the therapist sets the agenda for the session, provides information verbally or in written forms and handouts, and assigns homework to be completed by the client between sessions. The therapist moves firmly into a superior role and demonstrates professional expertise toward the client. These roles of teacher and student can disrupt the collaborative nature of therapy and may impair the establishment of an effective therapeutic alliance. A therapeutic conversation is better served by retaining the view that the client, not the therapist, is the expert (Anderson & Goolishian, 1992).

Guided Discovery

A Socratic dialogue is a cooperative inquiry (Klein, 1986). Guided discovery is a process designed to help clients search for their own solutions, set their own goals, and devise plans for moving toward those goals (figure 8.1). Therapy is not directive or manipulative but involves two people working together as a team, striving to expand options and find solutions. Therapy entails a conversation with two participants searching and exploring (Anderson & Goolishian, 1992). The goal is to focus on the self-discovery of problematic patterns and possible solutions (Mahoney, 1974).

Guided discovery can be examined in terms of its content and in terms of the process it takes during therapy sessions. It uses the stages of social problem solving as a framework for therapeutic discussion (Overholser, 2013). Clients can learn new strategies for approaching difficult situations. The

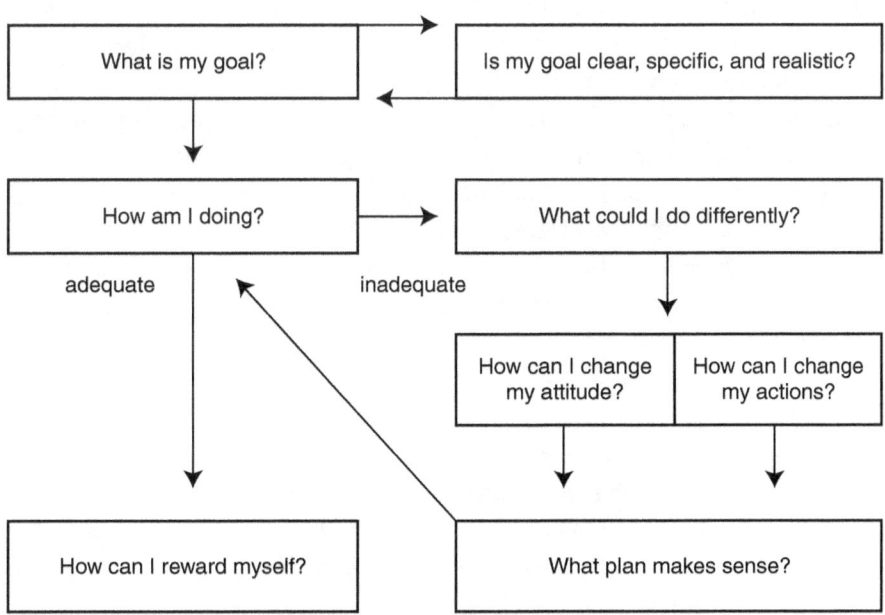

Figure 8.1

therapist remains careful to let clients make all decisions (Overholser, 2012b). Therapy can help clients confront, examine, and change misguided beliefs or destructive attitudes. Over time, therapy helps develop core beliefs that remain positive but realistic (Overholser, Braden, & Fisher, 2010).

Over the years, I have become less concerned about the accuracy of a client's views and more concerned about the utility of the person's beliefs. The truth value of a belief is not as important as the subjective impact that belief has on the person (Efran, Lukens, & Lukens, 1990). Therapy can help clients develop an adaptive attitude that views problems as a normal part of life. The therapist uses questions to guide the discussion, define a problem in a clear and manageable form, divide a complex situation into components, and clarify goals for positive change. The reliance on questions helps keep the dialogue conversational instead of educational. Socratic questions help stimulate the client's interest in a process of search and discovery (Hoyt, 1996).

A therapist can use questions to stimulate creative thinking, encourage clients to break out of their habits, and approach a problem from a new perspective (Efran, Lukens, & Lukens, 1990), both in terms of attitude and behavior. Guided discovery helps clients move from a strong conviction in their beliefs to a questioning mode more open to new ideas (Padesky & Beck, 2003). Then, the therapist can help the client make decisions. The discussion can help clients develop a plan, evaluate different options, anticipate potential problems, identify risks and benefits, evaluate the personal effort required, and estimate the probability of success. Finally, therapy can help clients put the changes in effect, try new responses to difficult situations, and monitor the effects on their mood and functioning and on the social ramifications of their new interpersonal style.

Socrates considered himself as a gadfly, annoying a horse but prodding it to continue moving forward, though without attempting to steer its path (Parker, 1979).

> If you kill me you will not easily find a successor to me, who, if I may use such a ludicrous figure of speech, am a sort of gadfly, given to the state of God; and the state is a great and noble steed who is tardy in his motions owing to his very size, and requires to be stirred into life. I am that gadfly which God has attached to the state, and all day long and in all places am always fastening upon you, arousing and persuading and reproaching you.
>
> (*Apology* 30–31)

This notion of an annoying gadfly can be useful in therapeutic and classroom settings. The therapist's questions aim to provoke a new reaction and help stimulate a change of attitude. A Socratic therapist can poke and prod, using questions to stimulate further exploration of an important topic while still allowing the client control over the path and direction of the discussion. Likewise, the instructor who serves as a gadfly may engage students by challenging their central beliefs and values (Regan, 1973). The therapist uses a variety of questions to prod the client, with the goal of uncovering knowledge and insights the client already possesses but that are latent in the depth of the mind (Kidd, 1992).

The process of guided discovery requires patience combined with gentle persistence from the therapist (Overholser, 2017). The client retains autonomy over the content and direction of the discussion (Seeskin, 1987). The process is similar to traveling with a well-respected tour guide. A Socratic therapist makes sure that the client will not get lost. A guide keeps the client safe but allows the client to make many of the decisions about destinations and when to take a break. Throughout the dialogue, the therapist reassures the client that they are making progress and moving forward with the discussion (Seeskin, 1987). The therapist helps encourage the client to continue searching and believing that useful answers are within reach (Seeskin, 1987).

Socrates viewed himself as an intellectual midwife, claiming:

> My art of midwifery is in most respects like theirs; but differs in that I attend men and not women, and I look after their souls when they are in labor, and not after their bodies; and the triumph of my art is in thoroughly examining whether the thought which the mind of a young man brings forth is a false idol or a noble and true birth. And like the midwives, I am barren.... I ask questions of others and have not the wit to answer them myself.... I neither know, nor profess to know, anything of these matters; you are the person who is in labour, I am the barren midwife.... I hope that I may at last help to bring your own opinion into the light of day; when this has been accomplished, then we will determine whether what you have brought forth is only a wind-egg or a real and genuine birth.
>
> (*Theaetetus*, 150, 157)

Socrates felt that many beliefs, when voiced, seemed like wind-eggs.

Collaborative Empiricism

Similar to guided discovery, the notion of collaborative empiricism derives from cognitive therapy. However, collaborative empiricism is much more focused on confronting the client's attitudes and expectations, searching for evidence to support or refute various beliefs. Collaborative empiricism highlights two central components: the therapist and client working together in a collaborative manner and a search for empirical evidence that can support or refute a client's beliefs (Overholser, 2011). In addition to the dialogue that occurs in session, clients can be asked to complete a wide spectrum of behavioral activities between sessions in order to maintain their mental focus and help them confront important issues.

Some clients struggle with major life decisions and ask their therapist to make the decision for them. For example, an adult female client wanted to know if she should marry her long-term boyfriend or end the relationship. This "either-or" of extreme choices derived from her mixed view of their long-term compatibility. A simple metaphor can help capture the process of some therapy sessions. The therapist acts in a manner similar to a parent helping a child assemble a jigsaw puzzle. If the parent takes over, the puzzle can be assembled quickly, but from the child's perspective, there is likely to be minimal enjoyment, no ownership of the end result, and nothing learned from the process. However, if the parent collaborates with the child, the parent can explain the basic strategy of turning over all pieces so the picture is facing up, gathering all corner and edge pieces, and assembling the border. The parent may refer to the picture on the puzzle box to see how it should look when completed. Together, parent and child can search for patterns in the bits, and the child can assemble the pieces.

Analogously, the therapist can help the client sort through his or her own thoughts, feelings, and inclinations, while being careful to avoid pushing the client down one path or another. Too often, beginning therapists will rely on a structured listing of pros and cons of each choice. Although such a tabular approach can be useful, many high-functioning clients have already grappled with the pros and cons. Both questions (during the session) and writing assignments (completed between sessions) can be used to propel clients forward.

Behavioral activities often involve asking a client to spend time confronting an important issue and writing down the client's thoughts, reactions, or conclusions. In this case, the therapist asked the client to write her personalized definition of love (seeking a universal definition that could apply to all people in a romantic relationship). Upon asking the client to write a definition of love, the therapist noticed the client pause, look askance, and not say anything. The therapist stated: "Let's be sure we have something for you to do that fits with where you are at right now. If this writing activity is not a good fit, tell me now. I would rather we drop it now and replace it with one of the other two ideas I had in mind as we were discussing your concerns." Given that opening, the client asked for a second option as a new topic about which to write. The therapist said, "For a different topic, how about you write a paragraph or two of personalized wedding vows. This would be an almost poetic, romantic tribute of your undying love, something you would tell your husband at the altar in the middle of your wedding." The client paused and asked for the third option. The therapist laughed and said, "Okay, but I am going to run this like an old-fashioned game show. You can keep option 1 or 2, or you can trade for what's behind the curtain, but if I give you the third option, you must accept it." The client smiled, thought for a moment, and said she would write her definition of love. When suggesting behavioral activities, the therapist's goal is not to solve the problem or remove the dilemma. Furthermore, the therapist is not trying to get the client to see the situation from the therapist's perspective. Too many therapists (and instructors) end up playing the "Guess what I'm thinking" game. If the therapist has an idea, it is best to share it with the client, perhaps framed as a genuine question: "Would this be helpful or unlikely to help?"

When using behavioral activities to help guide clients, the true Socratic goal is to get behind the client and push, hoping the client will aim in a useful direction. The therapist can have a range of options in mind, hoping to find the best writing topic to fit the client and the current session's themes. Whenever giving clients topics on which to write, it is usually best to offer a mixture of choices, helping to sort through the underlying concerns. A central aspect of cognitive therapy relies on helping clients see their lives from a different perspective. Sometimes this involves a shift of view across person, place, or time. In the case of the writing activities, the focus could have been framed as passionate vows of undying love, legal vows written as a prenuptial agreement, or as a sad apology and explanation for canceling the wedding. Later, as the client moved toward strengthening the relationship, the client was asked to write the speech she might give at her golden wedding anniversary, summarizing how her love had grown over the past fifty years. Again, the goal aimed to produce a cognitive shift from daily annoyances to lasting love.

Sometimes, a therapist makes a mistake and leads the conversation down a dead end. Similarly, in the dialogue *Meno*, Socrates went down a wrong path, thereby showing the slave boy not to trust blindly the suggestions offered by Socrates (Seeskin, 1987). The discussion should be viewed as an inquiry into something not yet understood (Brown, 1967–68). Plato was capturing common misconceptions, and he displayed a remarkable insight into typical and common mental errors (Goldin, Pezzatti, Battro, & Sigman, 2011). Plato was trying to show why it is so important to think independently instead of trusting the opinion of an expert (Day, 1994; Moravcsik, 1994).

Sometimes, guided discovery can be encouraged through enigmatic phrases. For example, a client who failed to appreciate how her childhood had shaped her view of romantic relationships was asked to write about the phrase "Sometimes, the future lies in the past." After a week of thinking and writing about this phrase, she was in a somewhat better position to move forward with a thoughtful dialogue in session, aiming to help her confront issues lingering from her childhood and how they continue to influence her choice of romantic partner and, alternatively, help her see that perhaps the best choice of a future romantic partner would be a return to her ex-husband. Finally, therapy helped raise the possibility that she might reenact similar patterns with a new boyfriend unless she learns to appreciate the overpowering role her past plays on the dynamics of any intimate relationship.

Whenever clients are upset about an issue, it is important to treat the topic as a sensitive matter. For example, a divorced client reported that she felt ugly and asked what the therapist thought about her looks. It would not have been appropriate for the therapist to respond with praise, compliments, or common platitudes about her appearance or attire. The therapist should not say "You are beautiful" or even "I think you look fine." No matter how attractive or unattractive the therapist might find the client, it becomes a sensitive issue and too often becomes almost a parody of cliché answers. Physical appearance involves a subtle personalized evaluation. Also, a novice therapist may be likely to suggest a new hairstyle, a makeover, or a new style of fashion. Each of these suggestions appears overly directive and misses the mark in terms of inner beauty and how the client feels about her self-worth. To get to deeper issues, the therapist could ask a series of interrelated questions, including: "What do you think makes a person attractive?" "What could you do to enhance your degree of attractiveness in those ways?" "What do you want to do to move forward from here?" Note that each question avoids beauty and appearance while subtly replacing it with the term "attraction," which can go much deeper than common standards of physical beauty. In addition, each question aims to promote independent decision making and self-evaluation in the client.

Effective listening develops empathy and helps the therapist understand the client's fears, frustrations, and fantasies (Graybar & Leonard, 2005). Effective listening can be guided by a skillful use of questions. For example, a passive male complained about remaining in a loveless marriage. He was dissatisfied with the relationship but unwilling to do anything about it. Through a series of questions, he was helped to explore his values, goals, and self-direction: "How do you view your wife?" "How do you think your wife sees you in the marriage?" "How do you think your son sees you in the family?" "How do you want your wife and son to view you?" "In fifteen years, when your son is grown and married, what type of marriage do you hope he will have?" "What can you do to help make sure that happens?" "What can you do now to start building a better relationship with your wife?"

Throughout the dialogue, it is useful for the therapist to focus on a sincere collaboration and not have a predetermined answer in mind when asking the client a question. Instead, a collaborative exploration is guided by the simple notion that this issue is a solvable problem, not an overwhelming catastrophe. For example, a female client reported that her daughter was dating a man who had previously brought violence into the home. He had been arrested and spent six months in jail; now he was due to be released. The girl's boyfriend had previously made threats of violence. The client reported her worries but seemed largely oblivious to the risk of harm and likelihood of danger. In such a high-risk situation, if the therapist remains nondirective, session time could be used to help the client express her worries and feel temporary relief. However, in lieu of remaining nondirective, the therapist made use of a Socratic strategy by asking a series of questions designed to expand the client's awareness and help her assume a more proactive stance. "Let's jump ahead three months. What do you think is more likely to happen; the boyfriend moves back with your daughter, and they live happily ever after, or the boyfriend gets angry, becomes violent, and seriously injures your daughter?" The client could see the risk. The therapist asked, "What could you do now to increase the chances of a good outcome here and reduce the likelihood of the violent scene?" The therapist kept in mind that the client is a competent adult and that, with a change of perspective, she would be able to identify a range of options that might help her get through a difficult situation.

It is important for therapy to focus on client autonomy, promoting an internal locus for the changes (Ryan & Deci, 2008). Psychotherapy works from inside the client's internal point of view (Ryan & Deci, 2008). Experienced therapists recognize the importance of clients' experiences as a guide to possible solutions (Williams & Levitt, 2007). Socratic questioning can help clients realize they have more talent or knowledge than they had thought previously (Stein, 1991).

The Process Within Psychotherapy Sessions

Therapy needs to focus more on process issues and less on desired outcomes (Ryan & Deci, 2008). Guided discovery helps clients clarify and test their own beliefs by using their own experience, observation, and experimentation (Padesky & Beck, 2003). For example, a divorced client described her current concerns. Last night, her ex-husband had stopped by unexpectedly. He told the client that he had just moved back into town but was between jobs and had no place to stay. He wondered if he could stay at her place for a few days. She brought this dilemma into therapy, expressing her mixture of feelings. When asked for the reasons for and against granting his request, she could easily see that she wanted to help, felt concerned about his well-being, and always wanted to be helpful to those in need. She was implicitly asking for permission to let him back into her home and into her life. However, here the therapist must resist the temptation to direct the client's life and decisions. Instead, the guided discovery process is enhanced by the therapist's selective use of questions (Padesky, 1993). When the discussion focused on reasons to deny his request, she quickly remembered the many reasons why their marriage had failed, how manipulative he could become, and his verbal abusiveness when things did not go his way. To the therapist, it seemed

GUIDED DISCOVERY

like a simple decision. However, this was not the therapist's decision to make. Additional questions were used to explore this situation:

> THERAPIST: "First, let me ask why you feel you should help him."
>
> CLIENT: "I feel I should do it. I know I'll feel guilty if I say no to him." (At this point, the client is moving toward becoming more willing to helping him.)
>
> THERAPIST: "Well, now let me ask the opposite—why should you refuse his request?" (Now, the client moves toward saying no to the request.)
>
> THERAPIST: "How will things play out if you let him stay for a few nights?"
>
> CLIENT: "I guess it would be okay, if he behaves."
>
> THERAPIST: "What was he like back when you two lived together? How easy or hard was he to get along with when you were married?"
>
> CLIENT: "Well, he could be a real jerk. He always had trouble holding a job, and he could have a temper, a bad temper, but it was just words. He never hit me."
>
> THERAPIST: "How will things play out if you say no now?"
>
> CLIENT: "He will get mad, maybe start yelling or even break things in my home."
>
> THERAPIST: "Okay, so regardless of what he has asked for, what could you do to be helpful to him?"
>
> THERAPIST: "Are there ways that you can be helpful to him without necessarily letting him stay at your home?"
>
> THERAPIST: "Where do you *see* things going from here?" (This initial question is deliberately wide open, so the client will share her views of the future, but it does direct her attention onto the likely events of the upcoming months.)
>
> THERAPIST: "Where do you *want* them to go from here?" (Note the verbal emphasis used to highlight the client's desires and clarify what is in the best interests of the client.)
>
> THERAPIST: "How else could you respond to his request?"
>
> CLIENT: "Maybe I could just set a limit of three nights."
>
> THERAPIST: "And what is likely to happen on the morning of day four?"
>
> CLIENT: "Well, I would hope he would move on, but sometimes he can get stubborn, even rude."
>
> THERAPIST: "How can you be helpful while not putting yourself at risk?" (Here, the therapist helps guide the discussion toward strategies instead of goals.)
>
> THERAPIST: "Do you have other thoughts about how to move forward, here?"
>
> CLIENT: "I guess I could give him money for a hotel room."

THERAPIST: "How much money would it take? Do you have the funds to support him?"

CLIENT: "No, not really. Maybe I could let him stay in my garage. It's really not that messy."

THERAPIST: "Do you expect this relationship will remain on friendly terms, remain as good friends, or be more than friends?" (This question is presented with a few subtle pauses to clarify the multiple-choice nature of the question.)

THERAPIST: "So you have a few ideas for helping him. What makes the most sense for you?" (This question establishes the client as the person in charge of the situation, not the ex-husband and not the therapist.)

CLIENT: "Maybe I could let him use my phone to call his old friends. Maybe one of them would help him."

THERAPIST: "What is likely to be best for *you*?" (Note the emphasis on the optimal plan for the client. Some clients are kind and generous individuals that may minimize their own needs or desires. By highlighting what is best for the client the therapist helps her aim her focus on the future, her own gains, and how she can move forward to make things happen in a positive manner.)

THERAPIST: "What's the difference between being kind and taking unnecessary risks?"

As the conversation continued, she began to see a range of possibilities, including loaning him some money, calling one of his old friends on his behalf to ask for a place for him to stay, or letting him spend a few nights in the garage instead of in her home.

Imagine, as an analogy, that the client and the therapist were out on a stroll together. Over the course of the discussion, the two walk in a slow arc; over time, they turn 180 degrees. This gradual shift of direction is very different than, for example, the therapist grabbing the client by both shoulders, shaking her, and demanding that she turn around.

Conclusions

Guided discovery is a central therapeutic strategy used in cognitive therapy (Scott & Freeman, 2010). The Socratic method relies on a process of shaping that helps clients gradually modify their responses (Calero-Elvira et al., 2013). Questions can be used to structure a process of guided discovery, helping clients reach their own conclusions and develop helpful attitudes (Neenan, 2009). However, based on a study that rated therapy sessions for the presence of guided discovery, some evidence suggests that guided discovery may not be effective when working with clients diagnosed with a personality disorder (Hoffart, Versland, & Sexton, 2002).

The Socratic dialogue can only be successful if it involves a joint venture with both parties searching for a new and better understanding of the topic (Friedlander, 1969). Therapy relies on a collaborative approach whereby therapist and client share the work of understanding problems and devising a plan for change (Tee & Kazantzis, 2011). The Socratic method prompts clients to reach their own conclusions and solutions (Clark & Egan, 2015). Therapist and client can work together to identify and develop strengths that promote personal resilience (Padesky & Mooney, 2012). According to the Socratic method, the goal is not to lead the thought processes and deliver a sound conclusion but simply to assist the person to reach a conclusion derived through logic and reasoning (Taylor, 1956). However, Socrates did not simply follow the line of discussion wherever it might lead (Beversluis, 1987). He gently steered the flow onto useful topics.

Over time, the Socratic method helps people become more confident in their ability to confront difficult situations and discover useful solutions on their own (Areeda, 1996). In a study of problem solving and the ability to transfer skills to new situations, learning by discovery was found to be quite helpful (McDaniel & Schlager, 1990). People are more likely to value the information if it comes from their own efforts and experiences (Turkcapar et al. 2015), and the new ideas are more likely to transfer to other situations (McDaniel & Schlager, 1990).

NINE

Self-Improvement

Helping Clients Grow and Mature

THE SOCRATIC METHOD aims to help clients become more aware of their own thoughts, moods, and reactions. In this age of wearable technology, too many people remain plugged into a never-ending array of news feeds and social-media postings. To benefit from psychotherapy, clients are best served by a traditional approach that promotes quiet self-reflection and a view of larger life goals. The Socratic method helps clients evaluate themselves from a broad perspective, identifying major life goals and evaluating their current behavior in terms of movement toward those goals. Clients are encouraged to take ownership for all aspects of their functioning. The process relies on self-evaluation that promotes responsible behavior and that has been guided by insight into a person's major life goals.

According to the Socratic method, self-improvement can be seen as a central goal for therapy (Overholser, 1996a), and this goal is compatible with many forms of psychotherapy. Ultimately, the goal of therapy is to help clients improve in key aspects of their behavioral, social, and emotional functioning. Furthermore, an unspoken goal of therapy is ultimately to remove the client's need for therapy. The client should become a well-functioning adult capable of independent decision making and productive daily habits.

According to the Socratic method, self-improvement has three primary ingredients: self-awareness, self-acceptance, and self-regulation. These components are interrelated. For example, self-acceptance is meaningless and superficial without a thoughtful and thorough understanding of the self one is working to accept. Likewise, self-regulation requires a solid understanding of oneself, one's life goals, and a willingness to make changes in one's daily routine.

The Pursuit of Self-Awareness

At the core of effective psychotherapy lies the attainment of thoughtful self-awareness. Socrates famously stated: "The unexamined life is not worth living" (*Apology* 38). In a similar manner, the phrase "know thyself" has been attributed to the Oracle of Delphi, and it captures the importance of knowing your strengths, your limitations, and not exceeding your limits (Seeskin, 1987). "Know thyself" has also been interpreted as meaning that you should know that you are only human and therefore have all the flaws and limitations that pervade human existence (Morgan, 1990).

The pursuit of self-knowledge is both the goal and the process of self-development. Socrates emphasized the value of being aware of what one knows and does not know. In addition, the Socratic approach aims to promote one's self-awareness of personal tendencies and desires (Versenyi, 1963). In the process of examining their lives, clients find opportunities to remove false beliefs about their life situation and gain a clearer and more realistic understanding of their circumstances (Ericson, 2000). To become happy and successful in life, clients must become aware of their own strengths, achievements, and natural tendencies (Ballard, 1965). Often, many positive aspects of a person are blocked by a lack of self-knowledge. Even worse, a tendency toward self-ignorance can lay the foundation for unsupported faith in one's beliefs and unfounded confidence in one's abilities. A movement toward self-knowledge begins, paradoxically, with an acceptance of one's ignorance (Zimmerman, 1980).

Self-awareness plays a central role in many forms of psychotherapy. Most of the interpretive forms of psychotherapy have emphasized the therapeutic goal of insight, whereby a person's apprehension of the underlying motives of his or her behavior will make possible rational and conscious control over various urges and tendencies.

Through lively dialogue with a skilled therapist, self-awareness can come to life. The Socratic method relies on conversations aimed at promoting self-examination and self-improvement (Woolfolk, 2015). A search for self-understanding helps a person clarify and confront personal values and priorities (Stalley, 1986). A Socratic discussion is always aimed at promoting self-examination (Reeve, 1989). To be useful, however, self-knowledge must extend beyond the specific individual and include an awareness of human nature in general (Griswold, 1986). Understanding oneself goes beyond a review of an individual's personality traits and includes examining the individual within the broader social context and role in society (Annas, 1985). These notions are closely aligned with the work of Alfred Adler and his emphasis on social interest as a goal for therapy (Overholser, 2010d).

Self-knowledge includes an awareness of personal desires and aspirations (Griswold, 1986). The Socratic method assumes that personal insights help people better understand their own psyche, their relationships with others, and their dealings with the world (Kellerman & Burry, 1988). According to the Socratic method, self-awareness involves an objective view of oneself, interpreted within the broader context of a person's life, circumstances, and development. From a certain vantage point, it can appear that many people lack in self-awareness and have failed to examine their lives. If we simply follow social media or watch television shows that track every move of various current celebrities, we may believe that these events matter and that these people deserve our respect. However, taking a more existential view, celebrities are largely irrelevant. Fifty years from now, it won't matter which team won the World Series. Next year, few people will remember which celebrity won the current season of *Dancing with the Stars*. However, a person's life, goals, and values are more permanent contributors to a feeling of contentment.

Many different schools of psychotherapy have confronted this very important question: How can clients enhance their self-awareness? Insight-oriented therapies attempt to cultivate self-awareness through a variety of strategies, including the interpretation of dreams, the exploration of symbols, and the production of personal expressions through art or dance movements, among other methods. Experiential therapists encourage clients to focus their attention on the present moment, while deliberately moving them away from considerations of the past or future. The current interest in mindfulness strategies reveals the benefits that can come from a client's focus on presently occurring subjective experience. Action-oriented therapies use behavioral assignments to help clients gather objective information about their own behavior and its effect on their social network. For example, a simple self-monitoring form can be used to track mood, socialization patterns, headaches, and triggers. Likewise, clients can enhance their self-awareness through structured diary forms or weekly writing projects that focus on specific topics instead of encouraging a rambling rehash of recent events.

Even when a client fails to complete the self-monitoring form, the activity can still be used to advance the therapy. For example, a male client did not complete a form designed to track his constructive activity and chores around his home. In session, the therapist was careful not to assume the role of the critical parent or harsh teacher who scolds a child for neglecting his homework. Instead, the therapist asked a series of questions to gather more information about the weekly activities as well as the obstacles the client encountered that interrupted or prevented the self-monitoring process. Perhaps most importantly, the therapist emphasized the sincere belief that the client was at a choice point and had the power to decide how to spend his time, moving toward one goal (completing a college degree and seeking full-time employment) versus a very different goal (dropping out of college to pursue a career as a freelance photographer). This discussion allowed therapist and client to explore broader topics related to these decisions, including the importance of money and the ability to find love and romance while navigating different career paths.

The therapist's questions can be used to facilitate exploration and self-awareness (Moss, 1992). In the Socratic approach, the therapist refrains from giving mini-lectures or introducing an educational format into the therapy sessions. The therapist also avoids the role of expert or teacher, aiming to stay in the more effective role of fellow-explorer.

Self-awareness is a continuous process guided by questions and inquiry (Ballard, 1965). While involved in weekly psychotherapy sessions, clients may begin their search for a better understanding. However, this is only the beginning of a lifelong search. The therapist too must be willing to continue with this process of searching and exploring throughout a lifetime. An important aspect of the Socratic approach manifests in the uncertainty of the therapist, the profound curiosity displayed by the therapist throughout psychotherapy sessions, and the therapist's willingness to continue learning at all levels. Throughout the process of self-exploration, the deeper goal is to encourage the process of self-examination (Evans, 1990), or self-evaluation, helping the client fully engage in the process of understanding their goals and values. It is important for people to understand their beliefs and values in order for these qualities to serve as guides for living (Brickhouse & Smith, 1994).

People benefit from time spent in introspection aimed at understanding their true selves (Brickhouse & Smith, 1994). To become self-actualized, a client must know who he or she is (Griswold, 1986). Unfortunately, people are less likely to work on personal-growth issues when they feel naively satisfied with their life and goals (Livingstone, 1938). Furthermore, most people display biased ways of processing information, especially about themselves (Strohmer, Moilanen, & Barry, 1988). There is a tendency to identify and agree with information that is consistent with a person's established view of his or her self (Strohmer, Moilanen, & Barry, 1988). Finally, because people often lack self-awareness, the journey toward self-awareness cannot be a solitary activity but one that requires a dialogue with others (Navia, 1985). According to the Socratic view, to know oneself includes the goal of becoming one's true self (Griswold, 1986). Across the flow of the dialogue, the verbal exchange systematically moves the client toward awareness, understanding, and integration across beliefs. Questions can be used to promote self-reflection and enhance self-awareness (Neenan, 2009). For example, a young adult client stated, "If I don't get into medical school, I will be a complete failure." This expresses the underlying belief that without medical school she will be seen as a failure as a person. This thought process included the sub-belief that without medical school, her parents would be disappointed in her. The therapist pushed further with questions designed to confront these underlying beliefs: "What would happen if you dropped out of school now? In that way, you would be choosing to drop out, but you would not flunk out. Would that make it any different?" "What would happen if you joined the work force for the next five years or longer and went back later to get into medical school ten years from now?" "What would things be like if you got into medical school now, glided through your training, conducted innovative medical research, and ten years from today, you were awarded the Nobel Prize for Medicine. However, it included a special clause saying you needed to retire from medicine forever. What would you do with your life?" Surprisingly, the client replied that she would happily become a stay-at-home mom. She had been chasing the dream of medical school because both of her parents were physicians, and she had been raised with subtle pressure to follow their career path. A self-reliant attitude helps clients choose proper behavior regardless of social pressure. With the help of these questions, the client began to see a different path for her future. She shifted her goals, reduced her self-induced pressure, and began to enjoy life, love, and romance with renewed vigor.

Self-Acceptance Derives from Self-Evaluation

Self-acceptance is central to successful psychotherapy. Self-acceptance involves the unconditional respect and value of each person, and it seems closely aligned with Carl Rogers's notion of unconditional positive regard and with Albert Ellis's concept of unconditional self-acceptance. A compassionate therapist can help clients grow beyond external conditions of worth that may have been imposed upon them by parents who displayed critical attitudes or rejecting behaviors during the developmental period. Self-knowledge allows for self-direction and integrity (Ballard, 1965), encouraging clients to develop their own unique style, interests, and skills.

Self-acceptance is intricately linked to insightful awareness and thoughtful knowledge about oneself. Without true awareness and evaluation, self-acceptance becomes empty and meaningless. Self-acceptance does not imply an unconditional acceptance and tolerance of improper behavior. It would not be useful if clients continued to engage in self-destructive acts or socially deviant behaviors. The intent is to facilitate a gradual process of self-discovery that promotes personal awareness and growth. The goal of therapy is not simply to force clients to change their opinions and attitudes but more importantly to help clients begin to learn strategies they can use to examine their thoughts and evaluate their goals in a thoughtful manner (Padesky, 1993). Thus, self-evaluation is based on thoughtful reflection and self-awareness.

For many clients, career aspirations are shaped by family pressures or societal influences. Thus, some clients have reported going to law school or medical school because of parental expectations instead of their own personal desire. Other clients have worked in a family business because of family pressure or for financial security, while secretly wanting to become an artist or a musician. For many people, personal aspirations and career goals have been influenced by family expectations, societal pressures, or convenient opportunities. These external influences can sometimes distort the client's own values and talents. For example, a young adult client was hoping to go to medical school, but she found herself struggling with many of the science courses that were required for her pre-med schooling. In session, she admitted to having minimal interest in biology and chemistry but having deeply enjoyed a recent theater class. Over the course of several discussions, she explored her interests, talents, and skills. She enjoyed helping other people but began to realize there were many different helping professions. Eventually, she became willing to oppose the family pressure to apply for medical school, and she was accepted into a graduate program specializing in drama therapy as an applied field. As a therapist, the goal of direct confrontation in session is not to destroy a client's dreams but to help each client find satisfying goals that fit that client's resources. Through a Socratic-inspired dialogue, clients can become more aware of their own natural inclinations and native talents. As their awareness expands, clients can begin to make beneficial use of their natural tendencies and talents. In some ways, lasting happiness involves building on strengths and finding a person's niche. In the *Republic* (4.434), Socrates explained that a cobbler or a trader would not make a good warrior or guardian and, furthermore, that such attempts to meddle with their natural tendencies would cause ruin. Everyone is unique, with different strengths and talents that align with different careers (Sayers, 1999). Therefore, each person should perform the job that is best suited to the person's natural abilities and temperament (White, 1979).

When examining areas of self-acceptance, both therapist and client should remain modest. Despite the goal of self-acceptance, it should be noted that excessive self-admiration can be a cause of numerous problems (Despland, 1985). Thus, the goal is to promote a modest and balanced view, helping clients respect their limits, work on their flaws, and utilize their strengths whenever possible.

Developing sincere self-acceptance can take a bit of time, especially with clients who struggle with low self-esteem or depression on a chronic basis. For example, a depressed male client was lonely but hoping to meet a woman and begin a romantic relationship. Unfortunately, his low self-esteem often prevented him from showing any initiative in most social events. He was asked to make a list of qualities that would make him a desirable person to date. As his therapist, the goal was less focused on promoting any dating activity and more focused on helping him explore and improve his view of himself. He needed help identifying his strengths, which was difficult given his natural tendency to focus on his flaws and weaknesses. Self-evaluation is a protracted process that includes awareness and reflection on one's strengths and weaknesses and is aimed at personal growth and environmental mastery (Ryff & Singer, 2008).

Self-Regulation and Self-Control

In an effort to remain true to the Socratic method, three terms are used somewhat interchangeably: self-regulation, self-control, and self-discipline. Self-regulation involves an ability to control behavior in the pursuit of meaningful goals and the tendency to live up to personal standards (Peterson & Seligman, 2004). The person's life is guided by rational decisions that help him or her focus on the big picture of life and meaning.

Socrates emphasized the practical utility of self-discipline, living his life in full rational control over his appetites and his emotions (Waterfield, 1990). Self-discipline is important when trying to develop any helpful habit. The goal of self-control is to help clients make conscious and deliberate choices that guide their behavior (Rosenbaum, 1993). It is most important to develop control over responses that are likely to interfere with adaptive functioning (Rosenbaum, 1993). Self-control can be enhanced by helping clients increase their frustration tolerance (Ellis, 1987). Clients are encouraged to develop new responses that may help them satisfy their motives in a socially acceptable manner (Rosenbaum, 1993).

Socrates emphasized the importance of rational self-control (Chessick, 1982). Socrates controlled his emotions and desires instead of being controlled by them (Tredennick & Waterfield, 1990). In many situations, self-discipline relies on personal restraint and endurance (Richmond, 1955).

Self-control is found when a person is able to exert personal restraint over pleasure and pain and learns to tame urges and passions (Reale, 1987). Moderation is used synonymously with temperance and can often be interchanged with balance or self-restraint (Melling, 1987). Self-control derives from knowledge and reason, not willpower (Reale, 1987). People can learn to use reason to control instincts and bodily urges (Reale, 1987). In contrast, a lack of self-control is seen when behavior is guided by animal instincts and bodily urges (Reale, 1987).

Self-control helps suppress maladaptive behaviors that could become excessive, such as overeating, alcohol abuse, or shopping. Self-control is based on logical decisions that exert deliberate control over emotions and appetites, including primitive urges for food and sex. For many people, physical urges and bodily desires can become a distraction that diverts attention from philosophical ideals (Robinson, 1995). It is useful to find acceptable ways for satisfying biological urges while ensuring these desires do not become excessive (Robinson, 1995).

Self-regulation involves developing mastery over urges and desires. When self-control is adequate, then external rules, restraints, and punishments are unnecessary (Taylor, 1956). Proper behavior must originate in the person's reason and voluntary action (Adler, 1941). Lasting satisfaction develops more slowly than the simple gratification of physical urges (Hampton, 1990), but this insight requires wisdom. The immediacy of physical gratification makes it appear larger or more important than modal refinement (Hampton, 1990). Clients can learn to use logic and reason to control urges or redirect their desires, focusing on long-term satisfactions and moving away from short-term pleasures. Pleasures and pains may appear more substantial than they truly are (Grube, 1966). Instead, it is wise to focus on long-term satisfactions (Ellis, 1994). Therapy aims to help people guide their behavior based on reason, not emotions, self-interest, or passive wishful thinking (Mason & Wakefield, 1955).

All people have the potential to be kind and generous (that is, altruistic) as well as the potential to become self-absorbed and miserly (Guisinger & Blatt, 1994). It becomes important for clients to develop interests in self-improvement as well as compassion toward others. However, a person's self-control may be thrown off because physical pleasures result in immediate gratification whereas moral pleasures accumulate slowly over a lifetime (Hampton, 1990). Self-control and personal discipline require training (Richmond, 1955). Self-control includes an ability to tame one's urges, whether lustful desires or emotional reactions. It helps to become aware of the different components within all people, including a rational side, a spirited energy built on self-respect, and a mixture of appetites or urges to gratify (Crombie, 1964).

A lack of self-control, or a weakness of will (called *akrasia* by the ancient Greeks), refers to behaviors that conflict with a person's better judgment. Thus, the individual needs to be guided by wisdom and a view to long-term satisfactions. It can be helpful to realize that physical desires are temporary and often insatiable, with overindulgence often followed by negative consequences, whereas the benefits of knowledge are lasting and free of aftereffects (Hampton, 1990).

Self-improvement involves helping clients identify their personal strengths and life goals. When these attributes have been identified and visualized, then questions can be used to push the client forward, taking small steps each day to move closer to these goals. For example, a middle-aged female client was struggling with depression, aggravated by the recent end of a romantic relationship. In one session, she described her volunteer work with a local Girl Scout troop. To encourage confidence in the girls, she often emphasized the motto "you always have choices." As part of her therapy, the client was asked how this phrase "you always have choices" might apply to her own life and current struggles. The simple use of her own words forced her to respect her goals, consider her options, and disengage from her emphasis on emotional reactions. The goal of therapy is rational self-determination, where individuals begin to make their own choices based on insight and reasoning (Nelson, 1980).

Therapy can help clients take control of their lives as well as their futures, by assuming personal responsibility for their choices, actions, and inactions. For example, an adult client was struggling with a troubled romantic relationship. In session, she was asked a series of questions to help clarify her goals and motivation: "What do you think this relationship might be like in two years?" "What do you *want* it to be like in two years?" "How much of this is under *your* control?" "What can you start doing now to make it more likely to develop into the kind of relationship you hope to see?" Over the course of the dialogue, the client was gently pushed and prodded to accept responsibility for her own future. She began making choices instead of waiting for her partner to act so she could react.

Self-improvement implies that the impetus for change comes from the client. However, some people are resistant to change, whether because of secondary gains, from bad habits, or out of a tendency for stubbornness. For example, an adult client reported too many emotional highs and lows, usually triggered by relationship problems, and her on-and-off romance with a young man. She expressed a desire to reduce her low periods and understood the value of finding a middle-ground reaction. The therapist explained that negative moods can be magnified by certain words ("horrible," "terrible," "catastrophe"). The therapist warned her that to achieve balance in the middle, it means she will need to work at reducing both extremes, the emotional lows and the euphoric highs. Finally, the therapist explained that positive moods can be magnified beyond their natural limits by certain words ("wonderful," "fantastic," "perfect"). She began to see how her view of her romance had become distorted along these two extremes.

The importance of balance in life includes having time for enjoyable activities with family and friends instead of devoting all of one's energy to work and chores. When a person's desires become too strong and focused on one goal, other areas of the person's life will weaken through neglect (Sallis, 1986). According to Socrates, "He whose desires are strong in one direction will have them weaker in others; they will be like a stream which has been drawn off into another channel" (*Republic* 6.485).

Sometimes it can be helpful to ask thought-provoking questions for which the therapist has no clear answer in mind. For example: "If you could go back in time, what advice might you give to yourself twenty years ago, say, when you were still in high school?" "Let's change it a bit. Now you are twenty years into the future. If you came back from the future to share your wisdom with us today, what advice do you think you would share?" "I realize this is a really hard question, so let's try it one more time. With the problems you have encountered recently, in twenty years from now, what will you remember about these events?" "What do you want to remember, in terms of how you deal with this messy situation?" Each of these questions remain completely open in terms of the answers the client could provide. However, these questions all push the client to view the situation from a different perspective and gain new insights through the discussion.

Self-control can help a person resist enjoyable or easy activities in favor of more important life goals (Mele, 1987). Self-control relies on a sense of purpose and direction when confronted with a difficult situation. As explained in a useful metaphor, when the wind stops, a sailor must rely on oars to move forward (Benardete, 1989). For example, an adult female client had recently completed a job-training program for adults, learning the skills needed to become a massage therapist. However, she still needed to study and pass a licensure exam. This exam posed a major barrier, and she felt frightened and overwhelmed. Instead of studying, she was falling back into her old habits, staying up late, watching too much television, and reading various online news feeds. Despite the upcoming deadline, she had not studied at all over the past three weeks. She made excuses for her inefficiency, ranging from a minor cold to feeling upset over the death of a celebrity in the news. It would be easy for the therapist to scold, push, or structure her daily schedule, but any attempt to reprimand or guide resulted in the client quickly reverting to the persona of an unruly teenage girl being scolded by a critical parent. Such an interaction could easily disrupt the therapeutic alliance and potentially cause missed appointments or the client dropping out of therapy prematurely. To confront the issue without creating a rift, the therapist asked a series of questions to help the client explore her own goals and values. "Where do you see things going?" "Which do you prefer, to find a full-time job as a massage therapist, while keeping jewelry designing as a good hobby, or a full-time job in jewelry but your finances remaining limited?" "Let's take a look ahead. What would things be like if you were to invest time each day in your studying?" "What would it be like during the studying period and when you reach the deadline for the exam?" The client thought for a moment and said: "I think I could do well. It would be hard, but I could pass the exam, get a job, and move forward with my career." The therapist then addressed the opposite possible future by asking, "Now let's look at the other side. What will things be like if you settle back into your old routine? You can stay up late, browse the internet, and watch a lot of television. How would that play out for you?" The client's expression became more serious, and she described living in a rut; without the certifications, there would be no job and very little money. To allow the client total choice and personal responsibility for all decisions, the therapist presented the alternatives in an honest and open manner. It is the client's views and opinions that matter in therapy (Anderson & Goolishian, 1992). The therapist asked, "Which plan works best for you? I realize that the first plan requires a lot of work and diligence, but you don't have to choose that plan. The second plan would be easy, and you are already on that path. Honestly, it is your choice, not mine or your family's. What makes sense for you?" Therapists hope to promote responsible decision making unfettered by social mores. When confronted with a difficult decision, most clients know the proper decision and simply need a bit of guidance. An interesting metaphor captures the process (Erickson, described in Gordon, 1978). When a stray horse wandered onto a farm, the farmer climbed atop the horse's back, held the reins, and said "giddy up." The horse knew the proper destination and simply needed a few gentle kicks to keep it moving forward. When the horse would stray

SELF-IMPROVEMENT

from a well-worn path, the farmer tugged the reins to keep its attention focused on forward movement. After a short ride, the horse turned onto its owner's property. This metaphor can help therapists to retain a focus on client self-determination, even when clients struggle to take the initial steps forward.

During the next session, the therapist explained to the aspiring massage therapist: "We have been looking at this situation as if the decision was either one option or the other, but in reality, there are many different choices for jobs and hobbies. Do you think it would be possible to find a job working in the jewelry industry or creative design, even if you were not a full-time jewelry designer?" Throughout the discussions, the therapist was careful consistently to encourage the client's strength and determination: "Whenever we talk about these situations, it seems clear that you can make a positive future for yourself. You are bright and talented. It doesn't matter to me if you choose a job in computers or music. I just want to help you make the decision that will be best and most helpful for your future. So what makes most sense to you at this time?" A simple tracking form was presented to help structure the client's daily activities (figure 9.1) and allow the client to make an informed decision about daily goals.

Activity

	Sunday	Monday	Tuesday	Wednesday	Thursday	Friday	Saturday

Figure 9.1 List 5–6 activities for which you hope to invest your time. Then, during the week, track either the number of minutes you were active with the chore or place a check mark to record the days for which you were active.

SELF-IMPROVEMENT

Actions Are Guided by Proper Motives

Self-control initially involves a conscious and deliberate effort to suppress deviant desires but progresses toward the elimination of these misguided urges and internal conflicts (Trianoksy, 1988). Self-control also involves the ability to redirect one's impulses toward rational goals (Annas, 1985). A focus on self-control is compatible with Freudian views of ego strength and the need to regulate primitive impulses.

In the Socratic method, the focus is not simply on a person's actions but on a person's *intentional* actions. Intentional behaviors reflect thoughtful deliberation about various options and the reasons to choose one course over another. Before a person acts, the behavior is guided by the person's intentions (Mele, 1987). Self-control involves a deliberate ability to emphasize the person's motivation in favor of desirable actions (Mele, 1987). The Socratic method aims to promote a natural harmony whereby the person exhibits desirable behavior because of personal desire, not rigid control (Weiner, 1993). The goal is a personal harmony in which positive actions flow easily and naturally in a habitual and satisfying manner of responding, instead of out of a regimented sense of self-control (Annas, 1993).

Conclusions

Psychotherapy according to the Socratic method provides a broad framework to guide treatment sessions. The goal is to help the person become as good as they can (McPherran, 1996). During his trial, Socrates explained his view of the best way to eradicate evil: "The easiest and noblest way is not to be disabling others but to be improving yourselves" (*Apology* 39). The goal of the Socratic method is to promote the optimal development of each individual's potential (Kellerman & Burry, 1988). Therapeutic sessions are likely to move beyond a focus on reducing acute symptoms or resolving specific problems. Instead, the client is viewed as a unique individual with important personal values, life goals, and insights into the client's own identity. The therapist uses a collaborative dialogue to help clients confront their beliefs and values, especially as related to virtuous behavior and broad goals.

The Socratic method helps improve a person's self-knowledge by helping clients explore their lives, goals, and most importantly values. These values should be found within the psyche of the individual and not imposed by others. When a therapist asks questions that confront values, the client is not expected naively to follow the therapist's lead but to seek, understand, and defend those values. In the same way, adults should not uncritically accept the values promoted by societal convention or media coverage.

The therapist gently encourages change that moves the client closer to a focus on long-term satisfactions. The goal is to increase the client's motivation for desirable and helpful actions. Along the way, there is a tendency to reduce enjoyment from undesirable behaviors and destructive actions.

Ultimately, the process of self-awareness and self-regulation will aim at moving toward broad life goals. In the Socratic method, the ideal focus of therapy is aimed at helping clients become aware of their life values, where they learn to work toward a good life, one characterized by virtue. Thus, there is less focus on daily stressors or minor problems, and the therapist maintains a focus on major issues such as personal integrity, moral character, maturity, and responsibility.

Self-discipline can be an important theme to confront with clients who have been diagnosed with a personality disorder, especially borderline, antisocial, or histrionic personality disorder. In addition, issues related to self-control can be directed toward specific behaviors such as overeating or habit control. However, it is often helpful for the therapist to retain a broad view that includes virtue ethics at the center of the conceptualization. In contrast to other forms of psychotherapy, the Socratic method readily confronts major moral and ethical issues in session. Ultimately, it maintains a central focus on a person's character, personal choices, and skills in practical reasoning (Annas, 1993).

TEN

A Focus on Virtue Ethics in Psychotherapy

THE PRESENT CHAPTER will provide an overview of virtue ethics, with the following five chapters confronting each of the core virtues in detail. An abstract topic such as "virtue" needs to be explored through reason and logic (Toulmin, 1950/1986). Although these issues can easily become abstract and philosophical, feeling far removed from daily experience, here we will remain closely anchored to common situations that arise in psychotherapy sessions.

Modern society is filled with distractions. Everyone seems plugged into some form of technology, with constant internet access, streaming videos, social media, news feeds, and 150 channels on cable television. When living at a frantic pace, it can become easy to feel aggravated by trivial events, such as slow-moving traffic, being stopped at a red light, or slow service at a coffee shop. Furthermore, many people fall into a trap of their daily actions becoming guided by the endless pursuit of money. It becomes too easy to be distracted by the pursuit of wealth, social status, and reputation (Sesonske & Fleming, 1965). A person's values are revealed through how the person lives (Stalley, 1986) and can be seen in the choices that are made every day. It seems that most people view themselves as good. Few people see themselves as evil, troubled, or vice ridden. According to Socrates, however, evil behavior results from ignorance (Kekes, 1988). The risk lies in people accepting their views of themselves uncritically (White, 1976).

Currently, the field of psychotherapy is focused on prescriptive approaches to treatment, in which each diagnostic condition is paired with its optimal approach to treatment. Although such strategies make some sense, there is a risk that clinicians overly focus on identifying each problem and aiming to fix it. The field of psychotherapy has accepted the standard diagnostic nomenclature of the medical model and largely has discarded a more nuanced view of human existence as a perpetual struggle between virtue and vice (Weiner, 1993). It must be remembered that clients are not "broken" and therefore do not need to be "fixed." Instead, therapy is best seen as helping clients grow, mature, and move toward a good life guided by virtue and reason. The quality of a person's life may be determined by the person's moral character (Reeve, 1988). Virtues are essential qualities to possess. According to the Socratic method, a life lived virtuously leads to a happy and rewarding existence (Norman, 1983).

Perhaps the most daunting aspect of the Socratic method is its attempt to understand the virtues. Socrates was intrigued by the virtues and would typically direct his conversations onto topics of morality and general beliefs about virtue and values (Lycos, 1987). He discussed the nature of courage with military leaders, and he explored the meaning of justice with the judges. Eventually, Socrates realized that the leaders and scholars of his time really did not know what they were assumed to know (Seeskin, 1987). For a trait to be considered a virtue, it must always be good and beneficial to the person who displays it (Reeve, 1988).

A common goal of a Socratic dialogue is to help the person care more about virtue than about wealth, possessions, or even his or her own body (Reeve, 1989). The virtues are more important than other things often misconstrued as good, such as wealth, physical strength, or beauty (Allen, 1970). Virtue is based on several qualities (Wallace, 1978): a difficult situation, knowledge of options, a voluntary choice to act in a certain manner, the choice based on logical reasons, and the responses developing into a persistent tendency (Petersen & Seligman, 2004).

Happiness and moral character are inseparable, interconnected, and necessary for a good life (Garrett, 1996). In one view, virtue in the soul is analogous to health in the body (Santas, 1979). A person's moral health is strengthened through the regular employment of the virtues (Ballard, 1965). Socrates made the claim that "virtues of the soul seem to be akin to bodily qualities, for even when they are not originally innate they can be implanted later by habit and exercise" (*Republic* 7.518).

Rational people appreciate the benefits of financial gain but do not value personal wealth more than their own well-being and moral character (McPherran, 1996). Anything should be valued by how it is used. The decision to view something as good or evil resides not in the characteristic, quality, or possession but on how the thing is used (Reale, 1987). Thus, wealth, fame, power, and even knowledge can be used in helpful or destructive ways depending on the character of the person (Navia, 1985). Likewise, physical health is important for living a satisfactory existence but not more important than leading a life of virtue and moral behavior (McPherran, 1996). It is essential to care more about a person's moral development than about superficial things such as personal finances (McPherran, 1996).

Socrates identified key differences between technical skill and philosophical wisdom. Technical skill is privileged in most structured treatment manuals. However, psychotherapy is not a simplistic methodology that can be applied via a cookbook approach to client struggles. Instead, in many psychotherapy sessions, philosophical ideas are needed to guide the dialogue. Thus, effective therapy helps people not simply change their behavior but aims to help them live according to proper insight, understanding, and life goals (Seeskin, 1987). Likewise, the Socratic dialogue does not simply confront a client's beliefs but examines his or her way of living (King, 1987). Everyday ethical behavior involves choices guided by sensitivity to moral issues, personal integrity, and social responsibility, all combined into moral character (Halberstam, 1993).

Although Socrates and Plato often refer to the care of the soul, it seems less problematic to use slightly different language. The term "soul" has various religious connotations, and for some people, depending on their religious affiliation, using that word may obstruct a full open-minded appreciation of the therapeutic work. Instead, it may be less objectionable to talk about virtue ethics as "character traits" (Meara, Schmidt, & Day, 1996) and as important aspects of one's "personality." To avoid the religious connotations when mentioning the soul, it helps to reframe virtue as health of the person's morality or character (Beckman, 1979). The focus remains on personal qualities inside the character of the individual (Jordan & Meara, 1990).

A brief note on terminology: When Socrates refers to a person's "soul," it is more useful to translate this into an individual's "mind" and "intellect" (Grube, 1966) or "moral character." The term "character" captures the integration of emotions, attitudes, behaviors, and intentions in a person (Bright, Winn, & Kanov, 2014). An individual can examine life as a long series of steps toward becoming the person he or she aims to be (Reiman, 1990). Actions shape a person's character, and a person's character largely guides the person's actions (Reeve, 1988).

Virtue is best understood as a form of excellence, an optimal state, or an ideal point along a continuum of personal character (Bright, Winn, & Kanov, 2014). Virtue refers to admirable personality traits that promote behaving in a desirable manner (Wallace, 1978). Socrates explained: "virtue . . . is the greatest good of man" (*Apology* 29). Likewise, a modern quotation attributed to the basketball coach John Wooden recommends: "Be more concerned with your character than your reputation, because your character is what you really are, while your reputation is merely what others think you are." Hence, a person is advised to care for moral character because it cannot be lost like material possessions can (Annas, 1981). Character is internal and under the person's control; reputation is external and somewhat independent of a person's true actions.

According to Platonic ideals, a good person cannot be harmed, because happiness depends on personal choices and voluntary actions, not external advantages derived from, for example, family of origin, wealth, or social power (Irwin, 1977). The only thing that can truly harm an individual is an act of vice (McPherran, 1996) because the only harm that has severe and lasting effects on a person is harm to the person's moral character. Furthermore, if the previous claim is accepted, then the only way individuals can be harmed is through their own actions.

Many people will find themselves in a situation that involves some test of virtue at some point during a typical day. Unfortunately, people often fail to see an opportunity to exercise virtue or choose to ignore it. People can get caught up in daily business and minor concerns, and in the process, they may lose sight of the bigger concerns. Furthermore, it can be troubling to ponder major life issues. Confronting virtue can trigger a sense of uncertainty about doing the right thing and the potential consequences of misbehavior, such as revenge, cowardice, or excessive consumption. If a client hesitates or seems uncomfortable with a focus on virtue ethics, it can be wise to refocus until a different situation arises. Also, some clients are quite responsive to writing their thoughts as an expressive activity completed between sessions. Most importantly, the therapist should always remain respectful of the client's views, even when they are vastly different from the therapist's own opinions.

Some personal experience with misbehavior can be useful for learning about virtue and the other less helpful options. For example, many people who become experts in obesity and addiction use their own past experiences to guide their understanding of the change process. Ideally, the therapist can help clients value their own misbehaviors as important learning opportunities; this is reminiscent of the dead ends in reasoning confronted by the slave boy in the dialogue *Meno*. Although the past misdeeds may become destructive if left unchecked, these behaviors can provide important opportunities from which to learn. These events can be discussed without the therapist adopting the pose of a moral proselytizer who has never stumbled along the path to virtue; the therapist instead remains an inquisitive partner in the search for the proper path. Both parties focus on the lasting goodness that can be accrued through a lifetime of good moral character.

As part of the philosophical foundation underlying the Socratic method, it can be useful to examine different views of the human condition. A perennial question has been confronted throughout history: Are people basically good or essentially evil? Some people, including numerous mental health professionals, would argue that people are basically good. Others, including some pioneers in psychotherapy, would argue that people are born with dark sides. Finally, many people might try to avoid the dichotomy and argue that it depends. Such a reply clearly raises the question, "If it depends, what does it depend on?" Many scholars have debated the issue: Are people born good, but harsh conditions can create evil tendencies? Or are people born evil but under the proper conditions learn to suppress deviant desires? Socrates expressed the view that people are inherently good: "to prefer evil to good is not in human nature" (*Protagoras* 358). This positive view of human nature underlies many aspects of the Socratic method.

Virtue and vice are best understood when paired together (Crombie, 1963). From a Socratic view, an important problem confronting society today is a lack of virtue. In its various forms, vice leads to high rates of crime, robberies and burglaries, drug abuse, greed, laziness, hatred, addiction, depression, and social isolation. In contrast, virtue promotes a better life. However, the therapist does not force the topic of virtue into a therapy session. Instead, the therapist may listen for recurrent themes and patterns discussed in the client's concerns and explore ideas related to virtue when they appear in the client's life situation.

Core aspects of virtue seem to reside in the person's subjective view of ambiguous situations and idiosyncratic definitions of complex ideas. According to the Socratic method, some people struggle with a weakness of will, whereby the person is in a difficult situation and knows the proper moral behavior but for whatever reason refrains from acting on it (Santas, 1979). The willingness to avoid responsible behavior because it involves some type of risk can be viewed as a personal weakness (Santas, 1979).

Common misbehaviors include such things as minor theft; overindulging in food, alcohol, or sex; gossiping about friends or coworkers; or being afraid to help out a friend because of risk of social rejection. It can be too easy to rationalize one's behavior as acceptable, using explanations such as "Others have harmed me in the past"; "Most people would do the same thing in this situation"; "I have done plenty already"; "It's not my fault—there were other people that could have helped." In therapy, it can be difficult to cut through these rationalizations. Sometimes, asking the client to look at the situation from a different person's perspective can help: "What would the situation be like if you were the victim here?" "How would you react if the victim had been your child?" Sometimes, it can be useful to explore potential consistency across people: "What would happen if everyone behaved this way?" In a similar way, constancy over time can reveal problems in behavior: "What would things be like if you acted this way every day for the next three years?" Finally, it can be useful to exaggerate the intensity of the action: "What if you had taken $5,000 instead of $5 from the register?" "What is the maximum acceptable amount one can steal from his or her employer?" Finally, it may be useful to change the target: "Would it be acceptable to steal from a church or hospital?"

According to the Socratic method, therapist and client work, struggle, learn, and grow together. Even therapists can have their own struggles. However, session time is not used to work on the therapist's concerns. Nonetheless, it can be useful for a therapist to keep in mind that client and therapist are in the process together (Weeks, 1977). This collaborative view helps keep the therapist from holding or acting on harsh and evaluative attitudes. Virtue cannot be taught, but it can be learned through thoughtful discussions and collaborative inquiry (Brumbaugh, 1975).

Experienced therapists respect each client's values and perspectives so as to avoid imposing their own goals on the client (Williams & Levitt, 2007). The therapist must be able to admit that everyone, including the therapist, has flaws and weaknesses, with areas of deficiencies scattered through the virtues. According to the Socratic method, effective living requires a willingness continually to explore ways of improving one's virtue and character. This notion of ongoing self-improvement applies to the client and to the therapist.

It can be a challenge to discuss virtue in therapy, in an open manner of collaboration and exploration. Virtue cannot be taught by didactic instruction or through observing examples; it can only be confronted and possibly learned through a genuine collaborative inquiry (Brumbaugh, 1975). The therapist must be careful to discuss virtue in session without imposing his or her own beliefs on the client. To accomplish this nondirective stance, the therapist must maintain a sincere disavowal of knowledge, especially when it comes to virtue. As long as both therapist and client remain true to the basic rule "say only what you believe," then there can be a sincere search for understanding and examining moral beliefs without either person attempting to win an argument. As long as clients say only what they believe, the discussion is trusted as sincere and honest (Mackenzie, 1988).

A virtuous person is motivated to act in proper ways because the person judges these acts to be good, not because of fear of punishment or rejection (Meara, Schmidt, & Day, 1996). Thus, beyond the actions that can be observed, a person's intentions are important in virtue (Meara, Schmidt, & Day, 1996). Virtue is a propensity to act in a desirable manner for good reasons (McDowell, 1997). Thus, virtue requires an assessment of the person's actions as well as the reasons or intent. Virtue requires the proper behavior conducted for the proper reasons and motives (Irwin, 1995; Kaplan, 1979; Trianosky, 1987). Thus, it is not virtuous to behave in a pleasant manner to win social approval, earn an award for volunteer of the year, or get a raise in pay. Proper behavior should not be guided by obedience to authority or conformity to social custom (Cornford, 1932/1981; Fagothey, 1976).

According to the Socratic method, the path to lasting contentment relies on virtue. Therapy may aim for a major philosophical shift, helping the client see that happiness does not depend on health, wealth, power, or fame. Too often, people develop distorted views that encourage a hedonistic lifestyle (Hampton, 1990). Socrates was concerned that too many people were neglecting their moral character and instead seemed focused on trivialities such as fame or wealth (Beckman, 1979).

Aporia

Aporia means that the discussion aims for a clear and final definition, even though it may never actually reach that point. Socrates typically explored the meaning of different virtues by holding a discussion with someone who presumably possessed the quality that was being examined (Crombie, 1964). The discussion would focus on a search for a definition, a discussion that usually ended in failure (Crombie, 1964). Thus, the goal is more to value the process of exploring important topics and pondering complex issues, not to reach a clear and definitive answer to life's most complex questions.

Plato's dialogues involved the persistent search for universal definitions of the virtues. The virtues represent an ideal form of good behavior that remains the same across times and cultures (Kohlberg, 1970). These conversations were usually classified as *apoeretic*, meaning they ended in a state of confusion, having failed to identify a viable definition of the virtue. Nonetheless, Socrates was not perplexed. Instead, the apoeretic state confirmed to Socrates that people did not truly understand the key issues that presumably guided their lives and careers. Despite ending in confusion, the dialogue created a sense of puzzlement that was used to encourage an open mind and the continued search for answers (Gadamer, 1980). Even though most discussions failed to reach any clear or useful definition of the virtues, people were likely to behave in better ways because of the process of inquiry into the virtues (Evans, 1990).

It is useful to explore virtue in some psychotherapy sessions, even if the discussion ends in aporia. Throughout his discussions in ancient Athens, Socrates would seek definitions for each of the virtues, but a final acceptable definition was never found. Nonetheless, the process of seeking the definition and exploring the topics was useful. Hence, we do not need to *know* as long as we are willing to *seek* the definitions, living a life dedicated to learning and rational exploration. Socrates was searching for a universal definition that would apply to all people in all situations. However, others (the Sophists) were content teaching situational ethics, whereby the right behavior depended on the current situation. Situational ethics could be used to support almost any possible action, good or bad, by imputing an ethical basis even when it was weak or nonexistent.

When we move from ancient philosophy to contemporary psychotherapy, the situation remains largely similar. The conversation might aim to uncover the client's implicit definition of key terms, especially those related to virtue, but there is no guarantee that a viable definition will be found. The conversation may aim for but does not expect to arrive at an end goal. Instead, the Socratic therapist values the process of searching for an improved understanding of complex abstract topics. Along the way, both therapist and client have opportunities to explore their views, values, and meanings. Both therapist and client can sharpen their views of what they know, what they believe, and how these beliefs may guide their behavior. Again, the therapist can use a series of questions designed to help the client shift perspective and see the same situation from a new and more adaptive view. In broad terms, therapy aims to promote health and balance in each client. To live by the ideals of virtue, the person needs to establish a harmonious balance between reason and habit (Despland, 1985).

Virtue Is Based in Wisdom

Genuine virtue requires wisdom (Ahrensdorf, 1995). Socrates was guided by the belief that no one can become a good person unless they have knowledge of the virtues (Bluck, 1955). Thus, the center of virtue lies in knowledge of what is good and what is harmful to the person (Stalley, 1986). In modern society, many people are swept away by insignificant objects and perverse pleasures (Kristeva, 1995). Virtue requires knowledge of what is good, natural, and beneficial for the client to aim toward (Versenyi, 1982).

Wisdom helps people examine their own lives and desires and guides their behavior toward those values that have lasting goodness for them (Despland, 1985). Thus, wisdom plays a central role throughout the Socratic method. To live a virtuous life, a person needs to comprehend the true meaning of justice, moderation, piety, and courage (Despland, 1985). Therapy can help clients begin to move away from current urges and pleasurable activities and begin to focus on long-term satisfactions. For most people, fulfillment requires patience and a far-sighted view of life aspirations (Legomsky-Abel, 1989). Clients seek treatment when they feel a need for help, advice, or guidance. Therapists need to respect the client while not necessarily accepting all of the client's behaviors. It is not appropriate for a therapist to push certain views or ideals on a trusting client. Instead, both therapist and client can use the dialogue to explore important issues and grow in a positive manner.

When initially making changes, a client may benefit from external guidance and structure, which can help illustrate the dangers of misbehavior. It can be useful to ask a client: "How would you behave if you were an A-list celebrity or the president of the United States, and there was always a crew of reporters and photographers following your every move? Would you behave in a different manner?" "How would you manage to stop yourself from misbehaving?" "Can we capture that view now, even though there aren't any reporters, and still use this perspective as a guide and a stopgap?" "How would you behave if you were in some strange military troop, so you might be able to act on these urges, but you had to submit a request in writing and wait forty-eight hours for the approval from a superior? Would you deal with these urges in a different manner?"

Virtue is proper behavior performed in a conscious, deliberate, and informed manner (Wallace, 1978). The behavior must be motivated by personal choice (Wallace, 1978). The ideal involves aligning a person's desires with the person's intellect or logical reasoning, so the person willfully chooses proper acts (Charlton, 1988). A person's character is displayed in the person's actions. Virtue is an ideal that serves its function in an excellent manner, as guided by reason (Taylor, 2002). Virtues can be constructed as forms of excellence and are composed of character strengths that have been displayed in thoughts, emotions, and behaviors (Peterson & Seligman, 2004).

Instead of discussing willpower or a weakness of will, it may be helpful to understand the components of virtue. Free will, or personal freedom, implies an ability to choose one's behavior and not simply be regulated by biological urges or innate desires (Charlton, 1988). It can be helpful to view actions in terms of their goodness or excellence, instead of labeling them right or wrong (Slote, 1992). Virtue ethics involves an ability to see the goodness of various choices (Slote, 1992) in a fashion not simply determined by personal gain.

The best way to evaluate virtue requires moving beyond the observable action in order to evaluate the person's desires, intentions, and motives in a difficult situation (Dent, 1984). One must understand the reasons behind the actions (Dent, 1984). Three important factors to consider when evaluating virtue: the intent or motive, the actual behavior, and the effects of the behavior, whether intended or unexpected (Dent, 1984). Thus, the person who lacks virtue may be lacking in any of these three components. From a Socratic perspective, there is a heavy emphasis on the internal, cognitive, rational aspects that underlie the individual's motivation. However, it does not necessarily follow that whenever a person intellectually understands proper ethical behavior, the person will always act in a virtuous manner. This assumption is termed "the Socratic fallacy" (Nehamas, 1999).

Intentions: Doing the Right Thing for the Right Reasons

Clients should not simply follow the crowd and behave in a manner similar to those around them. There have been some historical situations where other people were not living up to an appropriate standard of behavior (soldiers in Nazi Germany, American troops during the My Lai massacre).

A good person is not necessarily pleasant to be around (Santas, 1979). Socrates was known to be a person of high moral fiber, but he could be difficult in some situations. In contrast, though some people appear kind and helpful, they may be performing their acts under a social façade. When superficial people relax and let down their guard, a shallowness and emptiness that lacks true moral fiber can be revealed. Moral problems can be seen in a person's actions but also in his or her dreams, desires, and fantasies (Dent, 1975). It seems important to explore a person's intent, because virtue is a quality that resides in the mind of the individual. People should not act in a virtuous manner as a way of seeking social approval or esteem from others (Beckman, 1979). Not all acts that appear generous really deserve to be praised as virtuous. For example, some people will donate money to the poor simply because the charitable act functions as a tax deduction.

Virtue resides in deliberate intentional acts, not simply acting out of habit, ignorance, or accident. Thus, wisdom allows that a person must act in a virtuous manner for the right reasons and with deliberate intentions (Seeskin, 1987).

A FOCUS ON VIRTUE ETHICS IN PSYCHOTHERAPY

Therapy Relies on a Collaborative Exploration

According to Socrates, virtuous behavior requires knowledge of what constitutes virtue and therefore can be discovered through thoughtful philosophical dialogue (Kraut, 1984). This identifies a paradox: a central goal of the Socratic method involves helping clients learn, but therapists do not teach. There are no recipes for moral behavior (Despland, 1985). Instead, the Socratic method aims to help clients approach difficult situations in a more thoughtful manner (Despland, 1985).

A Socratic dialogue can help clients explore virtue in their lives. According to the Socratic method, the goal of the discussion is not to lecture people about the meaning of virtue but to help them find their own definitions of the key terms (Kraut, 1984). Any discussion of virtue can have strong subjective inferences or moralistic undertones. Throughout treatment, it is important to avoid preaching to the client. It is essential to maintain an exploratory nature throughout the discussions, guided by intellectual modesty and an openness to new ideas. Both therapist and client can explore the meanings and benefits of different virtues, searching for universal definitions of a cardinal virtue. The discussion may aim to learn from real-life examples encountered by the client, relying on inductive reasoning to guide the exploration.

People can lose sight of a meaningful life if they become focused on apparent goods instead of real goods (Adler, 1941). Thus, clients often value their personal possessions and become upset when these objects are lost, damaged, or stolen. They become angry when another person discards or abuses their beloved objects. However, a meaningful life cannot be found in an assortment of objects. It can be helpful to instruct clients that "stuff is stuff" and that objects can be replaced but that often it is better to learn that life moves along just fine without them. Clients can learn that the objects are not the "good" they are truly seeking (Adler, 1941). For example, a middle-aged male client was moving to a new town and discarding many old objects and mementos. He was sad over losing these objects and felt stressed over his move. However, when asked about how people survive when a tornado or hurricane destroys their home, he began to step back from his minor stressor. Then, the therapist pushed even further, asking the hypothetical question: "What would it be like if we were talking in the parking lot outside your apartment, and we received news that a tornado was heading directly toward the building? You now have five minutes to make your way up to your apartment, gather what you can, and get back down for a quick ride to safety. What would you do?" He thought for a moment and said he would save his dog and get out of the path of the tornado. Clearly, he could now see the irreplaceable value of life and the relative triviality of most things.

Daily reminders and inspirational quotes can help clients remain focused on the virtuous ideals that have been discussed in session. With some clients, it can be helpful to split the session time: "Today, let's be sure we discuss your concerns, but also, I'd like to save a bit of time to discuss what we were talking about last week, when we were exploring the meaning of courage in modern life. Would that be okay?" Questions can examine actions and motives. For example, clients can be asked: "If we could go back in time before this event happened, what would you do differently?" "What could you tell others about courage based on your experience these last few days?"

Virtue Involves Daily Habits

Therapy is often a slow and gradual process. It is not effective to share with clients information about optimal behavior. Instead, therapy involves a process of searching for knowledge that can help guide behavior (Seeskin, 1987). According to virtue ethics, "virtue" refers to a disposition to act in a certain manner (Driver, 1989). The virtuous behavior should be stable over time and consistent across situations (Peterson & Seligman, 2004). This notion was captured in a quotation attributed to Blaise Pascal: "The strength of a man's virtue should not be measured by his special exertions but by his habitual acts." Thus, people are most likely to make their lives meaningful and satisfying by frequently engaging in activities that are kind and supportive of other people, such as volunteering their time, giving money to a person in need, and expressing gratitude about something another person did (Steger, Kashdan, & Oishi, 2008).

In modern psychology, virtue can be framed in terms of acquired habits that have developed through frequent use across an extended period of time (Putnam, 1997). People develop specific character traits through practice until the actions become automatic (Fowers, 2005). Socrates claimed: "Virtues of the soul seem to be akin to bodily qualities, for even when they are not originally innate they can be implanted later by habit and exercise" (*Republic* 7.518).

At the core of the Socratic method, trivialities become trivial, and wealth, fame, and power appear unimportant (Kraut, 1992a). Socrates devoted his investigative discussions to the question of how to live a life characterized by virtue (Kraut, 1992a).

How can therapy help cultivate virtue? The goal is to develop good habits in clients. Virtue and vice can be seen as habits that are developed through frequent use (Fagothey, 1976). This view allows therapists to focus on specific actions and minor moral dilemmas, with the overall goal of helping clients develop a habit of personal reflection, choice, and determined action, even when confronted with a difficult situation. Therapy aims to promote small changes each week, but with a certain amount of repetition across sessions, there will be a gradual accumulation of skill and improvements in thoughtful responses.

People can develop virtue as a skill or a craft (Annas, 1993) that becomes stronger through exercise (Baumeister, Vohs, & Tice, 2007). Learn by doing the desired action, whether it means becoming brave by performing brave acts or becoming temperate by acting in moderation (Kohlberg, 1970). It can be useful to view the cultivation of virtuous behavior as analogous to replacing a bad habit with a good habit (Annas, 1993). It may make sense to change the behavior first and later confront the underlying feelings and attitudes aligned with the actions (Annas, 1993). For example, an adult male high-school teacher was happily married despite his desire for more frequent sexual activity with his wife. To satisfy his urges, he became captivated by online pornography, sometimes of a deviant nature. He wanted to discontinue his reliance on pornography but struggled with the addiction-like qualities of the sexual arousal. In session, a series of questions helped him explore his own values and goals. For example: "What would you tell a high-school student if you found him watching online pornography on a computer at school?" "What would you do if it was a teacher you had caught?" "Would the principal say never do it? Or just do it on your own time at home?" "What might happen if you were caught viewing pornographic material on your computer at home? How would your wife react?" "How would you deal with it if the computer froze on a very explicit image, then moments later your son walked in?" The goal was to create a sense of anticipatory guilt, encouraging the client to feel guilty before he committed the undesirable act. This strategy is similar to asking a person to remember their most severe hangover as a strategy for reducing alcohol consumption during a night out with friends. The client was able to distance himself from the urge to view pornography but asked the therapist, "How can I be sure I won't go back to my old habits?" The therapist continued to push forward via a series of questions: "Where do you want to go from here?" "What kind of person do you want to become?" "When you meet St. Peter at the Pearly Gates of heaven and he asks, 'Why should I let you in?', how will you answer him?" "You have time now to create a good answer with your life and your actions. You make choices every day that steer you down one path or another. Do you see yourself as a strong and virtuous person?" "What does it mean to you for someone to be virtuous?" "Do you tend to choose the virtuous path in every instance (virtue ethics) or does it depend on the specific situation (situational ethics)?" "Would you choose what is right to do even if it is bad for you personally?" These questions were not asked all at once but over the course of an extended conversation exploring the client's beliefs and values. A few questions explored the difference between virtue ethics and situational ethics. Instead of asking "What should I do?", it is more profound to shift the question to "Who shall I become?" (Jordan & Meara, 1990; Louden, 1997). An important life goal involves aiming at becoming a person of integrity (Ballard, 1965). Too many people will talk about truth, virtue, and honor but in reality fail to live according to these standards (Cushman, 1978). Clients should behave according to their lifelong values and moral integrity. It seems essential to ensure that reason rules over primitive desires and emotional energy (Stauffer, 2001).

The Socratic approach aims to promote virtue ethics. Situational ethics is quite limited in its moral value. By choosing a life aimed toward virtue, the individual may become less likely to achieve the external markings of material success (Macintyre, 1997). However, external indicators of success are not respected but instead are seen as fleeting and unimportant. It is much more valuable to become a person of virtuous character. It is important to view each person in terms of moral goodness, regardless of social status in the community (Despland, 1985).

Conclusions

The most important problem confronting society today (as well as centuries ago) may be a lack of virtue in the average person. If this controversial view is accepted, or even considered, then the proper solution lies in promoting a more virtuous daily existence. Furthermore, the optimal guides for effective living reside in the cardinal virtues, learning to behave in a manner that is just, wise, courageous, self-controlled, and God-fearing (Bostock, 1986).

Although five different virtues will be explored in the chapters that follow, there is a common essence shared by them (Penner, 1992). They all entail a view to the good life and a respect for the ultimate importance of a person's moral character. A person's virtue and morality should be viewed in terms of the person's intentions, not simply based on observable actions (Allen, 1996). A virtuous person does not act virtuous in an attempt to achieve fame or honor (Irwin, 1977).

Socrates was aiming for moral ideals that held universal relevance. A virtuous act should be the proper behavior for people who might find themselves in a similar situation (Kaplan, 1979). Hence, Socrates was opposed to ethical relativism, which refers to the idea that each behavior is evaluated as good or bad depending on the situation and its relation to societal demands (Fagothey, 1976). All ethical questions can then be answered by "it depends," which creates the risk that people will manipulate the decision to suit their own personal interests.

Virtue can be viewed as a choice (Strycker, 1966). Everyone desires good things for themselves (Taylor, 1992). There is an important distinction between short-term hedonism and long-term satisfaction (Rudebusch, 1999). Problems arise when people do not fully understand what is good for them, especially in the long run. Virtue ethics focuses on the long-term characteristics of a person, not the discrete acts (Louden, 1997). People can realize that virtue is more valuable than wealth or fame (Strycker, 1966). The goodness of some qualities will be determined by how the qualities are used. Thus, wealth is not good in and of itself but can serve as a tool that allows a person to do good deeds (Benardete, 1989). A virtuous person chooses proper behavior because it is virtuous, not because it may lead to money or prestige (Rudebusch, 1999).

The most important goal in life is to realize each person's true potential (Ryff & Singer, 2008). Living well includes remaining thoughtful and pursuing intrinsic goals (Ryan, Huta, & Deci, 2008). Happiness derives not from pleasure but from living well and pursuing virtue (Ryan, Huta, & Deci, 2008). Unfortunately, some people can become distracted because of misguided intentions, valuing money, prestige, and reputation more than their own moral character (Maxwell, 1984). When guided by a new perspective, physical pleasures are seen as worthless and transient, whereas intellectual pleasures are to be valued (Patterson, 1965). Thus, it is best for a person to satisfy their bodily urges just enough to keep them from becoming a distraction (Patterson, 1965).

ELEVEN

Wisdom

Can You See the Big Picture?

WISDOM PRESENTS THE psychotherapist with a broad and abstract concept that can be used to guide psychotherapy sessions (Hanna & Ottens, 1995). Wisdom includes a knowledge about facts and procedures, an awareness of uncertainty, an appreciation of cultural differences, and an understanding of changes that occur across the lifespan (Baltes & Smith, 1990). For many people, wisdom is a term that has been reserved for older adults who are capable of sharing advice on a wide range of topics. Although this commonsense view of wisdom is useful, it may not fully capture the depth and breadth intended by Socrates and Plato.

Beyond an insight into ideal functioning, people need a practical wisdom (*phronesis*) that helps them express virtue through action (Bright, Winn, & Kanov, 2014). There have been many attempts to clarify and define wisdom. One group of investigators (Holliday & Chandler, 1986) proposed five factors: First, wisdom includes a clear understanding of essential features within a broader contextual background. Second, wisdom includes a high level of skill in judgment and interpersonal communication. Third, wisdom includes general intelligence and ability to focus attention. Fourth, wisdom reflects superior interpersonal skills. Fifth, wisdom entails an ability to blend in with most social groups in a nonobtrusive manner.

Wisdom is distinct from intelligence (Hanna, Bemak, & Chung, 1999; Sternberg, 1998a). Being intelligent does not mean the person is wise (Taranto, 1989). In contrast to intelligence, wisdom confronts serious life problems (Sternberg, 2003). Wisdom includes a timeless view, a focus on universal qualities, and an ability to grasp human nature (Clayton 1982). Wisdom includes creativity, curiosity, an open mind, a desire for learning, and a broad perspective (Peterson & Seligman, 2004).

It may be useful to conceptualize wisdom as an expert level of insight, judgment, knowledge, and pragmatism when considering the more complicated and uncertain matters of human life and its abstract meaning (Baltes & Staudinger, 1993). Much knowledge lies inert and can only be accessed within certain contexts (Bransford, Sherwood, & Sturdevant, 1987). Technical knowledge is quite different from philosophical life wisdom. A person can gain technical skills by studying with a master, such as an apprentice working with an established carpenter, but cultivating the wisdom required for living a virtuous life relies on the lively exchange of ideas in a dialogue (Roochnik, 1996). Wisdom is less likely to entail any specific body of knowledge that can be possessed by an individual but instead is best seen as a lifelong quest to continue learning (Cushman, 1978). Because it does not seem feasible to understand more complex matters when self-understanding is limited, wisdom is aligned with an understanding of oneself (Navia, 1985).

Plato had a simple goal: a life organized by reason (Edman, 1928/1956). According to a Socratic view, wisdom confronts important issues related to living a good life. A lack of wisdom does not stem from a simple lack of information but from erroneous values (Stalley, 1986). Clients need to clarify important values and major life goals. According to Plato, wisdom is focused on attempts to understand the meaning of life (Birren & Svensson, 2005). Wisdom focuses on the fundamental pragmatics of life, that is, good judgment about important life matters that include areas of uncertainty (Baltes & Smith, 1990). Clients can benefit from realizing that most objects (personal fame, social acclaim, career advancement, financial wealth) are not necessary for a lifetime of happiness, whereas morality and virtue are (Reale, 1987; Vlastos, 1994). The value derived from qualities such as wealth will depend on how those qualities are used (Vlastos, 1994). Qualities that are typically considered positive and helpful in reaching a state of happiness (wealth, power, social influence) cannot be valued unless their purpose is guided by wisdom (Day, 1994). Wealth, power, and fame are worthless unless the individual knows how to steer these qualities toward a positive purpose (Csikzentmihalyi & Rathunde, 1990). Wealth, fame, and power are not inherently good or bad but depend on how they are used.

It is important for clients to realize that some desirable things are beyond their control. Even when people behave in an admirable manner, their fame and reputation are dependent upon approval from others (Irwin, 1995). However, virtue can be attained through the actions and attitudes of each individual. Unfortunately, some people seem to invest much of their time and energy trying to gain things that are really fairly trivial (Foot, 1997), such as fame or social approval. According to the Socratic method, what is good is good for us and beneficial in important and lasting ways (Taylor, 1956). Lasting happiness cannot be found in a pill, a shopping expedition, a bank account, or a videogame marathon. Wisdom is needed to redirect one's desires and appetitive urges toward more lasting sources of pleasure. It is important to move away from the temporary pleasures obtained through acts of vice and begin to focus on the more lasting satisfactions derived from virtue (Weiner, 1993). According to the Socratic view, happiness and pleasure must become aligned with virtue (Weiner, 1993).

Psychotherapy can help clients identify ideas for reaching major life goals. Wisdom includes sophisticated knowledge about fundamental aspects of living and guides the person when making difficult life decisions (Smith & Baltes, 1990). Wisdom involves knowledge of good and evil so as to help the person know how to act in order to get the best results (Miller, 1971). Virtuous actions require knowledge of virtue (McPherran, 1996). Socrates stated: "No man voluntarily chooses evil, or that which he thinks to be evil. To prefer evil to good is not in human nature" (*Protagoras* 358). Thus, evil acts and wrongdoing are performed because of ignorance, not weak will or sinful tendencies (Versenyi, 1963). Wisdom relies on reason to make choices that tame the passions (Godlovitch, 1981). Because of a reflective style, a wise person is not likely to be dominated by strong emotional reactions (Birren & Fisher, 1990).

Clients may need help removing barriers to wisdom. Socrates believed that all people will choose what they believe to be best for them. However, because many people do not really know what is good and best, they choose incorrectly, not from evil but from ignorance (Irwin, 1977). This explains why people can defend their actions (for example, a middle-class woman who occasionally shoplifts justifies her actions by explaining that these big stores overcharge on everything). They lack knowledge of good and virtue. Actions should be based on valid reasons, not self-serving rationalizations. Proper behavior cannot be guided by personal desires (Reiman, 1990). Everyone has desires. However, important differences are seen in what people believe to be desirable and good for them (Morgan, 1990).

The Socratic method aims to help a client become a reasonable person. A logical and rational approach requires a person have a valid reason for every judgment and decision made (Nelson, 1949). Virtue is a skill based in wisdom that helps a person consistently do the right thing for the right reasons (Annas, 1993). All virtuous acts depend on the action as well as the proper reasons for the behavior (Fowers, 2005). Virtue is not simply behaving in the proper manner but understanding why and being capable of explaining reasons and defending choices (Annas, 1993).

Some people become focused on daily events and minor concerns. It can be an ongoing struggle to rise above the minor concerns of the day and really focus on the important issues of life, death, meaning, and values. Sometimes it helps to view most struggles as trivialities. Daily life includes a mix of struggles. For many people, life includes worries about the health and safety of loved ones, difficulties finding or succeeding at work, and financial problems. The situation becomes even more troubling when a person has severe or chronic problems with physical health, emotional well-being, or interpersonal functioning. Many clients use valuable session time to review recent events and express their worries. However, this is rarely an efficient use of psychotherapy. Instead, when adopting the Socratic method, the therapist will strive to shift the focus onto larger and more lasting topics. Wisdom includes a view that most hassles are temporary and minor in the large scope of life events.

The Value of Ignorance as a Part of Wisdom

In an interesting paradox, wisdom includes a strong dose of ignorance. Everyone should retain a view that knowledge is fallible (Meacham, 1990). Wisdom includes an awareness of the limits of human understanding (Kitchner & Brenner, 1990; Taranto, 1989). Even the therapist lacks definitive answers and clear life goals. Nonetheless, the therapist, to be effective, must remain open to exploring, learning, and growing during the shared venture of psychotherapy.

Wise people remain aware of their ignorance and other limitations to their ability to understand life. Wisdom includes openness to learning and an awareness of not knowing (Briere, 2012). Most people who think they are wise probably are not (Kupperman, 2005). In contrast, it is more accurate and helpful to retain the attitude that "the more you know, the more you know that you don't know," a statement first attributed to Aristotle. It can be reflected through a simple word change: from "I know" to "I believe" something to be true.

Despite his claim of ignorance, Socrates endorsed the view that human excellence and the good life can only be attained through wisdom (Lesher, 1987). However, the challenge involves accepting the limitations and fallibility of most forms of knowledge. Wisdom includes an awareness of personal ignorance and an appreciation for how much the person does *not* know (Meacham, 1983). Instead, living according to the ideals of the Socratic method requires a lifelong process of searching for wisdom while tolerating doubts, questions, and uncertainties about one's personal beliefs (Meacham, 1983). Thus, the path to wisdom begins with an honest admission of ignorance (Navia, 1985). Knowledge is information that has been verified by objective evidence, but absolute certainty is quite rare; thus intellectual modesty is often appropriate. Certainty leads to ignoring or minimizing other sources of information that contradict any preexisting beliefs.

Searching for Happiness in All the Wrong Places

The search for wisdom may be blocked by an uncritical acceptance of current fad ideas, tendencies to go along with popular opinion, and an overreliance on modern technology (Osbeck & Robinson, 2005). Wisdom does not depend on public opinion or group consensus. If something is true, it is true. Nor is knowledge influenced by opinion. A Socratic discussion may help the person become free from relying overly on popular opinions (Seeskin, 1987).

According to Socrates, happiness is not determined by wealth or poverty (Santas, 1979). Thus, it is common to hear reports of depression, addiction, and interpersonal conflict in the lives of celebrities from entertainment, sports, and politics. Instead of fame or fortune, lasting happiness derives from the honest possession of virtues as part of the person's character (Santas, 1979). Furthermore, knowledge of "the good" is considered necessary and sufficient for a person to behave in a virtuous manner (Reale, 1987).

WISDOM

Wisdom is not the ability to remember a wide spectrum of particular facts (Meacham, 1983). Wisdom goes beyond merely accumulating knowledge; it also creates a major philosophical shift of perspective, enabling the person to see the world in a new way (Dorter, 1997). It may be helpful to view wisdom as more similar to a worker's tools than as the construction that is being built (McLaren, 1989), as more of a process of reasoning and learning (Arlin, 1990) than as a collection of facts. In addition, to be useful, wisdom should guide the person's behavior (Meacham, 1983). Wisdom includes practical knowledge that provides a guide for useful action (Csikzentmihalyi & Rathunde, 1990). Wisdom is not limited to specific facts but confronts how knowledge can be put to use (Meacham, 1990). Wisdom goes beyond problem solving and focuses on broad lessons learned throughout a person's life. Wisdom includes both the proper goals for action as well as the proper path to get there (Foot, 1997). Wisdom includes an ability to make thoughtful decisions, understanding how to live a good life, and transcending daily hassles in favor of important values. Wise people transcend emotional reactions when dealing with a challenging situation (McKee & Barber, 1999).

Wisdom encourages thoughtful reflection. There are many occasions when it is important to stop, think, and find the silver lining of a dark cloud. In a long-term longitudinal study of ninety-four women and forty-four men who were assessed when seniors in high school and again at age fifty-two, results showed that surviving a divorce can help many women enhance their practical wisdom and self-confidence (Wink & Helson, 1997). Clients can be helped to find the silver lining and seek the good that arises from the ashes of a bad event. For example, one older male client bemoaned his recent struggles because of his wife's disabling illness and the added responsibilities that were now placed on him. With help, he was able to appreciate his new expanded role in the family, for example, spending more time with his teenage daughters as they all learned basic cooking skills. He enjoyed the changes to his work schedule to accommodate taking his children to their social activities and sporting events. He valued the loving bond with his children and shifted his priorities in many ways.

It is easy to be nice when things are going well, but kindness, compassion, and generosity become much harder when problems arise. Pain, suffering, and loss can be used to transform personal experiences into wisdom if the person pauses to reflect on the experience in a thoughtful manner (Mulder, House, & Gregory, 2000). Some clients have been able to learn from their personal experience with trauma. For example, a middle-aged adult male had been in a car accident and damaged his spinal cord. Now he was confronting life with paraplegia, and he had adjusted surprisingly well. When asked for advice he might share with other patients, he expressed the life lessons he had learned. "Before my accident, I was something of a jerk to people. I took people for granted, and I used them for whatever I wanted. I don't do that anymore. Now every day, every moment, I see how much I need other people. Even with simple things, I need help. I am a much nicer person now. Because of my injury, I've changed. I'm a better person now."

According to the Socratic method, depression reveals a lack of wisdom. Depression is often triggered by some type of loss, but in some situations, wisdom can help the client view the loss as a natural and inevitable life event. Wisdom includes a focus on life's major concerns and not on trivial and ephemeral worries. For example, when a client became upset over the credit-card debt incurred by his wife, he was initially upset, sad, worried, distraught, and angry. However, his emotions were quickly put into perspective when he was helped to see that several thousand dollars of debt is trivial, especially when compared to a friend's recent diagnosis of cancer. Thus, some cases of anxiety or depression can be treated by helping the client step back from daily worries and minor problems in order to see the big picture, value the positive qualities in the individual's life, and not dwell on recent struggles. Wisdom helps resolve dilemmas and make difficult decisions, guide a personal life review, and raise important questions about life values (Kramer, 1990).

Wisdom promotes positive well-being of self and others and helps guide strategies for personal conduct (Baltes & Staudinger, 2000). Furthermore, wisdom includes an awareness of limitations to most knowledge and a realization that many aspects of life remain unknown and uncertain (Baltes & Staudinger, 2000). At the heart of the Socratic view lies the belief that virtue requires a knowledge of good behavior, and most people who lack virtue do so because they lack knowledge (Benson, 2000). According to Socrates, no one desires evil if they are able to view it as evil (Despland, 1985). Immoral actions are deemed involuntary because they are conducted out of ignorance (Guthrie, 1978).

According to the Socratic method, wisdom is the cardinal virtue. Without wisdom, the other four virtues would not be possible. Hence, this chapter explains the role of wisdom in modern society, helping both therapist and client shift away from a focus on memorization of isolated facts and appreciating the role of wisdom as a view toward life, meaning, and personal values. Because knowledge is fallible, wisdom includes a balance of knowing and doubting (Meacham, 1990).

The Importance of Life Events, Good or Bad

Wisdom develops with age—sort of. Oscar Wilde lamented, "I am not young enough to know everything." Wisdom derives from major life events. Because wisdom must be lived, it accumulates over many years and therefore is unlikely to be seen in youth. In therapy, it can be useful to help clients review their life history to explore any foundation for wisdom. Issues revolve around basic questions: "What major life events have shaped who you are as a person?" "When a stressful life event happens, is it possible for you to choose sadness or tolerance?" Major life events include the end of a long-term relationship, the loss of a loved one through death, and the loss of a job through unemployment or retirement. Is it likely that people learn more about life and wisdom from negative events than from positive events? For example, an adult male client had been successfully treated for a benign brain tumor two years earlier. Now, when he struggled with anxiety about his job, he found it helpful to remind himself of the real difficulties he had already overcome. During stressful weeks at work, he used daily reminders to maintain his perspective that job stress is not the end of the world. He made a copy of his medical report to keep on his desk as a subtle reminder of true stresses he'd already endured, in the hopes of holding on to his awareness of wisdom and life values during a distracting and busy week.

When negative life events happen, it can provide an opportunity to learn, change, and grow. Some people have a tendency to take for granted their spouse, children, job, home, and health. They may only stop to appreciate these things after they have been lost. However, the newfound appreciation may only be a temporary reaction to the threatened loss, and within a few weeks, the old patterns may reemerge.

Let me share a personal example. Many years ago, I was having dinner at a fast-food restaurant with my wife and two young children. I enjoy fast-food burgers if they are eaten hot and fresh, but I dislike them if they have become cool and limp. We received our order of food, found a booth, and sat down ready to eat. The moment I picked up my cheeseburger, my son, age three, announced that he needed to go to the bathroom. I put down my food, and off we went to find the restroom. As we walked down the hall, I was feeling quite annoyed, knowing that my food would be cold by the time we returned to the table. My son was at an age where bathroom rituals were a slow and involved process, taking five to ten minutes before we were again seated. I felt my dinner had been ruined. However, as we walked back to our table, we passed another table, with a father helping his son eat his meal. The father appeared to be beyond retirement age, and the son looked to be a young adult, with some form of severe disability. The son needed help with every mouthful. As I sat back down to eat my cold burger, I realized how trivial my situation was in comparison. In a few months, my son would become much more independent, and even at that point in my son's life, he was fully capable of eating a meal on his own. I felt sad about my own self-centered view and my feelings went out to this father and his son.

A central aspect of wisdom includes an appreciation for the limits of knowledge and the fallibility of human understanding (Meacham, 1990). It is humbling to notice how tiny and insignificant humans are in the universe, how little humans fully understand, how prone to error human beliefs can be, and how fallible all human beings are. For many people, the more they learn about a specific domain, the more plagued they are with uncertainty, doubt, and questions (Meacham, 1990).

Psychotherapy can help clients see the bigger picture of life, death, virtue, and quality of character. Clients are best served by moving away from a focus on petty issues and trivial problems. Several studies have interviewed patients who experienced a near-death experience. In one study of seventeen adults who had survived a serious and life-threatening accident or illness (Kinnier, Tribbensee, Rose, & Vaughan, 2001), patients reported a change of life perspective. After recovery, qualitative analysis revealed that the patients recommended not allowing minor frustrations or daily trivialities to disrupt their moods, and instead they aimed to savor the good moments in their lives. Furthermore, most of the participants (fifteen of seventeen) had become more spiritual and felt a closer spiritual bond with other people. They now devalued the pursuit of money and disregarded social comparisons and instead wanted to become more helpful to others. Wisdom encourages people to treat other people better (Garrett, 1996).

Clients benefit when they are able to appreciate the transitory and trivial nature of most problems. For example, a single parent of two children became quite distraught when her oldest son moved out of state. Now that her son lived far away, he was unable to visit over the major holidays, and he tended to call home infrequently. The client felt lonely, rejected, and somewhat angry at her son. However, during therapy sessions, the client was helped to see the situation differently. When she was able to see ways in which the situation could be different—and worse—it helped her change her view of this situation from dire to minimal. Her son was alive and healthy. He was not in a distant hospital seeking radical treatments for an incurable illness. He was not serving as active-duty military in a war-torn country. He was not imprisoned as a POW in a foreign country. Although he was unable to call often or visit home, he remained alive, safe, and healthy. More importantly, this discussion helped shift the client's perspective in a broad manner, and her new views were not exclusive to one specific situation. Instead, therapy aimed to help the client develop a broader view and a more pervasive shift of attitudes, which in turn helped her, among other things, appreciate the time she could spend with her other child. Effective therapy may require lifelong efforts to redirect a person's habitual views and begin to focus on the bigger concerns in life.

Wisdom refers to the general ability to reason logically and make useful decisions. According to Socrates, a good life derives from reason, not pleasure (Hampton, 1990), and no one desires evil (Santas, 1979). Using more contemporary language, no one chooses to act in an evil manner. Instead, they may mistakenly believe their actions can bring about positive gains.

Therapy can help clients appreciate the wonders of nature and the wonderful aspects of their lives before they are gone (see figure 11.1). Clients can detach from their current struggles in order to review their lives as a whole. Clients may reduce their distress when they stop to appreciate the value of little things. Clients can appreciate the ability to breathe without the need for mechanical assistance (because patients on oxygen or respirators cannot do so), the ability to choose what to eat and when to eat (because prison inmates and famine-ravaged countries cannot do so), and the ability to sleep in a dry bed (as homeless people cannot do). Overall, the goal is to reduce a focus on material gains and enhance an appreciation for social bonds and simple pleasures. Some clients do not stop to appreciate the big picture until death is near, and at that point it may be too late to make meaningful changes in their lifestyle or daily routines.

For many clients, a focus on their future deathbed scenario can be enlightening. It can be useful to ask a series of questions: "Do you think you could ever forgive the other person?" "Do you think you could ever reach the point where you could laugh at these events or at least shrug them off as no big deal?" "Let's jump ahead forty years or more. Suddenly we are both very old and sickly. You have lived a long life, but now you are quite ill and have only a few days left to live. At that point, how much will the events this last week really matter?" "At that point, will you view them as a catastrophe that ruined your life or as no big deal anymore?" "Is there a chance you could learn to look back at these events and see them as an amusing anecdote?" "What would you need to change for you to reach that point now and be able to see the humor of this situation?" "Realistically, in ten years, will you still remember these events?" "I remember an old quotation that says 'Time alone does nothing, but situations change over time.' So what would need to change for you to shift your view of these events?" "How long will it take to reach the point where you feel recovered from these events?" "How long are you going to let these recent events bother you?" "How long will you keep the memory of these events alive, rubbing your own face in the memory of what happened a few days ago?" "Is it possible to make the shift now and spare you that emotional burden?" "If we come back to the present day, but you knew that you only had six months left to live, how would you live differently?" "Would you still work ten hours a day on most days?" "Would you continue to watch television for six hours each day?" "How would you spend your time differently?" "How would you manage stress and conflict differently?" "What can we do in our sessions to help you begin making those changes?"

The sincere pursuit of wisdom is likely to create a change in the person's character (Cushman, 1978). The search for wisdom is not a disinterested intellectual debate. To be useful, the person must value the insights gained through wisdom, so the client believes it, feels it, does it, and lives it. Wisdom can help a person overlook minor hassles and see the big picture. For example, a middle-aged male client had been struggling with his divorce and adjustment to life as a single parent. He had made plans to spend his weekend doing yard work and cleaning his basement. While carrying out trash, an elderly neighbor invited him over for a beer, but he politely declined, explaining his need to complete several household chores. In session, this issue of priorities was discussed. He was asked to jump ahead forty years: what might people say at his funeral? He replied: "He kept a clean house and yard." He immediately saw how ludicrous this answer seemed and let out an abrupt, spontaneous laugh. He then gave a different answer: "I guess I would want them to say he was nice, friendly, helpful to everyone, and he appreciated the people in his life." Although this was a minor event, he was able to use it as leverage to shift his priorities and make changes in his daily behavior. Wisdom guides people toward what is important and away from trivialities, so people do not risk wasting their lives (Kekes, 1983). A person cannot live well without understanding the difference between important and unimportant things (Kupperman, 2005). The client began a major shift, seeing his previously "big goals" now as trivial obstacles and recontextualizing his tendency to put tasks ahead of people in his daily life. He began to view people and social bonds as more important life goals. During his final session, he noted: "I am always building my life and my contentment, and I can live in the present and enjoy life."

Wisdom should not be viewed in terms of blocks of information but as a process that examines which views are to be trusted and how they can be used (Meacham, 1990). Thus, a wise person is likely to examine various sources of information, remain cautious in making decisions, consider several different points of view, evaluate a mixture of available options, and anticipate the likely consequences of action (Meacham, 1990).

The Beneficial Impact of Wisdom

Problems arise when people value power, money, or social recognition more than the quality of their character (Stalley, 1986). Possessing wisdom includes an ability to avoid actions driven more by emotion than reason (McKee & Barber, 1999). Wisdom helps people focus on important and lasting goals. Wisdom can help a person remain calm and tolerant throughout most situations but become energized to fight when needed. A central goal of the Socratic method involves clarifying the person's values and aligning a person's life with virtue (Edman, 1928).

The therapist can ask questions that may help clients explore different issues aligned with wisdom. First, it is essential for clients to explore and understand proper goals for life, especially issues related to their own personal character and virtue ethics. Second, Socratic questions can be used to help clients develop ideas for obtaining their most important life goals. Third, in order to accomplish life goals, clients may need help in reducing common distractions and frivolous ideas. Fourth, cultivating wisdom relies on helping all people become aware of their own ignorance and limitations.

Wisdom as a Focus for Psychotherapy

The quest for wisdom is a lifelong process (Ardelt, 1997). Therapy can help clients appreciate the wonders of nature and the wonderful aspects of their lives. Wisdom may be cultivated from a thoughtful review of life events. In a study of 121 older adults who were interviewed as part of a forty-year follow-up evaluation, analyses using a structural-equation model revealed that wisdom had a profound impact on life satisfaction in old age and that the impact of wisdom was stronger than the power of each person's objective life circumstances (Ardelt, 1997).

A person's attitude is something like an amplifier of the emotions that are currently being experienced. Thus, the events may not change, but depending on the person's attitude, emotions can become more intense (I am furious) or less intense (I am not happy about what happened, but I will get over it). Therapy can help clients develop a more adaptive perspective. In session, the therapist can use the client's life events as opportunities to confront attitudes and expectations. Clients can be asked questions to explore their values: "What do you wish you had said during that heated argument?" "If we jump ahead fifty years from today, will you still remember these events?" "Will you care about these events?" "Will you let these events cause the end of your relationship, or can you tolerate them and move forward in a positive manner?" "What can you do to manage this situation in a positive manner?" "What can you learn about yourself from these events?"

Unlike a person's beliefs and opinions, knowledge cannot be changed through simple persuasion (Miller, 1971). Likewise, information obtained through the senses cannot be fully trusted. One sense cannot observe another sense. Each organ is restricted to its own experience. Therefore, knowledge does not rely on sensory perception (Cropsey, 1995). Wisdom relies on knowledge and reasoning, not empirical evidence. True knowledge can be obtained through reason (Miller, 1971). Thus, most transitory things are tangible or visible, whereas eternal qualities cannot be seen (More, 1928) except with the mind's eye.

Psychotherapy to Cultivate Wisdom

Considering psychotherapy sessions as cultivating wisdom in the client seems like an odd and overwhelming way to view therapy. However, when working from a Socratic approach, wisdom is a central goal for therapy. Without wisdom, clients are unlikely to develop attitudes in support of courage, justice, or moderation. Wisdom plays the central role among the virtues. People do not behave poorly because of a weakness of willpower but because they lack an understanding of good versus evil (Hughen, 1982).

Therapy can help clients with their important life decisions (Roemer & Orsillo, 2012). Wisdom can develop through adversity and by overcoming major life problems. Clients can be encouraged to appreciate the mixture of good and bad events that have occurred and that have contributed to shaping them into the people they have become. Clearly, this is the central underpinning behind existential analysis, as developed by Viktor Frankl. In modern times, we can all use the memory of the terrorist attacks on September 11 to remind us to value our friends, family, and good experiences every day.

It is easy to be happy and act friendly when everything is going well. It becomes much harder to enjoy life and remain helpful to others when problems disrupt routine. However, like a good sailor, it takes experience and skill to sail against the rough seas and large waves. Furthermore, when the wind stops completely, the sailor uses oars to keep moving under his own power; this is analogous to the self-guided search for personal insights and wisdom gained through a Socratic exploration (Benardete, 1989).

Conclusions

Socrates used dialogue to explore and improve a person's life goals, hoping to make improvements in Athens's social life, moral integrity, and daily functioning (Maxwell, 1984). Unfortunately, his followers, most notably

Aristotle, shifted the focus onto intellectual contributions that had less direct impact on daily living (Maxwell, 1984). Thus, whereas Socrates devoted his life to the pursuit of wisdom, others that followed him shifted their focus onto the expansion of knowledge (Maxwell, 1984).

Wisdom is the voice of reason, encouraging clients to rely on a combination of logic and common sense to guide their behavior. However, it is essential to view wisdom in terms of major life goals and a perspective that values meaningful actions. Wisdom is the central virtue (Brickhouse & Smith, 1997); without an adequate basis in wisdom, the other virtues the next four chapters will cover would not be possible. Virtuous character requires that the person hold a thoughtful understanding of the virtue (Fowers, 2005). Wisdom provides the foundation for virtuous behavior, and a lack of wisdom paves the way for destructive acts (Despland, 1985).

The development of wisdom relies on a critical examination of all beliefs (King, 2008). In the dialogue *Meno*, Socrates viewed himself as similar to an electric eel, stinging people awake. When a person's beliefs undergo a critical examination and possible refutation, the person moves closer toward wisdom because even if the beliefs are refuted, a central aspect of wisdom involves knowing what you do not know (King, 2008).

Wisdom takes time to develop (Kekes, 1983). Wisdom involves moving away from temporary fads and inconsequential notions in order to begin a lifelong search for timeless truths (Robinson, 1990). The search for wisdom requires daily effort and prolonged thoughtful discussion (Osbeck & Robinson, 2005).

Worksheet on Everyday Miracles

There are only two ways to live your life: One is as though nothing is a miracle. The other is as though everything is a miracle.

—Albert Einstein

It can be easy to get caught up in the activity and commotion of daily living. We may become so busy with chores or distractions that we hardly notice the many good things in our lives. Fortunately, if we stop and really look at our lives, we may be able to see the many wonderful things that happen every day. It can be useful to think of the unfortunate people who are unable to make the following statements because of severe medical illness, physical injury, living in extreme poverty, or being incarcerated.

I may take them for granted, but really I am thankful for these everyday marvels:
    I can breathe without the need of a machine to help me.
    My eyes work adequately so that I can see.
    My legs let me move around so I can walk.
    I can talk and express myself using words.
    My ears work so I can hear sounds.
    I have a home where I can live and sleep.
    I can go to a store to buy groceries so I have food to eat.
    I can turn on a faucet and easily get water that is safe to drink.
    I can spend my leisure time as I choose.
    I can go to bed when I feel tired.
    Please add to this list by writing statements about everyday marvels that you appreciate.

_____
_____
_____

Figure 11.1

TWELVE

Courage

Are You Brave Enough to Be Yourself?

COURAGE SEEMS LIKE an uncommon topic for most psychotherapy sessions. At an even more basic level, most people do not think of courage as playing an important role in their everyday lives. However, in many ways, a proper understanding of courage can help promote its prevalence in modern society. When viewed from the perspective of the Socratic method, courage becomes an important and even central goal for many clients.

The dialogues of Plato repeatedly display an interest in discovering clear and objective terminology. Socrates asks the Athenian general Laches: "What is that common quality which is the same in all of these cases, and which is called courage?" (*Laches* 191). However, Socratic hopes for clarity notwithstanding, the dialogue produces a state of confusion. Laches replies: "I fancy that I do know the nature of courage; but somehow or other, she has slipped away from me, and I cannot get hold of her and tell her nature" (*Laches* 194). Even when we think we understand various terms, abstract concepts can be difficult to define in a clear, consistent, and objective manner. Nonetheless, a dialogue still can be useful for confronting an abstract idea and exploring how it might be displayed in daily life. To continue with Socrates's search for the meaning of courage, after Nicias joins Laches and Socrates in conversation, Socrates offers a summary of their discussion, proposing that "courage is a sort of wisdom" (*Laches* 195).

Courage is a quality that, though ever-present, is barely noticed in modern society. For the most part, people can travel from home to work and go out for an evening without fearing for their lives. Despite recent acts of terrorism and gun violence, most aspects of life in the modern world are safe from imminent threat.

Courage can help overcome a variety of problems. Courage is likely to play a prominent role in the treatment of debilitating anxiety disorders (Putnam, 1997). However, a Socratic approach may not be necessary for the treatment of many anxiety disorders. Because of the wealth of data supporting short-term treatments for the anxiety disorders, simple exposure-based therapies can be effective. Exposure to the feared situation is an effective and potent treatment for most forms of phobia as well as for social anxiety, panic disorder, obsessive-compulsive disorder, and many cases of PTSD. Thus, a Socratic approach is more likely to play a background role in these sessions. However, such an approach may be more useful when clients are struggling with generalized worries or chronic social anxiety.

Understanding the Nature of Courage

Despite being a common term that is frequently used in casual conversation, developing a clear and useful definition of courage can be complicated. One research study sought to identify common acts of courage (Pury & Starkey, 2010). After reviewing almost one thousand narrative reports of courage as displayed personally by participants, most narratives were coded as unacceptable examples that did not qualify as acts of courage (Pury & Starkey, 2010). So what does courage entail? Mere boldness of action does not necessarily mean the actions are based in courage (Schmid, 1992). Acts of courage typically involve bold action and doing what is needed to protect an important life value. The brave person takes risks that can be justified. When a person confronts danger for entertainment or for a thrill, such actions are best viewed as foolhardy, not as acts of courage.

According to the present interpretation of the Socratic method, courage is a complex quality. It involves a potentially dangerous situation that could pose real harm, yet the person thoughtfully chooses to accept substantial personal risk, in the hopes of producing a worthwhile outcome (Rate, 2010).

Courage also involves the personal integrity and perseverance required to carry out these acts (Peterson & Seligman, 2004).

Courage is brought to bear in situations that pose some degree of risk or danger, situations most people might freeze or run away from (Seeskin, 1976). However, what is considered dangerous is greatly influenced by an individual's perception of difficulty, risk, and potential harm (Rorty, 1986). Courage is important when confronting physical threats, such as those faced by soldiers and police officers. However, courage is also important when confronting the social risks encountered by most people in their day-to-day lives, risks such as social rejection, saying something stupid, being the only one in the group to endorse a novel idea, or dressing in clothing that violates local mores.

Courage is important whenever a therapist is helping clients manage feelings of fear and anxiety. Fear may create a focus on safety and protection, preventing acts of courage (Wallace, 1978). Courage does not mean confronting difficult events without fear. The experience of fear and physiological arousal is normal and does not reflect either courage or cowardice. Fear cannot be controlled, whereas behavior in the face of fear can be a measure of courage (Foot, 1997). Courage is not found in fearlessness but in actions guided by wisdom (Versenyi, 1963).

Courage is based on the wisdom to determine what is best in the long run. Courage involves an awareness of a worthy goal (Devereux, 1977), and it can be more effective to act despite fear when pursuing an important goal (Fowers, 2005). Without a worthy goal, the willingness to take risks can be described more as thrill seeking, foolhardiness, or bravado than as courage (Fowers, 2005). Socrates stated: "He is to be deemed courageous whose spirit retains in pleasure and in pain the commands of reason about what he ought or ought not to fear" (*Republic* 4.442). Thus, courage requires the knowledge of what is to be feared (Schmid, 1985) because cowardly acts are dangerous to the person's moral character (Seeskin, 1976).

Wisdom is necessary for acts to be acts of courage. Courage involves knowing which situations are truly dangerous and which situations are trivial. According to the Socratic view, if a person has true knowledge of good and moral behavior, the person should automatically do what is right, regardless of fear or danger (Seeskin, 1976). Wisdom is key because both the hero and the coward act according to their opinion of which action will cause them the least amount of harm (Seeskin, 1976).

Courage requires the practical knowledge about how to manage a difficult situation. One must know when, where, and how to take an action that involves risk (Rorty, 1986). It also includes a realistic appraisal of one's limits and of human limitations more generally (Dent, 1981). Courage depends on wisdom in terms of insight into morality and virtue (Vlastos, 1994). It can also be considered as knowledge of what should and should not be feared (Allen, 1996); one need not be fearless but learn to fear less. To be considered an act of courage, actions are based on moral values and aimed at achieving goals considered important (Pury, Lopez, & Key-Roberts, 2010; Schmid, 1992).

Courage is displayed in bold action (Schmid, 1992). It is not simply knowing what should be feared but also requires holding true to one's beliefs when faced with fear, temptation, or coercion (Annas, 1981). When courage is present, the person does not allow fear or danger to deflect from the preferred plan of action (Dent, 1981). Courageous acts rely on the awareness of what is worth the risk versus what dangers should be avoided (Versenyi, 1963). Courage involves a voluntary choice of action that is conducted with deliberate and thoughtful intent, intended for a positive outcome (Devereux, 1977; Gruber, 2011). When combined with wisdom, courage allows the person the strength and determination to choose and continue to follow a course of action toward admirable goals (Santas, 1979). Courage allows a person to choose rationally the desired behavior, instead of reacting to fear and anxiety (Schmid, 1992). Despite a rational desire to leave or avoid a dangerous situation, the person displays the strength of will needed to suppress negative emotions and endure a difficult situation. Courage can be seen as perseverance despite the person's subjective experience of fear (Norton & Weiss, 2009). Courage keeps a space open for logical reasoning, which helps the person to choose the proper action even in the face of danger (Wallace, 1978). Thus, courage includes endurance (Devereux, 1977) and fortitude (Hunt, 1980; Schmid, 1992) when trying to accomplish a good and important act (Irwin, 1977).

Situations That Pose a Risk of Harm

People often associate courage with some form of life-threatening danger; that is, courage only comes into play during combat or when police officers or firefighters risk their lives to save others. However, Socrates moved courage beyond these contexts and into various aspects of everyday living (Gericke, 1994). According to Socrates, courage relies on an understanding of what is important and potentially worth fighting to protect. In contrast, when courage is lacking, a person avoids proper behavior because too much concern has been placed on potential dangers and risks that should be seen as trivial in nature (Wallace, 1978). Such ignorance disrupts the view of risks and dangers (Wallace, 1978). According to the Socratic method, courage involves maintaining proper behavior despite risk of social discomfort, disapproval, or rejection (Lopez et al., 2010).

Courage can help people manage the anxiety that accompanies a life of poverty (Irwin, 1977). Many clients struggle with financial limitations that create endless worries about their ability to pay their rent, purchase food, or buy gas or a bus pass. It can take courage to deal with daily struggles and still retain enough personal strength and integrity to be helpful to others.

Courage is important when a person is facing a major disease or illness (Irwin, 1977) or when forced to face a terminal illness (Jacobs, 2008). Based on semistructured interviews with twenty-one older adults (aged 67 to 94) who had been diagnosed with a chronic illness, common themes revealed the view that development of courage is a lifelong process (Finfgeld, 1995). Courage allows a person to face death with dignity (Lageman, 1989).

A lack of courage can most commonly be seen in the area of social situations. Social pressure can impair a person's natural tendencies at work, school, and in the family. Courage can be described as a willingness to confront social pressure, behaving according to personal values and speaking one's mind even when others disagree. It takes courage to stand up for one's beliefs when those beliefs are opposed by others. Courage provides the strength to oppose peer pressure (Taylor, 1956) and may help a person confront a risk of social rejection. However, in social situations and work environments, many people hold back from expressing unpopular views.

Some people seem afraid of confrontation, especially in the workplace. They may let coworkers continue engaging in some form of inappropriate behavior out of fear of confrontation and the possible social repercussions. Such acts of cowardice may include tolerating rude language from a colleague, enduring sexually inappropriate advances from a superior, or rigidly following corporate rules while neglecting the practical realities of an individual case.

A lack of courage also can be seen within some family dynamics. In some families, one family member sets the tone for acceptable behavior, interests, and activities. Other family members may follow this lead even when they personally hold different views. According to the Socratic model, people with courage will disregard social approval as a guide for their behavior (Schmid, 1992). Courage is necessary for the other virtues (Medina, 2008) because it provides the person with the inner strength often needed to act in a responsible manner.

Finally, courage includes a willingness to accept oneself, including one's weaknesses, flaws, and imperfections (Tillich, 1952). Awareness of these limitations does not weaken the client but instead can be used to motivate each client toward self-improvement. It can be important to develop the courage needed to be true to oneself and live according to one's standards and ideals (Medina, 2008). People often benefit from the courage to be sincere and authentic and not by trying to seek public approval or please others (Shklar, 1984). The courage to be true to one's self is important, especially during adolescence. At a basic level, courage is needed for an open exploration in therapy so clients are willing to confront their true self (Poland, 2008). Therapy often aims to help clients have the courage to be imperfect (Brouwers & Wiggum, 1993). At a much deeper level, to become a person of virtue, the person must hold certain principles and be willing to act on them (Hunt, 1980).

Promoting Brave Actions Through a Therapeutic Dialogue

Psychotherapy sessions can help promote courage. Clients can be helped to identify situations that would benefit from courage, confront their reasons for previously not acting in a courageous manner, and realign their focus from trivial harm to meaningful action. In this way, clients can begin to minimize the risks involved in certain situations while valuing the actions and keeping sight of admirable goals. A therapeutic dialogue is used to remove obstacles such as ignorance or misguided values that could obstruct the path toward courageous behavior (Schmid, 1992).

Positive self-statements can be used to cultivate courage. In a study of fifty adults who reported a fear of heights (Marshall, Bristol, & Barbaree, 1992), the participants were sorted into three groups: twenty-nine individuals who reported minimal fear, nine participants whose fear blocked them from continuing in the study, and twelve individuals who reported high levels of fear yet persisted in the activities and confronted their fear of heights. Analyses revealed that the individuals in the "courageous" group, who overcame their negative emotions while confronting the dangerous situation, used positive self-statements to maintain their focus and determination so they could persevere despite their fears. Effective psychotherapy can incorporate strategies based on cognitive restructuring to develop positive expectations and adaptive attitudes to guide behavior.

Common acts of courage may be seen when a person confronts social anxiety or other phobias. Clients may need courage to oppose social norms, confront peer pressure, and face the risk of ridicule. For example, an adult male client described his irrational fear of airplane travel. He reported the frequent belief "I think the plane will crash, and I will die." He was upset with himself because, though he didn't want to ruin the family vacation, he felt he was disrupting plans for a trip to Disneyworld because his fear blocked his ability to fly there. He realized he could tame his anxiety if he accepted the more important goal—he did not want to raise his children to have a similar fear. I explained the value of a coping role model who demonstrates a struggle but works to overcome it. "I am not going to let my anxiety ruin the family vacation"; "I do not want to become a bad role model for my kids."

Therapy often requires an individualized approach. Strategies for managing a fearful or dangerous situation must come from the person so he or she can take into account dark memories and past terrors (Kohak, 1960). Even current struggles can create excessive feelings of distress that block effective action. For example, an adult male client was struggling because of a mixture of stressful events that all were happening close together in time. He reported that he was currently underemployed, working only part-time hours. He was hoping to apply for jobs that matched his interests and paid a decent wage. However, he needed to get a better job sooner rather than later because his wife was currently pregnant with their third child. He had been applying for jobs throughout the area, determined to become a police officer, but many of these job options were limited by a recent hiring freeze. In session one week later, he reported that his landlord had sold the apartment building they lived in, and he and his family now had six weeks to relocate. He described his current struggles as being like the movie *The Perfect Storm*. He felt his small ship was destined to capsize: all three "waves" were about to hit him and his family. Instead of rejecting his view, the therapist built on that imagery and used it to create a shift in his focus. It was pointed out that in the movie, the ship sank because the captain and crew made poor choices: they held onto their cargo and continued along the same, slow path. If the ship's captain had made different choices, the movie could have ended differently. Thus, if the client expanded his job search to other allied professions (such as security guard, firefighter, or paramedic), he might be able to get through the "rough seas." However, if he stubbornly delayed searching for a new job or new housing, his ship could sink. Over a span of three sessions, the analogy was used to help the client steer a different path, one toward calm waters, and to develop the patience to wait out the storm. The therapist asked him to consider his life in fifteen years if he followed one of several possible paths. The first option involved continuing to seek jobs in his chosen field. If he remained focused on one line of work, most likely his financial struggles would continue because there were no relevant job openings within a fifty-mile radius of his home. The second path involved seeking jobs in other areas, even though the jobs may be boring. He was asked to consider what his life might be like if he accepted an office job or a job as a field inspector. Next, he was asked to consider jobs for which he might be qualified. Thus, instead of police officer, what would it be like to serve as an insurance claims investigator? This would be an area in which he might excel, and it could serve as a job that provided financial security even if it was outside his original career choices. Using the "perfect storm" metaphor, he could see that stubbornly holding onto one plan while neglecting the storm surrounding him and his family would likely end in disaster. However, if he broadened his view to include a range of options, he could chart a new course. It might create a detour, at least temporarily, until the storm had passed. When things settled down, he could return to a more satisfying and permanent plan for his family and career options. In one session, the Socratic notion that "no harm can come to a good person" was explored, and the client shifted his focus from his current stressors onto his strength and determination when confronted with adversity. We identified the potential strengths he could develop if he could manage to get through these events. He could begin to see the sunshine starting to peek through the dark clouds.

Family conflict can create some important and lasting problems. In some families, one member rises to dominance and claims leadership in the family. As an example, an adult female client felt endless pressure to attend all family gatherings, regardless of her own busy lifestyle. Despite being a successful professional, she was afraid of family conflict and the risk of rejection by her parents. Socrates demonstrated the strength needed to say "no" when others were pushing him to do or say something he felt was not right (Despland, 1985). A person should not worry how others might react (Seeskin, 1987). Instead, it is important to stand up for what is right, even when others disagree.

Effective therapy requires the courage to change. Clients are more likely to remain in therapy if they maintain at least a modest amount of courage. Such courage relies on the client and therapist believing that the client can withstand the scrutiny that is involved in psychotherapy and the client and therapist maintaining the belief that the client can grow stronger by completing a course of psychotherapy.

A therapist can facilitate courage by highlighting the client's strengths and by identifying past struggles in which the client has behaved with courage (Goldberg & Simon, 1982). For example, when working with an adult male client who is overly helpful and a bit timid, a Socratic discussion helped empower him and encourage his ability to deal with his family. A question that is overly direct is likely to fall flat: "When was the last time you displayed courage through observable actions?" It is much more useful to ask clients about their own experiences with similar problems in the past: "Have you ever had to deal with a situation like this before?" "Was there ever a time when things were resolved quite well?" "What was going on at that time?" "How did you manage to deal with it back then?" "Do you think you could try a similar strategy now?" Many clients tend to focus on their flaws and limitations and may not remember past efforts that were successful in managing a difficult situation. Thus, it can be even more helpful when the therapist is aware of a past event that involved successful coping by the client. More directive questions can be useful: "Do you remember a few weeks ago when we were discussing the disagreement you had with your cousin?" "How did you react?" "I know it was an uncomfortable situation, but you were able to remain composed and assertive; how did you manage to handle it at that time?" "Do you think you can do something similar now, with the current situation?" With thoughtful questions and gentle prodding, even timid clients can be encouraged to behave in a more courageous and assertive manner. When a therapist can highlight a client's strengths, the client can begin to develop the confidence needed to confront instead of avoid problems.

The process of inductive reasoning can be used to help bolster a client's confidence on the path to courage (Overholser, 1993a). When clients have managed one struggle, it can be used as a reference point for future coping efforts. It is helpful and even complimentary to ask a client: "Do you remember three weeks ago when you were having a similar problem with your neighbor?" "How did you handle the conflict at that time?" "I thought you were able to talk to him in a direct yet supportive way?" "Do you think you could use a similar strategy now with your coworker?" These questions were not blurted out all at once but were used over the course of the dialogue to help identify useful coping strategies while also enhancing the client's self-confidence.

Conclusions

Courage can provide a valuable target for psychotherapy with some clients (Overholser, 1999b). When fear and uncertainty are prominent, clients may be suffering from a lack of courage. Thus, therapy discussions about fear, anxiety, and courage can be useful for a wide spectrum of clients. Courage empowers an individual to display the other virtues (Bell & Campbell, 1995). Courage requires wisdom to see what is worth a battle, justice to do what is right for everyone, and moderation to fight only when truly necessary.

Courage is important in many social situations. Too many forms of social injustice have been allowed to continue because bystanders were afraid of the potential social repercussions had they intervened. It could be argued that bystander apathy stems from a lack of courage. Clients can become brave enough to protect self and others, even when they know they may be harmed in some way.

Courage should be guided by wisdom and moderation (Irwin, 1995). Acts of bravery are guided by reason and not diverted by fear (Irwin, 1995). Courage needs an evaluation of which dangers are worth the risk and which would be foolhardy to confront. Instead of a risk of death or injury, clients may risk their standing in their social group through embarrassment, rejection, or ridicule. A person can tame fear through a sense of purpose that guides important action (Goud, 2005). Courage is the power to choose reason over emotion, being willing to face danger and confront fear for an admirable cause (Wallace, 1978). Courage involves a rational choice of action when confronted with a risk of danger or suffering (Schmid, 1992). Courage can be found at the middle ground between cowardice and rash behavior (Putnam, 2010). Courage bridges the gap between a person's tendency to seek safety and willingness to confront opportunities for growth (Goud, 2005).

THIRTEEN

Moderation

Learning to Tame Your Desires

PSYCHOTHERAPY SESSIONS OFTEN focus on facilitating self-improvement and self-control in clients (Overholser, 1996a). Self-control can help a person restrain or redirect urges and desires (Trianosky, 1988). The Socratic view of moderation can be a useful guideline in treatment. The development of moderation relies on a rational control over passions and urges (Versenyi, 1963).

A therapeutic dialogue can guide a process of self-exploration to help clients evaluate their values and life priorities (Annas, 1993). Therapy can help clients develop self-control over their temptations, desires, and passions, in order to maintain an effective balance in their lives. People can learn how to act in ways that are beneficial for themselves and others (Miller, 1971). Over the course of therapy, clients can develop the wisdom, strength, and motivation to guide their behavior toward constructive goals consistently (Meara, Schmidt, & Day, 1996). The goal is rational self-determination derived through a logical self-contemplative dialogue combined with personal life experiences (Nelson, 1980).

According to Socratic teaching, most forms of excess stem from ignorance. Hence, moderation requires the wisdom (Curzer, 1991) to downplay the importance of transient physical pleasures (Gosling, 1973). Clients do not display patterns of excess because of a weakness of willpower but because they lack knowledge, wisdom, and appropriate life goals (Hughen, 1982). The aim of a Socratic approach is to bring desires into alignment with wisdom, with a focus on important and lasting pleasures (Weiner, 1993). To be effective, moderation must become integrated with wisdom so the person's beliefs and desires are fully integrated with life goals (Curzer, 1991). Wisdom involves helping clients see the trivial nature of most temporary pleasures, thereby reducing the potency of a desire. Wisdom helps clients distance themselves from their possessions and physical urges so they can focus on the lasting benefits of a virtuous character.

Psychotherapy sessions can focus on important life goals, values, and virtues. Because some physical pleasures and material gains are destructive, a person should not use pleasure or enjoyment as a guide for living (Grube, 1966). Socrates held the belief that when a person sees the unwavering value in wisdom as a lifelong pursuit, other temptations will lose their influence and become impotent and irrelevant (Bostock, 1986). People need to realize that some pleasurable things are not good for them (Gomez-Lobo, 1994). The only things that cannot be used to an excessive amount or reach a dangerous level are the virtues.

Clients are surrounded by temptations. Many potential sources of pleasure can seduce clients into ignoring their potentially harmful effects (Brickhouse & Smith, 1994). Many forms of excess are characterized by an overindulgence in physical pleasures and an excessive focus on material desires. Food, alcohol, and sex can all be carried to an extreme, turning something good into something bad, turning pleasure into pain, turning help into harm (Hughen, 1982). When taken to excess, a person's desires can become a weakness.

Excessive desires can take many forms, including drug addiction, overeating, pathological gambling, and excessive sexual activity (Orford, 1985). Even productive activities such as physical exercise and work habits can be performed excessively (Stephenson et al., 1995), becoming detrimental to one's physical health or social functioning. Almost anything done to excess can create a hazard.

Tendencies for gluttony seem to be common today. Although obesity has biological and genetic components, for some people, eating behavior is guided by the immediate satisfaction of basic urges. The standard intervention for weight-loss programs involves a balanced diet with sound nutrition, combined with reduced caloric intake and increased caloric expenditure. Changes should focus on respecting a healthy lifestyle, not just weight loss. Lifestyle changes provide a valuable pathway to lasting improvement.

Excessive urges for food, alcohol, drugs, gambling, or sexual activity can reach addictive levels (Orford, 1985). Short-term pleasure can create long-term problems. Disease models of addiction focus on biological predispositions that can be suppressed through drug treatments, but these disease models risk neglecting psychosocial factors in the etiology and treatment of addictive behaviors (Orford, 1985). Misguided values and a lack of personal restraint can play important roles in addiction.

Moderation can be a useful goal for therapy. In a research study of forty-two adults with self-admitted problems with excessive alcohol consumption, the participants learned how to drink in moderation, and this was found to be an effective treatment for alcohol abuse (Sitharthan, Sitharthan, Hough, & Kavanagh, 1997). Additional research has shown that patients trained in moderate drinking were able to maintain their new habit, still drinking in moderation at a thirty-month follow-up evaluation (Walitzer & Connors, 2007).

According to the Socratic dictum, people should strive for moderation in all things and attempt to eliminate excessive behaviors. A therapeutic focus on moderation helps clients find a balance between extremes without referencing the client's own excessive behaviors regarding food, alcohol, money, or emotions. The goal is a balanced lifestyle. A search for pleasure can be guided by intelligent thought (Taylor, 1956). A person's body is in a constant state of need, and the restoration of natural equilibrium creates a sense of satisfaction (Frede, 1993). Most people can benefit by simplifying their desires. For example, when a person is thirsty, a specific beverage is not required to satisfy the thirst (Penner, 1971). Problems develop when people consistently choose to act on the urge to satisfy their desires. The indulgence of sensual appetites can make these desires grow stronger (Dent, 1975).

The Pursuit of Pleasure, Possessions, Prestige, or Perfection

Almost anything can be taken to an extreme level. All forms of excess revolve around self-indulgence and short-term pleasures. It becomes easy to determine if something poses a danger when asked: "If you did this on a daily basis, how would it affect you?" Excessive desires often focus on the pursuit of pleasure, power, possessions, perfection, or prestige. Socrates described a metaphor of a man carrying water in leaky vases: "Night and day he is compelled to be filling them, and if he pauses for a moment, he is in an agony of pain.... The more you pour in, the greater the waste" (*Gorgias* 494). Like the leaky jar, most desires do not remain satisfied for long (Allen, 1984; Parry, 1996). Material desires become limitless and insatiable (Morgan, 1990). When left unrestrained, desires become stronger (Parry, 1996). When a person succumbs to the desires of excess, even good actions and qualities lose their beneficial aspects (Wilson, 1984).

Some clients are guided by an excessive focus on pleasure. Appetites and bodily urges focus on physical pleasures, and most people pursue these pleasant sensations (Hampton, 1990). A desire for pleasure does not usually include any built-in level of satiation, resulting in tendencies for gluttony and addiction (Benardete, 1991). A lack of moderation can be seen in the excessive pursuit of pleasure, perhaps through sexual promiscuity, drug abuse, or videogames. When decisions are guided by the desire for pleasure, the behavior often leads to excess (Edman, 1928/1956). An excessive focus on pleasure can be seen in the amount of time spent engaging in various enjoyable activities.

Some clients develop an excessive focus on possessions, with issues related to the accumulation of money or objects. Greed involves a fixation on money, power, and accumulation. In contrast to the cyclical nature of most physical desires, greed can become unyielding and limitless in its power to direct human behavior. Contemporary society seems to encourage an overemphasis on money, accumulation, and financial gain. Excessive consumption may result in hoarding, with a focus on the perceived value of objects others might view as worthless. Some people manage feelings of loneliness or frustration through hours spent shopping in stores or online. An overemphasis on purchasing may mask feelings of depression or desperation. However, ultimately money and material gains are not sufficient for lasting happiness (Irwin, 1986).

A lack of moderation can be seen in an excessive pursuit of personal accomplishments ranging from career ambitions to the vanity of physical appearance. Socrates was known to shame the people of Athens publicly for placing a higher value on money or social reputation than on trying to improve their moral character (Beckman, 1979). Problems arise if a client displays too much or too little self-esteem. In contrast, modesty involves an unexaggerated appraisal of strengths, weaknesses, and flaws common to all people (Ben-Ze'ev, 1993).

Some clients become consumed with the pursuit of perfection, never learning to be satisfied with performances that are "good enough." An excessive devotion to academic performance or occupational productivity can result in a neglect of health, rest, or social activities. The highly successful worker may be using dedication to the job as a misguided way of avoiding intimacy with family, friends, or romantic partner.

It can be useful to distinguish the basic necessities for living from unnecessary luxuries (Sayers, 1999). Socrates distinguished necessary desires (for example, for food and drink) from unnecessary ones (specific foods or certain drinks) (Morgan, 1990). It is normal, natural, and adaptive to satisfy basic needs for hunger and thirst (Nussbaum, 1986) as long as the needs are not carried to excess. Appetites for food, drink, and sex are natural, but they need to be guided so they are not carried to an excessive extreme (Irwin, 1995). Physical desires are triggered by a deficit (Allen, 1991), but after being sated, the person should not desire food or drink for a period of time.

Self-indulgence involves readily choosing pleasures that require minimal effort or personal sacrifice. Behaviors may be performed excessively until some form of harm occurs (Wallace, 1978). Tendencies for excess may stem from a lack of restraint. Self-restraint is the ability to resist harmful pleasures (McKim, 1988). A person who lacks self-restraint displays actions that are often guided by primary desires (Reeve, 1988). An excessive focus on satisfying urges can cause financial harm, social repercussions, legal problems, and health risks (Orford, 1985). The costs can be imposed in the short term or long term, and they may detract from the client or the client's social network (Orford, 1985).

Taming a Tendency for Excess

Therapy aims to help the client develop the ability to make a rational choice to forgo every temptation and pleasure. Instead of simply avoiding excessive consumption of food or alcohol, clients can learn to value a healthy lifestyle in which reason controls desires. People can learn to adjust their desires to match their circumstances (Irwin, 1986; 1995). When certain goals are blocked, the temperate person adjusts desires to match the satisfactions that are still attainable (Brickhouse & Smith, 1987). Therapy can help clients enjoy what they already have instead of constantly trying to obtain more.

Therapy can help clients to confront, challenge, and reduce their excessive desires, not just suppress their deviant acts. Therapy aims to replace destructive habits with more adaptive responses. Proper behavior requires desirable action guided by deliberate intent and good motives, and the action produces the desired result (Dent, 1984). Clients should not simply learn strategies for suppressing a deviant action. When focused on overeating, drug addiction, or sexual urges, clients can shift their focus. The long-term goal involves promoting an internalization of proper desires so that moderation becomes easier (Trianosky, 1988). After clients develop moderation in one domain, the new attitudes and skills can generalize to other areas. Clients learn to make rational choices over temptations, preferring reason over emotions, desires, and appetite.

Moderation is based in self-control (Gomez-Lobo, 1994) and in a rational choice over pleasure, desire, and temptation. Self-regulation involves personal control guided by reason instead of by primitive urges and unrestrained desires. Moderation is the ability to control powerful desires in order to suppress an overindulgence in pleasures (Irwin, 1977; 1996). Moderation often involves seeking a balance between two extremes (Hartshorne, 1987), whether it involves greed versus generosity, work versus play, or socialization versus isolation. The goal is not to eliminate desires but to aim for a balanced approach. When an activity is performed excessively, it can result in neglect to other areas of life. When a person focuses on satisfying desires, the desires can begin to enslave the person (Norman, 1983). Desires can be tamed by satisfying them without overindulging (White, 1979). According to Socrates, moderation relies on self-control and the personal ability to satisfy one's needs in a calm and indifferent manner, without resorting to either extreme of excess or total abstinence (Guthrie, 1971).

Finding a Balance Between Extremes

Problems arise when a desire is overindulged (for example, excessive eating, carefree purchasing) or excessively suppressed (extreme dieting, fiscal miserliness). Moderation aims for a middle ground (Hartshorne, 1987; Vernezze, 2008). Similarly, in many therapy situations the goal is to reach a midpoint between the extremes of deficiency and excess (Bright, Winn, & Kanov, 2014; Norman, 1983; Wilson, 1984). Reason should rule over

MODERATION

appetites and desires (Cooper, 1999) so that desires are expressed in a restrained manner, without being completely blocked or frustrated (Brickhouse & Smith, 1994). The goal of therapy is to aim for balance, whether a "balanced diet," a "balanced lifestyle," or a "balanced personality." The goal is to promote a balance across short-term desires and long-term satisfactions (Weiner, 1993). Clients can be directed away from temporary pleasures that may lead to future misery and instead directed toward lasting sources of life satisfaction (Guthrie, 1971).

Excessive desires can be moderated through a balance across physical activity, emotions, and basic appetites (Dent, 1975). For example, a client suffered from chronic depression that was exacerbated by his stressful lifestyle, excessively high standards, and unrealistic self-expectations. He was a single parent raising two children while also working full-time as a warehouse supervisor. In addition, he was taking college courses most evenings. Because of his busy schedule, he often neglected his own rest, hobbies, sleep, relaxation, and proper nutrition. He displayed workaholic habits and had little time for his family or friends. In therapy, he needed to confront his excessive devotion to work, performance, and productivity. The therapist used the analogy of a high-wire performer in a circus. The acrobat was able to remain balanced by extending and adjusting the weights at each end of a long pole. The therapist described the left weight as work and school responsibilities; the right weight represented family, children, and home life. To remain balanced, he needed to monitor the two domains. If one domain was emphasized too much, it meant other areas were being neglected, making it likely he would lose his balance and crash. Also, if he felt tired, sick, or hungry, it would become much more difficult to maintain his balance. This analogy helped him appreciate the benefits of balance across different areas of his life.

Problem drinkers can develop self-control skills to learn how to drink alcohol in moderation (Dawe et al., 2002; Vannicelli, 2001), although these findings are somewhat controversial. More generally speaking, clients can learn to identify their high-risk situations, set explicit limits, and develop alternate behaviors (Vannicelli, 2001). In one study, the beneficial effects of moderation training were maintained at an eight-month follow-up assessment (Dawe et al., 2002). Therapy can work to disrupt the automatic link between craving (subjective urges) and deliberate action designed to satisfy the craving.

When conducting therapy, it can be useful to explore prior periods of excess in order to examine both the positive and negative consequences. The therapeutic dialogue can examine several distinct domains where excess has disrupted the client's life (binge eating, intoxication, excessive spending). The therapist uses questions to guide a collaborative dialogue (Overholser, 1993a) so clients do not feel that they are being lectured and reprimanded for prior misdeeds. The therapeutic dialogue provides opportunities to explore consequences without having goals, standards, or expectations imposed upon the client. The therapist remains respectful and curious while exploring the client's views of proper behavior (Lutz, 1998) and the consequences of prior actions. The therapist is not a moral proselytizer who condemns clients for their misdeeds. Instead, it is more effective to begin discussion where each client is currently having concerns and gradually help the client move toward more productive tendencies. Throughout this dialogue, clients can learn to appreciate some of the problems caused by excess. The therapist does not attempt to "steer" the client down a particular life path but provides "guard rails" to keep the client from driving off the side of a hill (Legomsky-Abel, 1989).

Therapy can help promote moderation by exploring times when the client has remained moderate and restrained despite urges and opportunity. Clients can be helped to examine the consequences of restraint in terms of their problematic behavior's effect on others. Eventually, the client can learn to identify internal and external means of promoting self-restraint. Clients can learn to anticipate the probable negative consequences of future excess. The therapeutic dialogue can help clients learn to anticipate the risks, dangers, and side effects of their devotion to excess. When a person's desires are allowed to grow, they become difficult to satisfy, create feelings of frustration, and disrupt a person's life (Kraut, 1992b). For example, a married male client reported several recurrent problems with sexual indiscretion. He enjoyed flirting with young women, and occasionally he would have a brief affair. He realized there were potential difficulties with these actions, and his wife had already caught him on two previous occasions. It can be important for the therapist to set aside any personal opinions about sensitive topics such as infidelity, open marriage, or the excitement of a sexual conquest. The therapist asked a series of questions to explore the potential dangers of his actions: "How will your wife react if she catches you again?" "What might your minister have to say?" "What would your parents say?" Additional questions can help shift his perspective using role reversal: "How do you think you might react if it was your wife having the affair?" "In this age of hidden cameras, what will happen when someone catches you on videotape?" "How would your boss react if he read in the newspaper about your string of affairs?" "What would your son think if he walked in during one of these episodes with another woman?" Some questions can help shift the client's view by changing the time perspective: "Do you hope to stay married or do you want a divorce?" "What do you hope to see in your marriage over the next few years?" "What have you been investing in your marriage?" "How will you react if in fifteen years you learn that your son has followed in your footsteps and confides to you he is cheating on his wife?" "What will you say to him when he confronts you with the statement, 'You had affairs, what is so bad if I do it too?'" The goal of the dialogue was to develop a sense of anticipatory guilt that can be used to suppress potentially problematic desires. During these discussions, the therapist used a range of questions to explore different views without openly criticizing the client's behavior. Instead of focusing on the immediate feelings of excitement or pleasure, the client was repeatedly asked to look ahead in order to anticipate the potential negative effects of his behavior. The therapist aimed to develop the client's self-restraint through promoting his ability to anticipate the potential consequences of his acts.

The Value of Anticipatory Guilt or Regret

Anticipatory guilt may be used to suppress deviant desires (alcohol, food, shopping, infidelity). Clients are helped to reduce their focus on the anticipated pleasure from the act and instead to estimate the negative consequences that are likely to occur following the act. It can be useful to identify analogous situations that might provide a novel view of the events (Overholser, 1993b). For example, a client described her persistent tendencies for compulsive cleaning and washing. She believed that her acts were acceptable because they did not harm anyone else. The therapist explained the similarities between the client's statements and those commonly heard from drug addicts. In compulsive cleaning and many cases of drug addiction, logic is disregarded in favor of the avoidance of discomfort. The therapist asked the client, "If you behaved this same way every day for the next forty years, what would your life be like?" "How would you respond if your best friend developed this same habit?" "What if the problem was excessive drinking instead of excessive cleaning?" These questions helped the client begin to shift her view from the positive to the negative side of her behavior and begin to monitor the negative consequences that arose after her periods of excess. Also, she was helped to identify feelings of strength, determination, and self-control that arose when she was able to control her urges.

Most desires seek immediate gratification without considering the long-term consequences of the actions (Parry, 1996). Many clients need to learn to tolerate their unsatisfied urges via delayed gratification, partial satisfaction, or alternative outlets. Clients can shift from immediate and temporary pleasure to a focus on long-term satisfactions and an appreciation for the benefits of moderation. With a shift of perspective, clients may tolerate feelings of frustration and deprivation.

It can be useful to help clients appreciate the dangers of extreme reactions. Almost anything done to an extreme level can become maladaptive. The therapist can ask questions to identify examples of extreme responses from the client's own behavior or from that of friends and family members. Past negative effects of excess can be reviewed (for example, memories of a severe hangover can help reduce the interest in another bout of intoxication). The dangers of excess may be reviewed and personal experience with self-restraint identified.

It is often possible to identify periods of moderation in the client's recent past and to examine the consequences that followed. A distinction between short-term pleasures and long-term satisfactions can be useful (Rudebusch, 1999). Many addictive behaviors are focused on gaining fast but temporary feelings of euphoria. However, in the long run, most addictive acts are quite destructive to the client as well as to the client's family and friends. Clients need to look beyond their feelings of deprivation when short-term pleasures are denied and begin to anticipate, value, and work toward obtaining long-term satisfactions. Ideally, clients will begin to choose actions that maximize their pleasure and minimize their pain over the long term (Guthrie, 1971). When excessive behaviors are discontinued, clients can experience improvements in their physical health, emotional stability, time, money, and social functioning. The therapeutic dialogue can highlight the benefits and begin to identify the strategies the client used to maintain moderation.

Effective therapy moves the dialogue beyond the surface in order to confront the urge that underlies the focus on excess. A review of previous life events can usually reveal several incidents during which the client felt an urge to overindulge but was able to suppress that urge in favor of moderation. Past episodes of successful self-control can be examined for strategies and a sense of satisfaction. For example, an adult female client reported the abrupt termination of a romantic relationship. In response, she felt devastated, rejected, and alone. During the weeks following the breakup, she reported frequent crying spells, poor concentration, loss of appetite, and persistent anhedonia. The therapist asked what her reactions were during a breakup three years earlier. She described several weeks of sadness and self-blame but that eventually she regained her sense of stability. With help, she identified several people who were supportive and activities that helped her refocus on more pleasant experiences (for example, playing tennis with a good friend). The therapist asked what it might be like if her boyfriend had died instead of breaking up with her. She described intense sadness and uncontrollable tears. It would be appropriate for her to mourn the loss, but it would be excessive for her to jump into the open grave in a desperate attempt to pry open the casket. This analogy was then translated back into her recent activities, helping her see the benefits of moving on with her life.

Clients can develop skills in suppressing or redirecting their deviant urges. Sometimes, clients can set limits before entering a situation that holds the possibility of temptation, such as setting a monetary limit on financial losses before entering a casino or a two-drink maximum on alcohol consumption before entering a bar. Specific coping strategies can be identified, cultivated, and practiced to help fight off the urges and desires. Clients can learn to avoid extreme emotional reactions and repetitive behavioral patterns and develop an ability to untangle action from emotion. Excessive emotional reactions (crying, yelling, screaming) usually reflect an excessive cognitive interpretation, whereby a situation is perceived as horrible, dangerous, or threatening in a frightening way. When strong emotional reactions happen frequently, the problem may be internal (attitudinal) instead of external (situational). Moderation can help soften extreme or harsh reactions (Wilson, 1984). Clients may feel strong negative emotions (fear, anger) or persistent deviant desires (greed, addiction), but they do not need to act on these urges. Clients can be helped to translate these feelings into words and express their emotions and desires in verbal or written forms without turning impulsive and problematic desires into destructive actions.

MODERATION

The therapeutic dialogue focuses on promoting self-control in the client (Overholser, 1996). Socrates described the analogy of a chariot pulled through the sky by two winged horses (Guthrie, 1975a). One horse was well trained and behaved properly, helping the chariot gently fly through the air. However, the other horse was impulsive, wild, and unruly. A skilled charioteer was needed to control the two horses and guide the path of the chariot. The key to success involved using reason to serve as the guide and not allowing emotion or desire to steer the path. This analogy captures a picture of the internal struggle that is present in most people yet required to maintain balance in our lives. When desires are kept in moderation, the person attains a harmony or balance (Dent, 1975).

For most people, it takes persistence, daily effort, and frequent reminders to develop a new positive habit and to build the strength needed to fend off deviant urges. Usually, a situational cue elicits the basic urge. Then, the individual encounters a choice, either to move toward indulgence and possible excess followed by guilt or to maintain self-control and enjoy a more lasting sense of satisfaction. However, it is important to learn that new positive habits become easier over time and with frequent use. The more often a person engages in the new behavior, the more likely it will become a semiautomatic habit. The goal is to change from being a person who struggles to control urges through deliberate effort to a person who no longer desires anything excessively (Dent, 1975).

Clients are expected to experience a range of emotions. If emotions are blocked or suppressed, they could become weaker and lose their effectiveness when needed (Pappas, 1995). Alternatively, allowing an uncontrolled expression of emotions like anger can interfere with logical reasoning (Pappas, 1995). Some clients need to confront negative emotions without resorting to their problematic habits (Sitharthan, Sitharthan, & Kavanagh, 2001). Clients can learn to ask: "What do I hope to accomplish in this situation?" In terms of anger management, it is sometimes appropriate to feel anger, but it is not acceptable to act in a violent manner, using words or actions to harm another person. According to the Socratic method, a person continues to use reason to guide and control desires and emotions (Pappas, 1995). Reason helps suppress emotions and appetites until a time and situation where it may be appropriate to express them (Prior, 1991). Self-control involves the ability to control desires, impulses, and emotions until they can be expressed in the context of a thoughtful plan (Annas, 1985).

Conclusions

When a client's behavior demonstrates a form of excess, a focus on moderation can be helpful. Moderation can be seen as helpful and safe; excess tends to cause problems for self and others (Foot, 1997). Clients can learn to make rational choices when tempted by easy pleasures. Self-regulation requires that feelings, actions, and desires are guided by reason. If left unchecked, a desire for pleasure, prestige, or profit can become limitless (Kaplan, 1977). Indulgence breeds gluttony.

It usually takes persistent effort in order to develop the skills needed to suppress problem-causing desires and redirect the urges toward constructive behavior. With help, many clients can learn to redirect their desires onto more lasting satisfactions. The goal is to aim for moderation in all things and nothing to excess. Moderation involves using reason to guide desires and developing self-control to pursue the proper desires. The therapist relies on the client's logical reasoning to appraise the areas of excess from a more rational perspective. The process of reducing or eliminating excessive desires takes time (Curzer, 1991).

Moderation has been a controversial issue in the addiction literature. Many clients who develop an addiction to alcohol are treated effectively by using abstinence as the treatment goal (Rosenberg, 1993). It is useful to counsel patients to avoid any consumption of alcohol. The same guideline might apply to excessive gambling. However, it is not possible to avoid most other areas of excessive desire completely. Clients cannot entirely stop eating food or experiencing negative emotional states. Hence, moderation may be the optimal goal for many cases of excessive behavior. The goal is to promote a healthy gratification of normal appetites and desires (Cooper, 1999).

At a broad level, psychotherapy aims to promote self-improvement, and this may involve expanding the client's sensitivity to the cardinal virtues. The therapy process relies on inductive reasoning, helping clients explore their own life experiences in the promotion of helpful tendencies and the moderation of destructive ones.

FOURTEEN

Justice

Is It Possible to Be Fair to Everyone?

JUSTICE COULD SEEM like an odd topic to be addressed in a psychotherapy session. However, when viewed Socratically, it can be a useful goal in some clinical situations. Justice is relevant to a range of common clinical situations. Therapy sessions may include a discussion of justice and the related topics of anger, revenge, and forgiveness. Some people disregard justice because it conflicts with their greed, vanity, or pursuit of pleasure (Vlastos, 1971). Justice may be relevant whenever a client has encountered problems involving family conflict, workplace disagreements, and community relations. The discussion may evolve into a focus on assertiveness or anger management.

It is commonplace that justice derives from the law. However, when Socrates attempted to learn about justice, he discovered that the lawyers and judges of Athens knew little about the subject. Similarly, modern-day courts seem to follow certain prescribed rules but may nonetheless endorse judgments that can be viewed as lacking in true justice. Clients can learn to confront justice as a personal value that helps guide fairness toward all people. Therapy discussions emphasize the importance of fairness and forgiveness instead of resentment and revenge.

Justice is based on social responsibility (Peterson & Seligman, 2004) and a willingness to do what is best for everyone involved. Most aspects of society rely on fairness, equality, and cooperation in order to function (Rawls, 2001). Justice is relevant to the distribution of goods and implies a fair management and allocation of resources, including money, rewards, punishments, housing, and food (Pincoffs, 1986). Fairness means that all people should be treated equally and have their basic liberties protected (Rawls, 2001). A person in a position of authority should not take advantage of that position for personal gain (Pincoffs, 1986). Because social and economic inequalities are often attached to certain jobs and positions of power, there needs to be a focus on protecting the least advantaged members of the society (Rawls, 2001). There are numerous reports of people who hold positions of power taking advantage of their role, resulting in the disparate allocation of resources. Where justice is lacking, obstruction, divisiveness, and enmity can be rife in society (Prior, 1991).

For people to function in society, all citizens must develop a feeling of community toward one another (Kraut, 1992a). Citizens can step away from personal interests, transcend their own private point of view, and see themselves as part of a larger reality (Annas, 1993). These ideas are very similar to the work of Alfred Adler and his notion of social interest as a guide for psychotherapy. Justice entails cooperation (Pappas, 1995) for the betterment of society. Justice helps promote social harmony and friendship across people (Lycos, 1987). To behave in a fair and responsible manner, justice requires that the individual be able to identify with the concerns of other people (Reiman, 1990).

Justice relies on fairness and equality in the division of labor, the distribution of goods, and the assignment of authority (Rawls, 1971). Society would quickly crumble into anarchy were justice not the guide in most ruling decisions (Dobbs, 1985). Similarly, according to Socrates, the moral character of an individual who lacks justice decays.

Justice is a complex issue that influences behavior and decisions in a variety of settings. First, justice can be useful for making leadership decisions (who does what chore?). Second, justice can play a pivotal role in decisions about the distribution of goods (who gets paid how much?). Third, justice can play a role in legal proceedings (how is a person's guilt or innocence determined?). Fourth, justice is involved in restitution (what can rectify a situation after one person has been harmed by another?). Finally, justice plays a central role in negotiation (how can a middle ground be reached between two opposing views?).

At a basic level, justice involves making a decision about how to respond in a fair and equitable manner when confronted with a difficult issue or a controversial situation. In many cases, justice involves making a decision that guides interpersonal behavior. Common problems can arise at work and home, especially when a person in authority has decisions to make about the allocation of some type of resources.

Justice follows from thoughtful procedures being used to reach a fair decision based on proper motives. Just decisions are not based upon public opinion or social popularity but on rational decision making and sound judgment. As noted many years ago by William Penn, "Right is right, even if everyone is against it, and wrong is wrong, even if everyone is for it." Individuals should develop a habit of ignoring popular opinion or group consensus and learn to rely on reasoning to determine if their actions were just or unjust (Allen, 1980). Questions can be used to guide the decision: "When is it right to fight back?" "What makes this situation a big deal?"

Justice involves using reason and intellect to control appetites, desires, and passions (Lycos, 1987). Justice can be compared to carpentry (Parry, 1996): a carpenter may have tools and materials but, to produce a table, he or she needs to understand how they can be used. Likewise, a person may have the administrative, supervisory, or judicial power to make decisions that affect other people, but such power requires wisdom, logic, and reasoning to be just.

Justice is good in itself, not simply because it brings good results (Vlastos, 1971). Justice is not a quality of certain actions but a quality of certain people (Vlastos, 1971). Therefore, a person must act in a virtuous manner because it is the right and good thing to do, not because of social pressure or personal regret. A person acts with justice toward others and feels good about his or her actions even when there is no personal gain.

Justice is centered on what is good for others (Irwin, 1977). A decision must be fair to all parties involved in the outcome. The person making the decision should be impartial, even when the decision involves friendship, because an evil action can never be considered a good thing (Copleston, 1946/1993). To act in a just manner, the person should see the situation through the eyes of everyone who may be affected by the decision (Reiman, 1990). For the ruling authority, decisions should be based on what is best for the entire community; for an individual, decisions should be based on what is best for the parties involved (Lutz, 1998). There should be a clear focus on the common good, not personal gain, in order to protect the interests and well-being of everyone involved in the outcome of the decision.

JUSTICE

When in a position of power or authority over others, it is essential to remain dispassionate, rational, and focused on what is best for all parties involved in the situation. The authority figure should not do what is easy nor react out of anger. A parent or teacher can ask: "Will this situation matter in ten years?" "Is it a big deal to others?" "Is it worth a battle?" "Can we stop to understand the situation from the other person's view?" Clients can be helped to set aside their own personal dislike of a neighbor or coworker to avoid getting caught up in workplace conflicts and cliques. Instead of participating in a work conflict, a client can be guided to behave like a concerned parent trying to help an unruly child. By offering constructive feedback that is not hurtful or defamatory, all parties can move forward on the assumption that the situation can be resolved in a productive manner. The goal is to help the client become a better employee, combining teamwork and leadership despite the conflict.

A fair person should focus on the process and not on self-serving outcomes. It is important to behave in a just manner, regardless of whether anyone is watching and even if the result brings no positive outcome to the person making the decision (Annas, 1981). Some fair decisions may even result in a negative outcome to the decision maker. A virtuous person will act virtuously even if the results are detrimental to that person (Irwin, 1977). In acting justly, sometimes a person's own desires may be frustrated (Reeve, 1988).

Socrates lived by the laws of Athens. He accepted the court ruling that found him guilty, he accepted his sentence, and he refused to escape from prison despite encouragement from friends. Justice helps guide a person to focus on the long-term outcome of an action instead of being drawn to transitory feelings of pleasure.

Justice Means Being Fair to Everyone

Justice involves the fair distribution of goods and the fair division of labor (Prior, 1991). Justice involves fair decision making. John Rawls (1971) proposed a comprehensive theory of justice. The tenets are as follows: It must be agreed that society relies on cooperation across all people and that life is improved by joining a social community. The goals and interests of various individuals must come together in a cooperative manner for society to function. For social institutions to continue, the people must trust the decisions that are made, and goods (wealth, liberty, opportunity) must be distributed in a fair and impartial manner. Each person must have an equal right to attain the basic liberties, and if goods are distributed in an uneven manner, they should favor the least advantaged groups. However, justice in a society entails certain duties from all members of the social group. Thus, members of society have a duty to not harm others, not cause others to suffer, and to help others when they are in need.

It is important to remain fair and impartial (Lycos, 1987). Justice is central whenever decisions are made about the fair distribution of goods, supplies, or resources such as rewards, benefits, honors, duties, or burdens (Mikula, 1980). It can be difficult to make decisions that are fair to everyone and that remain balanced, impartial, and honest. Decision making should avoid a forceful dogmatic style ("because I said so") and instead seek input from all parties involved. It is important to ensure that just decisions are beneficial to those who are affected but may not have a say in the decision (Parry, 1996). Ideally, the best decision is made for the benefit of all, even if the decision maker receives no personal benefit. Decisions should be made in a fair and unbiased manner. It is important to treat everyone in the same manner, with no special considerations for self or friends and family (Pincoffs, 1986).

Unfortunately, at times an external appearance of justice can be misleading and in fact serve as a cover for corrupt behaviors (Despland, 1985). In some cases, behaving in an unjust manner demonstrates a willingness to sacrifice one's own character for the attainment of material possessions (Gerson, 1992). When a person commits an unjust act, the person's inner core suffers (Versenyi, 1963). This is a form of harm a person can only do to him- or herself (Versenyi, 1963).

Justice Is Not Revenge

When harmed or offended in some way, many people feel an urge to seek revenge against the offending party. When people spend time ruminating about a conflict with others, they are more likely to want revenge than forgiveness (Bono & McCullough, 2006). However, justice does not include actions that bring harm to anyone, even a person's enemies (Annas, 1981).

Forgiveness is usually a better option than revenge. Socrates does not accept the view of justice as returning evil for evil (McPherran, 2011). "We ought not to retaliate or render evil for evil to anyone, whatever evil may have suffered from him" (*Crito* 49).

"Justice is the excellence of the soul, and injustice the defect of the soul" (*Republic* 1.353). For our purposes, we can consider "soul" as synonymous with moral character. Acts of revenge should be avoided because they damage the moral character of the offender more than they harm the intended victim (Skemp, 1986). Socrates argued that a person should never commit an unjust act, even as retaliation for harm that has been incurred, because doing so will harm the person committing the unjust act (Allen, 1996). The only meaningful way that a person can be harmed is by committing an immoral action that thereby harms the individual's moral character (Prior, 1991). In this age of online reviews and anonymous reporting, it can be useful to ask: "Am I proud of my behavior here, or am I hiding behind a cloak of anonymity?" People should show respect and compassion toward others, even when other people might misbehave in some manner. For example, a male client was angry because his neighbor had recently filed a grievance about debris littering the client's property. The client mentioned that he was considering using antifreeze to kill a decorative tree in the neighbor's yard. The therapist interrupted the client, explaining the problems that arise "when you let another person's poor behavior drag you down to their level" and emphasizing the value of self-direction and rational control over emotions.

Justice guides assertiveness training and anger management, helping people stand up for their rights while not violating the rights of others. For example, when working with a client who had displayed tendencies for antisocial personality, the therapist confronted his inclinations for violence and retaliation. In one session, the client stated: "Like Marty McFly—don't call me chicken. If you trash me, I'm going to trash you double." He went on to describe recent activity in his adult soccer league. When a defenseman on the opposing team celebrated after blocking the client's shot, the client viewed it as "an insult to my manhood" and thought to himself, "I'm going to make you pay." Twenty minutes later the client checked the opponent so hard it broke the man's jaw. This stimulated an exploration of anger, justice, and revenge. The client expressed the view that "it's only wrong if you get caught" and "anything you can do and get away with without getting caught is perfectly legal." The therapist was able to use questions to turn this philosophy for living back on him: "So according to your view, if someone breaks into your home tonight and steals everything you own, it is okay if they get away without leaving any evidence?" The therapist used questions to cultivate empathy in the client and tried to help the client see the situation from the perspective of the other person, not simply his situation from his own view. The client's anger had become excessive, and justice was not guiding his decisions. Whether expressed in spoken words or limited to private thoughts, anger is often fueled by statements such as "How dare you!" or "You can't do that to me." Instead, clients can remain calm and composed by retaining the view that most problems are not a big deal. Clients can be asked to behave as if they were being videotaped and as if their actions could be viewed by others, including the police.

When therapist and client view some common struggles from the perspective of justice, it may be easier to see current conflicts as being minor in the greater scheme of things. Many disagreements can appear trivial when examined philosophically. Questions can be used to help the client move beyond the specific situation and begin to appreciate a change of perspective.

Socrates promoted justice over revenge. In the dialogue *Crito*, Socrates asks for Crito's view of doing evil in return for evil. A bit later, Socrates states, "we ought not to retaliate or render evil for evil to any one, whatever evil we may have suffered from him" (*Crito* 49). The end of a romantic relationship can stir up a desire for revenge. For example, an adult female client had been "dumped" by her boyfriend, and she expressed a desire for revenge. She remained quite angry and wanted to act on her feelings. In session, she admitted that she knew the code for her boyfriend's answering machine, and she would call to check his messages, looking for any from new women he might be dating. She also described sneaking into his apartment to check his bedroom for signs of another woman in his life. When she became convinced that he was indeed dating someone else, she became furious and wanted revenge. She began placing numerous calls to him at his job, in the hopes of getting him fired.

During an angry outburst in session, she described fantasies of minor and serious acts of injury, including calling him at work repeatedly and finding out whom he was currently dating so she could vandalize the woman's home. She denied that these fantasies reflected her feelings of anger and her desire to act aggressively toward him, claiming to be seeking justice for misdeeds. In session, she was asked to define justice and revenge. Throughout the discussion, the therapist's goal was to clarify that the essence of revenge is the intent to harm the other person. The conversation continued to explore the client's definitions of justice and revenge. She focused on the fact that her ex-boyfriend had been the one to leave her, creating tremendous emotional stress and loneliness. She demanded justice for his perceived misbehavior. She proposed that justice involves making a person pay for what he or she did, conflating justice and vengeful punishment.

The client could see that she needed to confront and adjust her definition of justice. Eventually, therapist and client were able to look at the client's anger toward her ex-boyfriend and see that her plans were actually aimed at revenge, not justice. This cognitive shift allowed the sessions to redirect onto her broader issues related to anger, such as her recurrent experiences of social rejection, and she began to confront her own pervasive fears of abandonment and loneliness. In applying the Socratic method, decisions are optimally based on logic, and the best decision is helpful for all people, not just a select few. Decisions should not be based on greed, anger, or revenge.

Clients can learn from a difficult decision without holding a grudge. For example, a client often fretted over minor annoyances at work and resented the special treatment given to a less qualified employee simply because of his marriage to the boss's niece. In session, he was asked a series of questions to evaluate the importance of the situation: "Is it worth a fight?" "Is it worth getting fired from the company?" "I can understand your concerns, but in the bigger scheme of things, is it horrible?" "I don't want to minimize the problem here, and it is easier as an outsider for me to look at it differently, but what have family members told you to do?" "If you were an undercover reporter, what would your secret investigation say on the 11:00 news?" "If you filed a case in the court of law, what would your argument be?" "How would a jury react to your accusations?" "What questions would the opposing counsel throw at you to disrupt your case?" "How would you handle it if you were the one, not your coworker, getting preferential treatment?" Throughout this exchange, the therapist had to remain careful to not minimize the client's distress while still helping the client see the situation from a different perspective.

Acts of injustice harm the person committing the acts, damaging the person's character and interpersonal relations. For example, an adult female client expressed fear of her ex-boyfriend, who had made threatening phone calls. In session, she mentioned considering buying a gun. She said if her ex-boyfriend showed up at her apartment, she would be able to recognize his voice, and she would shoot him through the closed door. In session, justice was discussed, helping her see the value in living by her own ideals and standards instead of letting the deviant actions of another person bring her down to that person's level. Socrates makes a bold claim: "Doing injustice is the greatest of evils" (*Gorgias* 469). As the dialogue continues, Socrates states, "Neither you nor I, nor any man, would rather do than suffer injustice; for to do injustice is the greater evil of the two" (*Gorgias* 475).

The Beneficial Effects of Punishment When Deserved

When an offensive act has been committed, it is important for the person who committed the offensive act to admit the error and accept the punishment. Punishment is seen as the treatment that intends to remove injustice from the person's moral character (Santas, 1979). Socrates sees the value in proper punishment: "When my sons are grown up, I would ask you, O my friends, to punish them . . . if they seem to care about riches, or anything more than virtue; or if they pretend to be something when they are really nothing" (*Apology* 41–42). When working with clients who have admitted to crimes but were never caught, it can be useful to confront their reactions, explore possible feelings of guilt, and encourage an honest confession. There are benefits derived from proper punishment, along the lines of common platitudes such as "Confession is good for the soul" and "The truth will set you free." Ideally, clients can accept punishment to become free from a guilty mind.

In his discussion with Polus, Socrates asked a series of question: "Is it not a fact that injustice, and the doing of injustice, is the greatest of evils?. . . and further, that to suffer punishment is the way to be released from this evil . . . and not to suffer is to perpetuate the evil?. . . To do wrong then, is second only in the scale of evils; but to do wrong and not be punished is first and greatest of all?" (*Gorgias* 479). These views are aligned with Socrates's perspective on the virtues (Santas, 1979). If a person suffers from injustice, there is no blame imposed upon them. However, if a person acts unjustly toward others, the person is at fault and has caused harm both to the victim and the person committing the unjust act (Santas, 1979).

Justice focuses on a person's relations to others and to the broader community (Gardner, 1995). Committing acts of injustice is harmful to the individual as well as to the broader community (Irwin, 1995). Socrates compared punishment as a treatment for vice as analogous to medical treatments designed to remove the source of a disease (Allen, 1984). Thus, punishment is not designed as retribution for past crimes via giving harm for harm and does not intend to make an example via deterrence but serves as a remedy to make bad men better (Allen, 1984).

The Unity of the Virtues

The virtues work together in a unified manner. Virtue must include the harmonious integration of emotion, attitude, and action (Fowers, 2005). Justice involves the integrated balance across reason, aspirations, and basic appetites (Cooper, 1977). Thus, justice requires reason to serve as the guide for a person's desires and emotional energy (Mackenzie, 1981). Justice creates a harmonious whole across elements, guided by wisdom, enforced with courage, and tempered by moderation. When combined with wisdom, a person experiences harmony across the different elements of virtue so that beliefs, passions, and desires are aligned toward moderation in thought, emotion, and action (Curzer, 1991). Justice includes a mixture of wisdom, courage, and moderation (Irwin, 1995).

Justice relies on the courage to fight back, the wisdom to know if the situation is important or trivial, and moderation to strike a balance across emotions and across people. For example, an adult male client felt he was being treated unfairly at his job. When he decided he'd had enough of the unfairness, he resigned and immediately felt depressed. In therapy he was helped to confront the decisions before him: fight the situation with legal help or move forward to find a new job. Clearly, he could pursue both paths, but his frustration and resentment were now disrupting his ability to focus on new job applications. In session, he reached the decision to learn from the situation, gain a better understanding of what is required to become a good supervisor, and avoid letting his frustration sour him into a bitter complainer.

In justice, reason rules over the other elements of the person's psyche (Stauffer, 2001). For example, a client struggled because of frequent conflicts with his teenage son. The son refused to help around the house, displayed an entitled attitude, and often seemed to ignore the father's demands by fussing with his cell phone. To manage the situation and deescalate his building anger, therapy helped the client set aside his emotional reactions and focus on serving as an effective and loving parent. The client was confronted with a choice: he could turn these events into a battle, or he could ignore it and move on. Therapy helped him focus on possible solutions instead of dwelling on feelings of rejection and disrespect, which would only lead to escalating threats of punishment.

If a person is offended by insulting words, it helps to realize it is the person's own interpretation that leads to feeling offended (Marinoff, 1999). Wisdom helps modulate justice. Most situations can be seen as trivial (getting a B instead of an A) when viewed from a different perspective (a person is diagnosed with cancer and lacks insurance).

Justice benefits from a middle ground; too much force can lead to aggression, and too little results in timid behavior. Justice can provide the courage needed to fight back or speak out against injustice. A subjective sense of moral outrage is not an inherently bad reaction. Instead, a sense of outrage can be used as a cue, providing information that something needs to change and creating the motivation to confront an uncomfortable situation (Meara, Schmidt, & Day, 1996).

It is useful to aim for a middle ground whenever feelings of anger arise (Vernezze, 2008). For example, a client worked as a postal delivery person and was frequently stressed and unhappy on the job. In session, he was helped to see that he was not overworked and that his coworkers were not being disrespectful toward him. His stress had derived from his own negative and biased views of the job and of his coworkers. He was helped to see that the other workers were simply doing their jobs, perhaps at a slower pace than he did his own work. Instead of focusing on their slow or sloppy work, he began to appreciate the control he had over the quantity and quality of his own work. Furthermore, he began to value his stable job, steady income, comfortable home, and pleasant times with his family. It became easier to tolerate or even appreciate the work of his coworkers. He began to notice they had similar complaints about the job, fatigue, aches, and finances. Understanding the experiences of his peers helped the client soften his views and reduce his anger.

Conclusions

When in a position of authority or power over others (as boss, supervisor, teacher, landlord, or parent), justice is essential to form the foundation for all decisions. The person in a position of power should base all decisions on fairness and equality for all parties who may be influenced by the decision. Furthermore, in some cases, the decision may not result in a favorable outcome for the decision maker.

Clients can learn how to resolve conflicts in a fair and civil manner. Wisdom helps people step outside of their own view in order to understand the dilemma from the perspective of the other person. Courage helps a person to fight when a battle is imminent but also promotes the ability to determine when a battle is worthwhile versus when the situation is trivial and can be ignored. Justice relies on moderation to help the person find a middle ground acceptable to everyone.

FIFTEEN

Piety

Do Spiritual Beliefs Have a Place in Psychotherapy?

PIETY CAN BE an odd topic for psychotherapy sessions, and it can be controversial to confront a person's spiritual beliefs during therapy sessions. Especially in today's sociopolitical climate, where religious beliefs are frequently challenged, it can be an awkward topic. Furthermore, the current scientific climate and the emphasis on the empirical foundation for psychotherapy may discourage efforts to include such a private and subjective issue like spiritual beliefs (Prest & Keller, 1993). However, there has been something of an upsurge of interest in spirituality as it relates to psychotherapy. A variety of studies (Nasser & Overholser, 2005; Weber & Pargament, 2014) have examined the role of spirituality in mental health. Furthermore, religion, spirituality, and piety are important topics for many psychotherapy clients.

Socrates was executed after being accused of impiety and corrupting the youth of Athens. Despite the accusation of impiety, Socrates held strong beliefs about spirituality. Socrates opposed the gods and goddesses of ancient Greece because they committed acts of lying and bribery (Morgan, 1990). In contrast, the higher power explored by Socrates was universally good, incapable of causing harm or evil to humans (Vlastos, 1989).

It is useful to clarify several related terms: religion, spirituality, piety, and faith. Religion typically refers to a set of beliefs aligned with a specific religious denomination. Spirituality can describe a person's awareness of spiritual matters and sensitivity to a higher power. Piety is closely aligned with spiritual faith but may extend into action, that is, that the spiritual beliefs one holds have a visible impact on one's behavior. Finally, faith involves trusting beliefs about a divine reality even when direct observation and empirical proof are not possible (Rotenstreich, 1998). When discussing piety, there is an important shift in the views regarding supporting evidence. Beliefs about spirituality do not depend on objective proof but on faith (Nash, 1988). As commonly used, faith refers to beliefs that are maintained when there is no supporting evidence. Having faith means that you do not *know* but are willing to move forward despite a lack of absolute certainty. The goal is not to make a believer out of an atheist but to help people to explore and appreciate their own views of spirituality.

Despite the lack of empirical support, there has been interest in psychotherapeutic circles in religion and spirituality because these beliefs may become involved in guiding people and helping them through difficult times. Furthermore, from a pragmatic view, discussing piety in session can be helpful to some clients. The pious individual engages in self-improvement to enhance the condition of their "soul" (Kachi, 1983), or moral character.

Piety refers to a spiritual foundation in the person's view of life and life's meaning. Various terms are used to capture spirituality, holiness, or an appreciation for a higher being. Some forms of psychotherapy welcome spirituality into the treatment plan. When Viktor Frankl developed his views on existential analysis, he kept a strong focus on helping clients find meaning in their lives. When reading Plato's dialogues, it makes sense to view the term "soul" as referring to a person's conscious intellect and moral character (McPherran, 1996). It is hoped that people will behave in a responsible manner when they place importance on their beliefs in a higher power (Wolz, 1974). However, intense religious convictions can result in intolerance of divergent views.

Piety is a difficult topic to discuss in an unbiased manner. Many interesting topics appear controversial, but they are unavoidable when exploring the Socratic notion of piety. The basic Socratic dictum claims that people should only say what they truly believe (Vlastos, 1991). Therefore, throughout this chapter (and this entire book), I am trying to write only those notions I truly believe. The suggestion that a therapist should behave with intellectual modesty becomes very important whenever religious views are being discussed. The therapist can listen, learn, explore, and support the client's personal beliefs in spirituality and faith. Therapeutic discussions of piety should be guided by the client's personal beliefs. The therapist should refrain from expressing any personal views about religious beliefs.

Piety is not aligned with any particular religion or religious doctrine. Instead, it revolves around a basic view that life on earth is limited. Even if people cannot "know" what happens after a person dies, it is beneficial to hold a view that there continues to be some form of existence. In a nondirective and exploratory manner, clients can benefit from discussions about their personal spiritual beliefs, and clients can make their own thoughtful decisions about how much their daily behavior should be guided by those beliefs. The therapeutic discussion of piety can only be useful if it is complemented by the other elements of the Socratic method, especially the sincere disavowal of knowledge from the therapist (Overholser, 1995a) and a willingness to use a series of questions to explore and discover new ideas along the way (Overholser, 1993a).

Piety can become a controversial topic if it is aligned with one specific religious denomination. It would be inappropriate for a therapist to present religious views aligned with one specific religious group, especially if the client is not a member of that religious community. Thus, it seems essential to shift the focus from religion so that the discussion remains focused on broader issues related to spirituality, issues that transcend any specific school of religion. Other scholars may remain skeptical of piety as a topic within the field of psychology because it lacks a strong empirical foundation. However, if the cautious researcher maintains a focus on the client's beliefs in spirituality or the afterlife, the investigations can be no different than the empirical study of any other kinds of beliefs or subjective experiences.

There are situations in psychotherapy where it becomes important to understand and explore a client's views on mortality. The role of spirituality and piety becomes most closely aligned when working with religious clients, when helping clients through a suicidal crisis, or when confronting issues related to illness and death. However, there are many other situations where exploring spirituality can help clients shift away from a focus on daily hassles and minor concerns. According to the Socratic view, eternal peace eludes us during life because of bodily demands such as hunger and thirst (Nash, 1988). Even worse, work, finances, and interpersonal conflict can provide endless distractions from more important philosophical ideas.

Piety and faith can be appropriate topics when working with religious clients. Because I see clients through a religion-based charity clinic, it is common for me to ask my clients questions such as: "How often do you attend church services?" "How long has it been since you last attended a church service?" "Do you ever visit a church or a chapel when it is quiet and empty, not just for a service?" "How often do you pray or spend time talking to God?" Obviously, the type and format of questions would need to be oriented toward each client's religious affiliation and preestablished beliefs.

Throughout history, there have been views of piety that center around a lifetime devoted to isolated prayer. The monks of Meteora, Greece, come to mind. However, from a more useful Socratic perspective, piety cannot be found in isolated self-reflection or daily meditation alone. Piety does not involve personal sacrifice or self-centered beseeching a higher power for personal assistance (Vlastos, 1989). Socrates did not view piety as quiet prayer or personal sacrifice aimed toward some form of material reward (McPherran, 2011). Instead, a personal sense of piety may be facilitated through daily communication with God, by listening with one's head and heart, not with one's ears. In contrast to the typical view of prayers and requests, the person may find solace not by asking for help but by asking for guidance as to how to help others.

In psychotherapy sessions, the focus may be on spiritual beliefs but not religious dogma. Faith resides in a nondenominational belief that a higher power exists. It may be useful to explore the logical consistency within a person's set of religious beliefs, but even then, there is a tendency for religious beliefs to become somewhat unshakeable. Thus, the therapist is unlikely to challenge or attempt to refute a client's beliefs about death, spirituality, or religion. Instead, the therapist may look for ways to use these beliefs for therapeutic gain.

Piety includes a belief in a higher spiritual power that is an ideal form of goodness (Kachi, 1983). According to the Socratic method, piety is not narrowly focused on religious beliefs but instead includes an awareness of the mysteries that exist throughout the universe and within the psyche of each person's mind, as evidenced in unconscious processes and intuition (Prasinos, 1992). Many clients find benefit from spiritual faith even when their beliefs have become removed from a particular religious tradition.

Piety and faith can be useful topics when working with suicidal clients. When a client has entered a suicidal crisis, the client is likely to spend extensive time thinking about death, especially the client's own death and the deaths of people close to the client who have already died. Suicidal clients may be pondering when, where, and how to end their own life. The suicidal client's thoughts might focus on the reactions likely to be experienced by family members and friends. There could be a sense of enjoyment through the passive-aggressive act involved in some suicidal acts. These thoughts are not helpful, and they may even push the client further along the suicidal path.

A client's view of death becomes highly relevant whenever a client has entered a suicidal crisis. The traditional approach to suicidal urges involves a focus on depression and an exploration of hopelessness. However, the treatment of suicide risk has lagged far behind the treatment of depression, and there is little guidance to help the therapist confront hopelessness and pervasive pessimism in therapy. In contrast, it can be helpful to shift the focus and explore openly a client's views about death and dying. A skillful therapist can explore the client's views and direct the discussion onto the client's spiritual foundation and possible belief in some form of existence that continues after a person's body dies.

Is Death the End or a New Beginning?

Impending death can push a person toward more spiritual thoughts. A client's thoughts about death and dying can become important when a client has been diagnosed with a terminal illness or is grieving the loss of a loved one. When death is near, people are usually frightened about what may lie ahead. However, humans lack objective knowledge of what happens after a person's body dies. Therefore, fear of death is irrational and unfounded, based on knowledge that is not truly available (McPherran, 1985). Instead, whether or not spiritual beliefs can be tested empirically, it can be helpful to retain some faith in a spiritual existence.

Fear of death comes from ignorance: no one really knows what happens after a person's body dies (Brickhouse & Smith, 1994). Socrates makes the claim: "No one knows whether death, which men in their fear apprehend to be the greatest evil, may not be the greatest good" (*Apology* 29). Much later, Socrates explains his view: "There is great reason to hope that death is a good; for one of two things—either death is a state of nothingness and utter unconsciousness, or, as men say, there is a change and migration of the soul from this world to another. Now if you suppose there is no consciousness, but a sleep like the sleep of him who is undisturbed even by dreams, death will be an unspeakable gain" (*Apology* 40). Socrates continues with his line of reasoning: "But if death is the journey to another place, and there, as men say, all the dead abide, what good, O my friends and judges, can be greater than this?" (*Apology* 40–41). Thus, Socrates proclaimed that death could be a peaceful state of sleep or the greatest of all blessings, but in reality we simply do not know (McPherran, 1996). According to Socrates, "Death may be the greatest of all human blessings" because death may provide the way to release the soul from the body (Ahrensdorf, 1995).

If a person's soul continues to exist after the death of the body, it will continue to exist whether or not the person believes in an afterlife (Patterson, 1965). Alternatively, if there is no soul and the death of the body means the end of life, then no persuasive argument can change that fact (Patterson, 1965). Thus, according to the Socratic method, discussions about piety and a possible afterlife existence have a potential impact on a person's mood and current behavior (Patterson, 1965). By increasing a person's faith in an afterlife, the person may retain hope during desperate times and may view immoral acts as less desirable because of the potential everlasting consequences.

Sometimes it can be useful to encourage clients to read popular books related to their concerns. This is not done as a form of bibliotherapy or formal self-help but is more aligned with building bases for later discussion. For example, a recent book (Alexander, 2012) described a neurosurgeon's personal account of his near-death experience. While in a week-long coma and pronounced brain dead by medical colleagues, the physician had an experience that resembled a mystical journey to a peaceful afterlife. When his health returned, he wrote about his experience traveling toward what he described as heaven. Sharing this book with clients can open discussions of life after death and of the overall meaning of a person's existence. Without imposing views on a client, a therapist can encourage some clients to read materials aligned with the client's own religious views and personal beliefs. Clients can then be asked to share their reactions by writing about their thoughts or discussing them in therapy sessions. The discussion can explore the client's faith in spiritual life and existence after death.

Spiritual faith can bring an attitude of calm acceptance of self and others. "No evil can happen to a good man, either in life or after death" (*Apology* 41). According to Socrates, the greatest harm a person can encounter is harm to one's moral character, and only an individual person can harm his or her own character. External circumstances cannot harm a person's moral character (Brickhouse & Smith, 1994).

When helping clients who are struggling with depression and suicidal urges, it is often helpful to ask a short series of questions, including: "Do you believe in an afterlife?" "In your view, what happens to a person after they die?" "Do you have traditional views of heaven and hell, or do you have different views of the afterlife?" "Do you feel that a person's behavior and actions while alive can play a role in determining what happens to them after they die?" "Do you feel that death by suicide can influence what happens to a person after death?" Even when the client is not suicidal, it can be quite helpful to reestablish a spiritual foundation for many clients. Useful questions include: "Does your behavior while alive influence what happens after you die?" "Does it matter if a person dies by suicide?" According to the Socratic method, a person's fate after death depends on the person's actions performed throughout life (Crombie, 1962). In his discussion with Callicles, Socrates stated, "Death, if I am right, is in the first place the separation from one another of two things, soul and body . . . whatever was the habit of the body during life would be distinguishable after death . . . when a man is stripped of the body, all the natural or acquired affections of the soul are laid open to view. . . . Behold them enduring forever the most terrible and painful and fearful sufferings as the penalty of their sins. . . . The best way of life is to practice justice and every virtue in life and death" (*Gorgias* 524–27).

Explore but Do Not Lecture

In all aspects of the Socratic method, it is important for the therapist to avoid the role of expert or teacher. This issue becomes especially important whenever approaching topics related to piety or religious beliefs. The role of expert can be minimized when a therapist fully accepts the notion of Socratic ignorance (Overholser, 1995a). The disavowal of knowledge becomes most prominent whenever topics related to piety or spirituality are discussed in therapy or elsewhere. It is more than likely that the therapist has never experienced the afterlife firsthand nor that the therapist has engaged in private discussions with God, Jesus, Mohammed, Buddha, or even the Pope or the Dalai Lama. Instead, like everyone else, therapists are limited to their own beliefs, views, and opinions about spirituality. The therapist keeps in mind that personal beliefs about religion and spirituality are fallible speculations. Discussions about piety should never approach the level of a lecture or sermon. It helps to remain tolerant of diverse views because even religious and political affiliations reflect personal opinion, whereas intense convictions may result in intolerance (Halberstam, 1982–83).

The Questions Are More Important Than the Answers

When working in the Socratic mode, questions are more important than answers. Socrates's contribution to piety might best be viewed as using the Socratic method to value spiritual beliefs and explore each person's values, while also accepting there is no religious dogma underlying the Socratic approach (Despland, 1985). Views of piety can be approached with modesty and ignorance, using questions to explore ideas and challenge opinions. When people seek to understand spiritual beliefs, the issues remain active in the person's mind, helping guide their behavior toward lofty ideals.

Socrates remained skeptical of the beliefs held by his contemporaries and challenged the rational foundation for their views of piety (McPherran, 1985). Instead of accepting the established dogma, Socrates focused more on the process of exploring different views about piety and, along the way, creating a pious identity for each person (Anderson, 1967). Wisdom helps clients open their minds to the broader view of life within the expansive universe. People who have survived cancer or life-endangering accidents sometimes develop a more spiritual view as well as a closer bond with all of humanity. Philosophical discussion can be used to explore ideas about how best to live and how to die (Hadot, 1986). A discussion of spiritual faith can be important whenever clients are confronting thoughts of death or dying. For example, in cases of complicated bereavement, some clients find solace in thoughts of their loved one finding peace and relief from pain in the afterlife. Clients can be asked to write a letter to their deceased loved one or a letter to themselves written from the perspective of the departed.

The goal when discussing piety in session is to examine qualities that seem important for all people, such as compassion and tolerance for others, generosity, and a willingness to retain a faith in a higher power, especially when a client is feeling overwhelmed or burdened by life problems. Regardless of the specific doctrines provided by any specific religion, these qualities help improve the social bonds throughout a community. Piety does not necessarily mean hours alone spent in silent prayer or church attendance; it can be seen in compassionate acts toward others and in respecting the miracle of life.

A focus on spiritual faith can help lift clients above recent struggles and current worries. For example, an adult male client was approaching middle age but struggling with his physical appearance and the aging process. He became quite upset whenever he noticed his wife admiring photos in an online catalog whose images included those of attractive young men modeling new clothes. He expressed feelings of jealousy over their age, hair, clothing, and muscles. He started wearing some of his old clothes from his days as a high-school athlete, trying to regain his youth and athletic physique. He purchased hair dye to color his hair and beard. Unfortunately, he felt troubled by the wrinkles around his eyes and was considering treatments to remove the wrinkles. In session, he was asked: "Jump ahead forty years. When you have become old and gray, will you still be jealous of men in their twenties?" "Would you still be focused on your body and your appearance?" "How can you shift your view now?" "When standing at heaven's gate, will St. Peter evaluate you by your muscles and your physical appearance?" "Is heaven going to be like a new exclusive nightclub, where only beautiful young people with designer clothing are allowed in?" "I know we are just speculating, but as we sit here now, what do you think will determine your outcome in the afterlife?" The therapist shifted the focus from transitory and trivial events onto bigger issues pertaining to morality and piety. Piety helps a person focus on the proper priorities and move beyond emotional reactions to common stressors. However, the real goal was to confront topics related to maturity, wisdom, and virtue ethics, as these were relevant to daily decisions being made by this client.

Some therapy sessions explore a client's views on death and dying. Socrates had no empirical proof of an afterlife. His views relied on simple logic. According to Socrates, if death would be an escape from everything, then death would be beneficial to wicked people (Despland, 1985). "If death had only been the end of all, the wicked would have a good bargain in dying" (*Phaedo* 107). It would be improper if wicked people were able to escape from their miserable acts through a death that ends all existence

(Ahrensdorf, 1995). Thus, it becomes important to remain virtuous while alive. According to the Socratic method, the primary life goal is to refine moral goodness because only the individual can harm one's own character through immoral acts. People should use their time while alive to purify their souls or improve their moral character.

The notion of piety can readily go beyond faith and spiritual beliefs to include compassion, tolerance, patience, and forgiveness. Piety involves spiritual work for the benefit of other people (Vlastos, 1989). Thus, some spiritual leaders devote their lives to charity work, helping the sick, poor, or disabled. A modern example would be the life of Mother Teresa, who left a life of family wealth to pursue charitable work. Piety means the individual strives to benefit others (Weiss, 1994) through personal gifts of time, love, and acceptance, regardless of the recipient's station in life.

Compassion is more than an attitude and can be expressed through simple acts of kindness and helpfulness toward others. For example, an older adult male client came to session and shared an inspirational quotation he had read recently and that he found to be quite helpful: "Without God, there will be failure." The therapist asked about the difference between religion and spirituality and about how similar or different might the major religions be if they were compared in terms of religious dogma versus spiritual beliefs. The client was able to shift his focus from organized religion to improving his own faith in a higher power. Then, he was asked how he could begin using his faith as a guide for struggles in everyday living.

Some clients begin to appreciate the spiritual aspects of other people in their lives.

THERAPIST: "When was the last time you were able to see God's presence in someone else?"
CLIENT: "Just yesterday. I was playing with my grandson."
THERAPIST: "So with some people it can be easy to see God's presence. However, how would it have gone if your grandson had vomited in your new car?"
CLIENT: "I guess I'd have cleaned it up. I wouldn't have yelled at him. I doubt I would have even gotten mad at him."
THERAPIST: "Do you think it would be possible to see the presence of God in people who annoy you, or even anger you, like someone who cuts you off while driving in heavy traffic, or a rude store clerk, or the telemarketer who calls just after you sit down for dinner?"

These questions are intended to stimulate thought by confronting difficult situations. The client is not expected to have clear and definitive answers to each question. Furthermore, the therapist does not have a predetermined answer at the moment the question is being asked. Instead, these questions are used as discussion points to help the therapist and client both search for piety, love, and forgiveness in their attitude toward others.

According to the Socratic view, piety helps people ask themselves how they would behave if they were to change roles with another person (Vlastos, 1989). Such a notion appears closely aligned with the Golden Rule and other views that promote kindness and gentleness toward others. At the core, there is an encouragement to maintain a sense of peace and kindness in one's heart. These gentle attitudes can help promote an attitude of patience, tolerance, and forgiveness.

Conclusions

Piety can be a useful topic in psychotherapy sessions. Many people get busy with work and household chores and lose connection with their spiritual beliefs. Discussions about piety should be approached in a gentle and exploratory manner. Most clients have been raised with some type of religious affiliation, but this does not mean that the therapist needs to become well versed in comparative religion. Instead, if the therapist remains curious about the client's views, beliefs, and opinions, these issues can be explored in a supportive manner.

Some clients find solace in their religious beliefs and spiritual faith. Often, it can be useful to encourage clients to become or remain active in solitary prayer, peaceful meditation, or organized church activities. It can be useful to ask a client: "How can you display piety on a daily basis?" There are a variety of strategies that can encourage clients to build upon their preexisting beliefs, such as, for Christians, attending Bible study classes, joining a church choir, or visiting the hospital chapel in the evening when seeking to be alone with thoughts and prayers. Clients may mention a passing interest in one of these activities, and the therapist can gently encourage the client to "give it a try" during the days before the next session. Such activities can be used to encourage a thoughtful approach to the client's spiritual life.

PIETY

Piety was removed from the short list of cardinal virtues in one of Plato's later dialogues (Weiss, 1994) because its qualities arguably are already contained within the other four cardinal virtues (Allen, 1970). Apparently, Plato reconsidered his views and concluded that piety was not distinct from justice (Annas, 1981). However, when examined closely, piety adds important vows and personal sacrifices that extend beyond social justice (Annas, 1981). A person's beliefs serve as the primary guide for most actions.

Piety can help each person to develop a disposition to respond with compassion and nurturance. People can strive to understand and accept other people even with their inevitable faults. By treating others with kindness and respect, they will be more likely to bring these same qualities to their own social interactions.

As the Socratic view of piety moves away from church affiliation and religious dogma, an interesting rationale can be observed. It becomes easier to appreciate the philosophical, not theological, foundation underlying the Socratic view of piety. According to the Socratic method, piety is a cognitive function that is likened to wisdom. To maintain a life guided by piety, the individual needs to focus on the bigger picture relative to living a meaningful life. It is more important to live well than simply to live for a long time (Taylor, 1956). Piety involves stepping away from desires for pleasure, wealth, or honor in order to focus on wisdom (Morgan, 1990) and a more philosophical view of life.

SIXTEEN

Psychotherapy from a Socratic View

PSYCHOTHERAPY AS INFORMED by the Socratic method is an abstract process requiring patience, flexibility, and creativity from the therapist. In most cases, it is much easier, simpler, and more efficient (in the short term) to take a directive stance with clients. Thus, it becomes all too easy for novice therapists to embrace the role of expert and share advice, give directions, assign homework, and solve specific problems for their clients. However, psychotherapy, at its core, lies in its ability to help clients change their views, perspective, and attitudes. This is a much more complex process, one that requires time, patience, and a sincere investment in the process of therapy. It is somewhat surprising that even Albert Ellis (1982) recommended that the therapist should remain flexible and curious and avoid a one-sided dogmatic style. With the current focus on effectiveness and efficacy research, there has been a neglect of process issues in contemporary psychotherapy.

The Socratic method can provide a strong philosophical foundation compatible with many schools of psychotherapy. It seems possible to use principles derived from the Socratic method to provide a broad framework for psychotherapy sessions. The sessions are used to help clients explore their own struggles, search for possible solutions, and confront areas that need to be changed. Most often, the focus remains centered on the client's life, attitudes, and emotions. Clients can learn that by changing their attitudes and expectations, they can better manage the daily struggles encountered by most people. Furthermore, if the client fully adopts a Socratic approach to life, the client's daily struggles tend to be viewed as relatively minor in the larger scope of life, living, and values. Clients are helped to view their concerns in terms of long-term life goals and with respect to how they can make lasting improvements in their functioning.

The Socratic method includes four processes and two topic areas that provide the substantive content for the therapeutic dialogue. The two primary topic areas can be broken down further, with self-improvement subdivided into three general domains and virtue ethics then subdivided into five cardinal virtues. The Socratic method can create an integrative approach that remains compatible with many other forms of psychotherapy while nonetheless creating several important shifts in style and content.

Psychotherapy, according to the Socratic method, aims to produce a major philosophical shift in the attitude and perspective held by both therapist and client. Therapy is heavily entrenched in cognitive restructuring, with a dominant focus on adaptive attitudes and a comprehensive view of life. In this way, it becomes important for the therapist gently to sidestep the client's concern over recent events and problems that might be considered trivial from the proper vantage point.

Clients often begin treatment with complex problems and intense worries. For example, one client wrote: "What will I do now? No one wants to hire me. No one wants to date me. What is wrong with me? I have screwed up everything. My life is a mess, and all I seem to do is complain." It becomes the job of the therapist, in close collaboration with the client, to use the tools of the Socratic method to untangle this complex network of problems and help the client begin to take steps in a more positive direction.

Four primary components are used to guide the Socratic dialogue. The first is *systematic questioning*, which has become the primary tool for the Socratic therapist (Overholser, 1993a). A wide range of questions can be used to stimulate discussion and encourage the client to move toward adaptive coping options. Therapy can promote an internalization of the questioning process (Areeda, 1996) so that clients will continue to pose questions about important and ambiguous topics.

Second, *inductive reasoning* underlies the logical approach used by a Socratic therapist (Overholser, 1993b). The discussions aim to learn from the client's life experiences and seek potential solutions to common life problems. Instead of the therapist lecturing to the client, the two parties join together as a team to explore, understand, and learn from the client's own personal experiences. In addition, analogies are often used to provide a visual image that captures key elements that can be learned and applied in the client's life.

Third, therapy sometimes involves a search for *universal definitions* (Overholser, 1994). In this way, the discussion shifts from a review of recent events and begins to confront larger issues that are relevant to the current problems; this can have a more general and lasting impact on the client's perspective. Some discussions naturally lead to an exploration of definitions. Whenever clients use important terms and evaluative labels, therapy can explore and revise the definition of those key terms.

Fourth, both therapist and client retain a willingness to *accept their own ignorance* of many aspects of life and functioning (Overholser, 1995). Intellectual modesty is beneficial when sincerely endorsed by both therapist and client. Such modesty underlies an attitude of curiosity, promoting a search for new information. It retains a willingness to view one's beliefs as hypotheses to be tested and avoids the tendency to "upgrade" one's beliefs into fact or dogma. Too often, conflict arises when beliefs have been upgraded and opposing sides begin to argue, debate, and fight to support their own views. When both sides can retain a more modest, provisional, and pragmatic approach to their ideas, the willingness to share, discuss, and understand the other side's view can develop. Such an open-minded tendency is often beneficial.

In addition to the four central components, psychotherapy can be facilitated through the use of *guided discovery* and *collaborative empiricism*. These strategies have been endorsed by prominent experts in the field of psychotherapy, and they help promote teamwork in therapy and autonomy in the client. A shaping process is used gently to encourage a series of gradual changes in the client's speech (Frojan-Pargo, Calero-Elvira, & Montano-Fidalgo, 2011) and implicitly in the client's attitudes and expectations. Socrates, by contrast, was focused on a critical review of the person's logical reasoning and coherence across beliefs. Other than the occasional inductive example, empirical support did not play a strong role in Socrates's efforts to endorse or refute various beliefs. However, it is helpful to view the Socratic method as empirical even if it is not experimental (Kazantzis et al., 2014) because of the strong reliance on inductive reasoning and the focus on learning from the client's own life experiences.

The Socratic method emphasizes the collaborative nature of psychotherapy discussions. In a manner analogous to depth perception, which requires two eyes aimed at the same object but originating from different points, the therapeutic dialogue starts from two different places and finds the area of convergence. If the two people disagree entirely, they will close one eye and ignore the alternative view completely. It is most helpful to focus on the area of agreement, respecting the value of two views where neither one is right or wrong.

There are two primary focal points for the therapeutic dialogue. First, therapy sessions may focus on self-improvement as a goal for psychotherapy (Overholser, 1996). Self-improvement includes simple strategies to expand and improve the client's self-awareness. Psychotherapy often relies on two basic dictums affiliated with the Socratic approach: "know thyself" and "an unexamined life is not worth living" (Lageman, 1989). Self-acceptance relies on a thoughtful self-awareness and a review of personal strengths and limitations. Self-regulation requires clients to develop self-control skills, ensuring that emotions and behaviors are guided by logical reasoning and long-term planning.

Second, sessions may aim to promote virtue in the client, as seen in everyday situations that allow for an expression of some virtuous act (Overholser, 1999a). It can be a real shift in focus when a therapist moves the discussion from specific problems or recent events and introduces issues related to virtue ethics. However, the discussion of virtue helps broaden the potential efficacy of therapy. Furthermore, a focus on virtue ethics can help clients make major and elegant changes in their views of life, self, and others.

In contrast to many forms of contemporary psychotherapy, the Socratic method shifts the focus of therapy sessions. Most forms of therapy begin with the assessment of psychiatric diagnosis and remain aimed at reducing symptoms of emotional distress. Psychotherapy using the Socratic method instead often focuses on cultivating a more balanced approach to life. These strategies are compatible with current views on positive psychology, which aim to cultivate persistent feelings of gratitude and a search for meaning in life (Seligman, Parks, & Steen, 2004).

Throughout the sessions, it is important for the therapist to remain fluid and flexible with the goals and the strategies. Thus, the Socratic method is not fully compatible with the current push for empirically supported treatments that typically rely on manualized approaches to sessions. The client should have clear input into the basic goals for therapy. However, some clients may not fully understand the psychosocial nature of acceptable goals. In such cases, the therapist can negotiate and help redirect the therapeutic aims onto important therapy goals. All psychotherapy sessions should be uniquely adapted to the strengths and weaknesses of each individual client. It can be extremely difficult to prepare a structured manual that can effectively guide psychotherapy sessions. Some of the most powerful discussions cannot be planned and organized before the session. Instead, it is often helpful for the therapist to be willing to explore a range of topics while keeping the focus on big issues (self-improvement, virtues) and without becoming bogged down by recent events, trivial concerns, or emotional reactions that have been bothering the client. Too many people become focused on their own career, family life, and personal struggles, and in doing so they fail to appreciate the bigger issues pertaining to life decisions, moral choices, and virtue ethics (Annas, 1981).

The Socratic method relies on a semistructured approach to psychotherapy sessions. When conducting a series of psychotherapy sessions, a plan guides the flow of topics addressed across several sessions. However, within each individual session, there is room for flexibility and spontaneity. Sessions are not structured using an agenda preestablished by the therapist at the start of each session. There is a risk that a structured agenda derives too heavily from the mind of the therapist and could risk reducing the client's input into the discussion topics. Thus, the therapist has the complex task of keeping the therapy discussion on target for the major issues while allowing a wide latitude of topics to be discussed in each session.

The therapist does hold a general plan for the therapy as a whole. However, even this overall plan for therapy should remain fluid and interact with the client's long-term goals and important desires. Sometimes, the larger framework rests squarely within the confines of the Socratic method; that is, it aims at cultivating self-control skills or confronting courage as a virtue relevant in modern society. However, at other times, the larger goal may extend beyond the typical Socratic focus and may center around helping clients approach life in a calm and mature manner or finding personal contentment on the path toward romantic love.

At the start of each session, the therapist can review a brief summary for topics that had been covered in the past sessions and share ideas for issues to be discussed in the current session. Across a series of sessions, clients can be helped to approach life problems in a new and more adaptive manner. Sessions are interactive, with two partners exploring ideas and general attitudes toward coping and resilience. Psychotherapy sessions can be used to explore topics that seem relevant to a client's needs. The therapist retains a belief that clients often need an opportunity to discuss and explore sensitive issues with a supportive therapist, but the therapist avoids taking the lead in steering the conversation or becoming overly directive in the discussion.

Therapy Relies on a Strong Therapeutic Alliance

Effective therapy requires good rapport. A skilled therapist pays attention to subtle indicators of the therapeutic relationship with every client throughout every session. Whenever expecting clients to share their vulnerable moments of beginning the process of change, therapy relies on a strong and supportive therapeutic alliance. Rapport and alliance are central to all forms of psychotherapy. Many clients were raised in a manner that may have promoted feelings of neglect or rejection. They are likely to benefit from a therapeutic atmosphere based on support and understanding. Therapists can be helpful by listening to clients as they share their life stories (Graybar & Leonard, 2005).

Psychotherapy is more than a bag of tricks. Instead, at the center of effective psychotherapy is always the relationship between therapist and client. An effective working alliance often includes an emotional bond, active involvement in sessions, and an agreement on therapeutic goals and planned tasks (Hill, 2005). Furthermore, supportive listening provides the essential bond that helps form the therapeutic relationship (Graybar & Leonard, 2005). For example, at the end of a difficult but productive therapy session, an older male client explained there was a chance he might be moving out of the region, and he asked if he could nonetheless continue our therapy sessions. He commented: "I value our discussions. You make me think, even about some things I'd rather not think about." The quality of the therapeutic alliance is a good predictor of treatment outcome (Castonguay et al., 1996). A supportive therapeutic alliance has been found important in the effectiveness of both psychotherapy and pharmacotherapy (Krupnick et al., 1996).

As best as possible, the therapist aims to understand the client's struggles from the unique perspective of each client. Were the therapist to minimize the perceived magnitude of the problem ("It's not that bad"; "you can handle it"), the client may work even harder to convince the therapist that the situation really is bad. However, if the therapist accepts the client's perceived severity of the problem and works to see the situation from the client's vantage point, then the client can feel less distressed, more supported, and aligned with the therapist as a teammate.

The Socratic method can be applied with many different clients and disorders. A Socratic approach can be useful when working with clients who have an eating disorder (Vitousek, Watson, & Wilson, 1998) and clients who are struggling with persistent memories of childhood trauma (Garrett, 2015).

Because the therapist explores ideas but does not present arguments, a Socratic approach can help reduce a risk of the power struggle sometimes seen when client motivation is low (Vitousek, Watson, & Wilson, 1998). Clients can be asked to complete simple writing projects between sessions, such as the worksheet on positive attitudes included at the end of this chapter. These writing activities can help encourage clients to examine and change their own attitudes in more positive and adaptive ways.

Conclusions

Psychotherapy requires an attitude of patience and an attentive and supportive therapist who encourages positive growth in each client. The underlying view is that all people need the proper conditions for ongoing growth. Psychotherapy according to the Socratic method focuses more on the process than on the outcome. If process issues are aligned with the ideals of the Socratic method, then a positive outcome is likely to follow. The therapist tends to downplay the importance of structured treatment manuals and time-limited therapy. Instead of a focus on diagnosis and prescriptive approaches to treatment, the Socratic therapist believes the client is not broken and therefore does not need to be fixed.

Therapists can facilitate a process that is jointly led by therapist and client working together to make improvements in the client's life, coping skills, and life view. Therapy involves removing false and incompatible beliefs, clearing the way for the person to develop more reasonable views and logical beliefs (Versenyi, 1982). Effective therapy can help clients become their own cognitive therapist (Kazantzis et al., 2013). An emphasis on logical reasoning allows a person to make life choices guided by logic and knowledge instead of by current moods or the strongest desire at that moment (Annas, 1981).

When fully adopted as the framework used to guide psychotherapy, the Socratic method can facilitate creativity and collaboration in every session. The Socratic approach can promote rapid change when clients begin a major philosophical shift in values and priorities. The sessions can address important issues related to virtue ethics and life meaning, thereby minimizing the discussion of recent events or trivial worries. The therapy sessions revolve around a lively exchange between two people, collaborating in a search for new information and different perspectives. The sessions remain fluid and flexible and do not rely on the rote application of a manualized process.

A purely Socratic approach might be limited because the focus is overly cognitive in nature. The goal is to enhance reason through a logical dialogue. The Socratic approach places a heavy focus on intellect and reason, possibly overestimating the ability of most people to refine their logical influence over their emotions and desires (Chessick, 1982). Therefore, psychotherapy according to the Socratic method works best when blended with other therapeutic styles. As seen throughout this text, the Socratic method seems compatible with the seminal works published by Sigmund Freud, Carl Rogers, Alfred Adler, Aaron Beck, Albert Ellis, William Glasser, Donald Meichenbaum, Viktor Frankl, and many others. Furthermore, the Socratic method provides a broad conceptual framework that a therapist can use as the basic theoretical underpinnings of therapy. The other schools of therapy may help provide different treatment targets or different intervention strategies. However, many trained psychotherapists bring a preestablished theoretical foundation that may only allow for the Socratic method as a small component instead of as a major restructuring of their approach to therapy.

Worksheet on Positive Attitudes

The happiness of your life depends on the quality of your thoughts.
—Marcus Aurelius

Right now, do you believe the following statements are True or False as related to you?

True	False	If I try hard, I can accomplish my goals.
True	False	I believe that things will go well for me in the future.
True	False	Even when I have problems, I know that things will get better.
True	False	Everyone makes mistakes; no one is perfect.
True	False	I believe that I can make my future what I want it to be.
True	False	I feel that I can handle most problems.
True	False	I am thankful for the good things that I have in my life.
True	False	Even when I am having problems, I know that I can tolerate them.
True	False	My current problems are not too bad.

It is important to increase adaptive attitudes that are honest, realistic, positive, and helpful. Statements are usually not helpful if they are overly positive and become unrealistic. We do not want statements that are untrue. Please write several of your own positive statements:

Positive, Realistic Attitude	Do you really believe it?	
	Yes	No
	Yes	No
	Yes	No

Begin each day by searching for a grain of happiness, something good in your life. Whether big or small, positive things can help you focus on the goodness that surrounds you. Describe one positive finding below:

_____
_____
_____

SEVENTEEN

Conclusions

Where Do We Go from Here?

PSYCHOTHERAPY REMAINS A strong and vibrant field. There are many situations where psychotherapy can help clients make important changes in their actions and their attitudes. By making a progressive series of small changes, clients can begin to notice improvements in mood, interpersonal functioning, and their enjoyment of life. However, effective therapy requires time and a solid bond between therapist and client.

In this age of accountability, there has been a strong emphasis on treatment-outcome research. Although there are many reasons to value well-controlled research on the effects of psychotherapy, there are risks as well. Research studies are designed in a highly structured manner. Certain types of clients are accepted into the study, while many others are rejected. Some clients may be excluded from treatment-outcome studies because their problems are too severe or because they meet criteria for more than one psychiatric problem. There are many studies that rely on analogue samples, undergraduate students, online surveys, treatments administered online via materials posted at a website, and even mTurk surveys. The use of samples of convenience may be fast and efficient, but the methodology often becomes overly simplified and far removed from the realities of clinical practice. The participants may express low levels of cognitive or emotional symptoms, but they are not on the same plane as psychiatric inpatients or clinic outpatients who intentionally seek help to overcome their struggles with some form of diagnosable mental illness. Personally, I remain reluctant to trust the findings derived from any study that relies on an analogue sample (for example, college students) using an analogue methodology (for example, treatment provided by online reading material) and for which the results depend on the insight and honesty of normal participants who complete a packet of self-report questionnaires at one assessment interval.

Research studies are typically designed to examine the effectiveness of a highly structured intervention. Such structure fits well with medical treatments, especially the administration of new medications given in a specific dosage. Also, some structured therapy strategies may be delivered in a highly regimented manner, for example, the treatment of phobia in a university clinic or a smoking-cessation program (Baker et al., 2007). However, most types of psychological treatments delivered in clinic settings are conducted in a fluid and flexible manner. Thus, there remains a gap between most published research studies and the actual clinical services provided in many different settings.

Cognitive-behavioral therapy provides a strong foundation upon which to build a therapist's core skills in psychotherapy. The foundations of CBT help provide a range of intervention strategies to guide the process of change. An even more comprehensive view of the mind and psychological problems can be obtained through an integrative approach that incorporates ideas and strategies from many different schools of psychotherapy. Turf wars do not help advance the field. Specific terminology becomes localized within one ideology. Different writers may stop communicating, and the sharing of ideas becomes constrained.

Every year for the past thirty years, I have taught a year-long graduate seminar on cognitive-behavioral psychotherapy. In addition to class meetings, my students are supervised in their delivery of outpatient psychotherapy sessions. For the past fifteen years, I have also been fortunate to teach a semester-long undergraduate course on schools of psychotherapy. Over the course of the semester, lectures explore the seminal ideas developed by various pioneers in the field, including Sigmund Freud, Carl Jung, Alfred Adler, Carl Rogers, Viktor Frankl, William Glasser, and Fritz Perls. Also, contemporary experts are reviewed, from Aaron Beck, Albert Ellis, and Don Meichenbaum to Irv Yalom and Salvador Minuchin. Finally, important historical figures are discussed, including Jean-Martin Charcot, Pierre Janet, and Paul Dubois. I have come to appreciate each of these experts and their valuable contributions. Because of my extensive background reading in

CONCLUSIONS: WHERE DO WE GO FROM HERE?

preparation for this course, I find myself relying on a wide spectrum of strategies when in session with different clients. I feel it is a mistake for contemporary psychotherapists to focus early in their training on one school of psychotherapy. I also find it valuable to use the Socratic method as a useful and comprehensive framework for guiding my plans for treatment.

I see a risk that the process and style of psychotherapy are changing. The split between scientists and practitioners continues to divide the field and force graduate students to make choices that determine the path of their career. Today, it seems difficult to meet the ideals of the Boulder model. Despite numerous reasons to adopt a scientist-practitioner lifestyle (Overholser, 2007a; 2010c; 2012a), it remains difficult for most psychologists to integrate the science and practice of psychology.

Most of the research studies published in the premier journals tend to emphasize high-quality research methodology. Most published studies rely on well-controlled but somewhat simple methodology. In addition, because of the pressure on faculty members to publish on a frequent basis, there is often an emphasis on efficient collection of data using samples of convenience, and these findings may not generalize to clinical settings. Some studies lack the external validity needed to shine light on mental illness or its treatment. A true blend of science and practice can help integrate and expand our understanding of clinical problems.

Some faculty members have discontinued their involvement with clinical practice or conducting research on clinical samples. Over the years, they risk lowering their insight into the complexities involved in clinical practice. When organized around efficient research, the assessment often relies on standardized questions, and the intervention uses a structured manual that guides a trainee across a fixed number of sessions. However, many clients receive services in clinics that differ from the published research studies.

One should respect and not disregard the collaborative and exploratory nature of therapy sessions. The Socratic method has widespread applicability for guiding psychotherapy sessions. In addition to psychological treatments, the Socratic method can be used to facilitate classroom discussions (Overholser, 1992) and clinical supervision (Overholser, 1991; 2005a). When conducting psychotherapy sessions, a Socratic approach can be especially helpful when clients are resistant, rebellious, or difficult to engage. However, there are limitations to the use of a Socratic approach to therapy. Clients who lack skills in complex cognitive processing may not be ideal candidates for such an approach. Different strategies are likely to be more effective with child clients or elderly who show signs of cognitive decline. When logic and reason appear insufficient to help a specific client, behavioral strategies can be useful (Hauck, 2001). The Socratic approach is also limited by the dearth of research to support its use. There has been very little research designed to examine the potential benefits of a Socratic style. Instead, remaining true to the historical figure of Socrates, the Socratic method relies on a strong theory, common sense, and a series of examples that have been explored in an inductive manner.

The Socratic method aims to integrate ancient philosophy with contemporary approaches to psychotherapy. This is often a difficult task, lacing together two fields that rarely communicate with each other. It can be surprising to read deeply in the two fields. It is rare to find scholars of ancient philosophy cite publications from modern psychotherapy. It is equally difficult to find any author who has published on contemporary psychotherapy while citing literature from the classics. I am a bit discouraged by contemporary authors who write about the Socratic method without citing works from philosophy or the classics. I am curious about their ability really to retain a sincere alignment with the Socratic method as it has survived over the centuries. Moreover, psychotherapy according to the Socratic method has lofty goals that quickly become abstract. The overarching intent of the Socratic approach involves bringing the various aspects of a person's life and psyche into harmony. In most cases, this process involves strengthening the person's logical reasoning and helping tame or redirect the person's more primitive urges (Simon, 1978). Thus, an important issue confronting psychology involves appreciating a client's strengths and weaknesses and viewing the therapy more in terms of process than in terms of outcome, goals, or steps (Weeks, 1977).

There are several key dilemmas facing psychotherapy in modern society. First, contemporary psychotherapy must confront the different views about what the optimal role of the therapist should be. A psychotherapist can be seen as an expert with knowledge of optimal coping skills, as a teacher in an educational format, or as a healer using a pseudomedical model. Alternatively, the therapist may be viewed as an inquisitive peer, a friendly collaborator, an experienced guide, or a fellow explorer in the pursuit of knowledge. One of my clients referred to me as his "healing partner," a term I continue to value and respect. I believe that I have learned more about mental illness and its treatment from my work with the brave clients who have shared their personal life stories with me in the privacy of a therapy session than I have from treatment manuals, research studies, or class lectures.

When exploring topics related to self-awareness and virtue ethics, the therapist risks problems if he or she adopts a didactic style. Instead, it seems especially important to explore issues and confront the limits of current understanding. Therapy is most likely to be effective when the therapist respects the individual life views of each client, promotes an honest and collaborative approach, and avoids the role of expert/teacher (Vitousek, Watson, & Wilson, 1998).

Second, contemporary psychotherapy must confront the issue of evidence to support its effectiveness. How much does psychotherapy benefit from a strong evidence basis? In the process of gathering empirical support, do we risk losing the subtle nuances integral to effective psychotherapy? Can empirical support be replaced by or supplemented with years of clinical experience and case examples? Psychotherapy according to the Socratic method does not have empirical support. It seems likely that future research could examine the effectiveness of a Socratic therapy as compared to a different form of treatment. However, it should be acknowledged that Socrates himself would not be convinced by the presence or absence of empirical support. Scientific inquiry is currently aimed at the expansion of knowledge, not wisdom, but science becomes more valuable when it aims to clarify and develop solutions for the problems of living (Maxwell, 1984). Maxwell quotes Albert Einstein: "Knowledge exists in two forms—lifeless, stored in books, and alive in the consciousness of men" (Maxwell, 1984, p. 58).

Third, contemporary psychotherapy must confront the optimal structure of therapy sessions. Are treatment manuals useful guides or rigid dogma? Novice therapists sometimes develop the view that treatment manuals can provide a strong foundation for psychotherapy skills. However, psychotherapy is a process, and skill develops across many years of practice. Psychotherapy is very different from auto repair; there is no *Chilton's* manual to fix the client or repair a client's psyche. There is a risk that published treatment manuals designed around treatment-outcome research create a "gap" because such research remains far removed from the complexities of clinical practice. Research relies on nomothetic principles, but psychotherapy is best when treated as an idiographic process.

CONCLUSIONS: WHERE DO WE GO FROM HERE?

It can be difficult to conduct Socratic therapy in an agency that is regulated by time-limited approaches. There is a risk, with the current emphasis on short-term care as mandated by managed-care corporations, that therapists will become technicians using manualized treatments that emphasize content, to the neglect of process issues (Graybar & Leonard, 2005). A manual goes against the nature of Socratic dialogue, which needs a lively, spontaneous, and fluid exchange between two contributors. However, it should be acknowledged that structured therapy manuals have been found useful for many therapists, whether for leading a group-therapy lesson plan or in organizing an intervention as part of a treatment-outcome research study.

Fourth, contemporary psychotherapy must confront the goals for effective treatment. According to the Socratic method, psychotherapy benefits when the goals move beyond a simple reduction of acute symptoms. By helping clients become involved in meaningful activities, therapy can help clients find and create satisfaction and meaning in their lives (Steger, Kashdan, & Oishi, 2008). It is important to live a satisfied lifestyle with contentment earned by working toward important life goals (Ryan, Huta, & Deci, 2001).

It is only in rare circumstances that the role of psychotherapist can be compared to a mechanic working to fix a broken car. Instead, in most situations, an effective psychotherapist functions as an advocate for personal growth, cultivating important characteristics such as maturity, flexibility, tolerance, responsibility, integrity, and virtue. Therapy can help clients move away from a focus on daily events and potentially trivial problems. It is important to maintain a balance across the major domains of life (Kashdan & Rottenberg, 2010).

Manuals are often written by expert scholars who have moved beyond clinical practice, no longer conducting therapy sessions each week. Some manuals appear rigid, with guidelines carved in stone. In contrast, Socrates opposed the written text, suspicious that writing can easily become authoritative dogma that forecloses any debate or challenge. Perhaps it would be best to combine structure and flexibility. A well-designed treatment manual can provide the structure for some sessions. The principles of the Socratic method can provide guidelines for the therapy process, helping explain how to explore important issues and promoting guided discovery. Perhaps a blend of a preplanned structure with spontaneous interpersonal interactions and genuine interest in each client as a unique person would be the optimal solution.

CONCLUSIONS: WHERE DO WE GO FROM HERE?

Empathy and collaboration are key ingredients for every session with every client. Instead of a manual, perhaps a map might be a more useful metaphor. If the therapist acts as an experienced guide, a map can help chart the course. The client has input into the preferred destination as well as the pathway taken to reach that destination. Sometimes, an unplanned detour becomes the most interesting aspect of a journey. Throughout the present text, the goal has been to reach a sincere integration of ideas that culminates in a realistic view of psychotherapy according to the Socratic method. The Socratic method aims to promote critical reasoning skills, social responsibility, and general value of morality and virtue (Schmid, 2002).

I have chosen in this book to omit three additional elements of the historical dialogues of Plato and the views attributed to Socrates. First, Socrates believed in innate knowledge, whereby all people are born with core knowledge about matters that transcend time. Perhaps this knowledge base could be called instinct, but it extends further into meaning and values, perhaps akin to Jung's notion of archetypes stored in the collective unconscious. The notion of innate ideas creates some interesting possibilities (Baillargeon, 2008). Thus, what was typically considered to be learning was actually just remembering inborn knowledge that had remained dormant until accessed through current life situations. Innate knowledge is a topic in developmental psychology research. If this notion is used in psychotherapy sessions, then clients can be trusted that they already know the difference between right and wrong behaviors and that they also understand the value of good versus bad choices. Therefore, it is not the therapist's role to make decisions for the client but to help clients make their own decisions after thoughtful reflection and a willingness to explore the situation from a variety of perspectives.

Second, Socrates was uncertain as to any form of individual human existence after death, but apparently Socrates viewed the soul as immortal. Therefore a person's knowledge carries with them throughout time. Thus, if there is some form of reincarnation, it may help explain the innate knowledge that guided Socrates's view of learning.

Third, Socrates proposed an interesting theory of personality, which played a major role in the development of Freud's views. Socrates proposed a tripartite model of the psyche, with domains in charge of the person's emotional energy, the basic desires or appetites, and the logical reasoning to control all decisions. According to Socrates, the human was similar to a charioteer (seen as reason) trying to steer two winged horses, one well taught (spirit) and one unruly (desires). Three parts to an individual's psyche: a rational part that understands the person in context of the broader situation, a spirited part that brings the forceful energy to guide different behaviors, and a passionate part that expresses the person's desires (Schmid, 1992). There are several important similarities between Plato's view and the psychoanalytic structure of the id, ego, and superego proposed by Freud.

The Socratic method provides a strong foundation for psychological treatments. Instead of becoming overly anchored with certain ideas and specific problems, the Socratic method provides a broad ideology that can encompass a vast array of developmental issues and severe problems.

Certain problems may be most relevant for the treatment sessions that have been guided by the Socratic method. In my professional experience (unsupported by empirical data), the Socratic method can be extremely helpful when working with clients who are seeking help because of longstanding problems with depression (Overholser, 2003b), anxiety, and interpersonal relationships (Overholser, 1997). However, this list of relevant problems is restricted to the types of clients with whom I typically work. Future scholars may explore the applications and limitations of the Socratic method through empirical research, treatment outcome studies, or surveys of mental health professionals.

Socrates presented a limited view of human functioning. The Socratic method is heavily based on cognitive change. There is less focus on emotions and physical aspects of human behavior, except as nuisance factors that distract a person from grander thoughts. Socrates has been criticized for his excessive focus on intellectual factors and neglect of emotions and volition as relevant to behavior (Nehamas, 1986). The Socratic method is guided by the underlying belief that clients will act in appropriate ways once they see the rational foundation that underlies self-improvement and virtue ethics (Nehamas, 1986). However, it may be idealistic to hope that clients will gravitate to good behavior and moral integrity while the modern world remains overcome by noise, commotion, and distractions.

Emotions provide important information and play a crucial role in guiding reactions and informing people; emotions are part of the construction of the reality of our lives (Greenberg, 2012). Thus, it becomes important to help clients learn to listen to their emotional reactions, not to suppress,

CONCLUSIONS: WHERE DO WE GO FROM HERE?

control, or ignore them (Greenberg, 2012). Instead, a goal of Socratically informed therapy is to increase awareness of emotional responses, express emotions in a responsible manner, and reflect on the experience.

Certain clients may be more appropriate than others for therapy guided by the Socratic method. Adults often know how to make effective use of their therapy time. In fact, most adult clients seem to have a good basic understanding of the unspoken rules of psychotherapy sessions. Clients come for their sessions with the expectation that their therapist will listen, remain supportive, and ask a lot of questions. Often, clients do not want and do not expect their therapist to solve problems for them. Clients are interested in talking through their difficult life decisions, especially when their dilemma revolves around something major (should we stay married and work on our relationship, or has it reached the point where we need to cut our losses and seek a divorce?). Even when clients ask the therapist for specific advice ("So what do you think I should do?"), it is common for the client to add their own disclaimer ("I know you can't answer this for me").

The Socratic method works well with clients who are cognitively intact and appear to be at an average level of intelligence. However, the Socratic method is a cognitive intervention that can become focused on abstract philosophical issues. More structured forms of therapy may be more useful for clients who have suffered from some type of cognitive impairment, whether through a traumatic brain injury, some form of dementia, or a developmental delay.

My own clinical work typically includes psychotherapy sessions with a range of adult outpatients. I no longer work with children or teenagers. However, based on my own past experience and that of younger colleagues, the Socratic method could be quite useful when working with adolescents. This is speculative, but perhaps future work can examine the benefits of the Socratic method with adolescents. Because many adolescents struggle with identity issues, conflict with authority, and peer relationships, the Socratic method may provide a useful forum for the teen to explore his or her own views and values.

A common attitude plays a central role in the practical application of psychotherapy according to the Socratic method: patience. Limited time is the biggest reason for poorly conducted clinical interviews (Fletcher, 1980a; 1980b). It becomes difficult to adhere to the guidelines of the Socratic method when a therapist feels rushed because of a limited number of sessions, restrictions on therapy time, or their own impatience. Instead, when feeling pressured to move quickly, it becomes much easier to step into the role of didactic expert and lecture the client on adaptive behavior skills.

The Socratic method may be useful with clients who are struggling with depression, anxiety, and personality problems (Overholser & Fine, 1994b). However, the Socratic method is not appropriate for all clients or all situations. Many aspects of the Socratic method touch on fairly abstract issues and often require complex cognitive processing. A Socratic approach may not work well with children, individuals lacking higher cognitive complexity, or adults in a state of cognitive decline. There are also some specific clinical situations that need to be tended to quickly, such as when a client expresses a high level of active suicidal ideation. Furthermore, for some clinical disorders, research has supported the effectiveness of structured psychological interventions. Thus, some problems can be addressed in a structured manner (for example, exposure with response prevention for OCD or prolonged exposure for PTSD). In contrast, the Socratic style seems well suited to chronic problems related to poor emotional regulation or tendencies for dysfunctional interpersonal relationships.

A final word of caution: Socrates was not known for his diplomacy. He asked difficult questions. As he listened to the person's answer, he often expressed, in a direct and spontaneous manner, his concern, confusion, and dismay over the flawed responses he was receiving. When he realized the other person did not fully comprehend the topic, Socrates exposed the person's ignorance in a public forum. Socrates was thus loved by some people of Athens but hated by many others. It is worth remembering that Socrates was sentenced to death because he had corrupted the youth of Athens, teaching the younger generation the importance of questioning authority. It makes sense that youth would enjoy watching their elders become confused, revealing the ignorance of the city leaders (Seeskin, 1987). The youth would imitate the Socratic style of dialogue, asking questions that challenged authority and revealed flaws in the established ideas (Seeskin, 1987).

In many ways, by fully adopting the Socratic method, a modern-day professional risks alienation from the local professional community. Most people, especially tenured faculty, would rather settle into their own niche of scholarship and believe they have the answers to many of life's great puzzles. In my experience, which confirms that of Socrates and Plato, most experts lack the awareness needed to identify the limits of their knowledge and accept the expansive breadth of the unknown. It is unfortunate whenever pride limits a person's willingness to continue learning, exploring, and discovering. Mental health professionals who adopt a Socratic style should remain cautious and sensitive when exposing their own lack of knowledge and that of other people.

Final Thoughts

Despite the value of the Socratic method, it may not be a good fit for all therapists or all clients. For many clients, psychotherapy requires time, patience, and gentle persistence. Psychotherapy is an individualized process for both client and therapist. It is important for a therapist to find the proper mixture of ideas and strategies that fit well with his or her own personality traits, life experiences, and typical clientele.

It seems possible to integrate the Socratic method with other forms of psychotherapy, especially cognitive therapy and rational-emotive behavior therapy. The cognitive-restructuring approaches focus heavily on self-statements and cognitive processes. In addition, the Socratic method can move the therapy even further, allowing the focus of sessions to grapple with virtues, which are relevant to many—but not all—clients.

The Socratic method provides a comprehensive and integrative framework that can help structure therapy sessions. The therapeutic dialogue can focus on recurrent themes, and it thereby moves beyond a traditional behavioral approach. Therapy sessions can examine potential solutions to various life problems, but the dialogue attempts to understand possible causal factors, examine broader underlying issues, and confront core themes related to life, self, and virtues.

Therapy is a collaborative process that relies on exploration and discovery. I frequently emphasize to the trainees I supervise the importance of understanding clients and their struggles before considering strategies for change. A therapist should not try to change what he or she does not understand. It is important to work with the person to get inside the psyche, share subjective experiences, bring a phenomenological view to psychotherapy, and promote change from within. Carl Rogers's emphasis on empathy is useful; the therapist aims to see the world through the client's eyes. Such an internal perspective may be the only way a therapist can understand what problems are important and what issues need to be confronted.

Therapy often requires patience, persistence, a bit of playfulness, and an awareness of the types of process issues that arise in most sessions. Patience is useful because growth requires time. When efficiency is a priority, the Socratic method may be neglected (Clark & Egan, 2015). The process may be analogous to the work of a gardener, who plants some seeds, pulls some weeds, and hopes to foster the proper conditions for growth.

References

Ablon, J. S., & Marci, C. (2004). Psychotherapy process: The missing link. *Psychological Bulletin, 130*(4), 664–668.
Ackermann, R. (1972). *Belief and knowledge*. Garden City, NJ: Doubleday.
Ahrensdorf, P. (1995). *The death of Socrates and the life of philosophy: An interpretation of Plato's* Phaedo. Albany: SUNY Press.
Adler, M. (1941). *A dialectic of morals*. Notre Dame, IN: University of Notre Dame.
Alexander, E. (2012). *Proof of heaven*. New York: Simon & Schuster.
Alford, B., & Beck, A. T. (1997). *The integrative power of cognitive therapy*. New York: Guilford.
Allan, D. (1940). *Plato's method of dialectic*. Oxford: Clarendon.
Allen, R. (1970). *Plato's* Euthyphro *and the earlier theory of forms*. New York: Humanities Press.
Allen, R. (1980). *Socrates and legal obligation*. Minneapolis: University of Minnesota Press.
Allen, R. E. (1984). *The dialogues of Plato, Volume I*. New Haven, CT: Yale University Press.
Allen, R. E. (1991). *The dialogues of Plato, Volume II*. New Haven, CT: Yale University Press.
Allen, R. E. (1996). *Plato:* Ion, Hippias Minor, Laches, Protagoras. New Haven, CT: Yale University Press.
American Psychological Association, Committee on Training in Clinical Psychology. (1947). Recommended graduate training program in clinical psychology. *American Psychologist, 2*, 539–558.
Anderson, D. (1967). Socrates' concept of piety. *Journal of the History of Philosophy, 5*, 1–13.
Anderson, H., & Goolishian, H. (1992). The client is the expert: A not-knowing approach to therapy. In S. McNamee & K. Gergen (Eds.), *Therapy as social construction* (pp. 25–39). New York: Sage.
Annas, J. (1981). *An introduction to Plato's* Republic. Oxford: Clarendon.

REFERENCES

Annas, J. (1985). Self-knowledge in early Plato. *Studies in Philosophy and the History of Philosophy, 13*, 111–138.

Annas, J. (1993). *The morality of happiness*. New York: Oxford University Press.

Ardelt, M. (1997). Wisdom and life satisfaction in old age. *Journal of Gerontology: Psychological Sciences, 52B*(1), P15–P27.

Areda, P. (1996). The Socratic method. *Harvard Law Review, 109*(5), 911–930.

Arlin, P. (1990). Wisdom: The art of problem finding. In R. Sternberg (Ed.), *Wisdom: Its nature, origins, and development* (pp. 230–243). New York: Cambridge University Press.

Armstrong, D. (1989). *Universals: An opinionated introduction*. Boulder, CO: Westview.

Austin, S. (1987). The paradox of Socratic ignorance (How to know that you don't know). *Philosophical Topics, 15*(2), 23–34.

Baillargeon, R. (2008). Innate ideas revisited. *Perspectives on Psychological Science, 3*(1), 2–13.

Baker, T., McFall, R., & Shoham, V. (2008). Current status and future prospects of clinical psychology: Toward a scientifically principled approach to mental and behavioral health care. *Psychological Science in the Public Interest, 9*(2), 67–103.

Ballard, E. (1965). *Socratic ignorance: An essay on Platonic self-knowledge*. The Hague: Martinus Nijhoff.

Baltes, P., & Smith, J. (1990). Toward a psychology of wisdom and its ontogenesis. In R. Sternberg (Ed.), *Wisdom: Its nature, origins, and development* (pp. 87–120). New York: Cambridge University Press.

Baltes, P., & Staudinger, U. (1993). The search for a psychology of wisdom. *Current Directions in Psychological Science, 2*, 75–80.

Baltes, P., & Staudinger, U. (2000). Wisdom: A metaheuristic (pragmatic) to orchestrate mind and virtue toward excellence. *American Psychologist, 55*(1), 122–136.

Bartlett, R. (1996). On the *Symposium*. In R. Bartlett (Ed.), *Xenophon: The shorter Socratic writings* (pp. 173–196). Ithaca, NY: Cornell University Press.

Baucom, D., & Boeding, S. (2013). The role of theory and research in the practice of cognitive-behavioral couple therapy: If you build it, they will come. *Behavior Therapy, 44*(4), 592–602.

Baumeister, R., Vohs, K., & Tice, D. (2007). The strength model of self-control. *Current Directions in Psychological Science, 16*(6), 351–355.

Beck, A. T. & Emery, G. (1985). *Anxiety disorders and phobias: A cognitive perspective*. New York: Basic Books.

Beck, A. T., Rush, A. J., Shaw, B., Emery, G. (1979). *Cognitive therapy of depression*. New York: Guilford.

Beckman, J. (1979). *The religious dimension of Socrates' thought*. Waterloo, Ontario: Wilfrid Laurier University Press.

Bell, J., & Campbell, S. (1995). *A return to virtue*. Chicago: Northfield.

Bell, A., & D'Zurilla, T. (2009). Problem-solving therapy for depression. *Clinical Psychology Review, 29*(4), 348–353.

Bemporad, J. (1996). Caring for the psyche: Classical origins and modern paradigms. *Journal of the American Academy of Psychoanalysis, 24*(2), 353–363.

Benardete, S. (1989). *Socrates' second sailing: On Plato's* Republic. Chicago: University of Chicago Press.

REFERENCES

Benardete, S. (1991). *The rhetoric of morality and philosophy: Plato's* Gorgias *and* Phaedrus. Chicago: University of Chicago Press.
Benson, H. (1990a). Meno, the slave boy, and the elenchus. *Phronesis, 35*, 128–158.
Benson, H. (1990b). The priority of definition and the Socratic elenchus. *Oxford Studies in Ancient Philosophy, 8*, 19–65.
Benson, H. (2000). *Socratic wisdom*. New York: Oxford University Press.
Benson, H. (2011). Socratic method. In D. Morrison (Ed.), *The Cambridge companion to Socrates* (pp. 179–200). Cambridge: Cambridge University Press.
Ben-Ze'ev, A. (1993). The virtue of modesty. *American Philosophical Quarterly, 30*(3), 235–246.
Beutler, L., Williams, R., Wakefield, P., & Entwistle, S. (1995). Bridging scientist and practitioner perspectives in clinical psychology. *American Psychologist, 50*(12), 984–994.
Beversluis, J. (1974). Socratic definition. *American Philosophical Quarterly, 11*(4), 331–336.
Beversluis, J. (1987). Does Socratic commit the Socratic fallacy? *American Philosophical Quarterly, 24*(3), 211–223.
Birren, J., & Fisher, L. (1990). The elements of wisdom. In R. Sternberg (Ed.), *Wisdom: Its nature, origins, and development* (pp. 317–332). New York: Cambridge University Press.
Birren, J., & Svensson, C. (2005). Wisdom in history. In R. Sternberg & J. Jordan (Eds.), *A handbook of wisdom* (pp. 3–31). New York: Cambridge University Press.
Bishop, W., & Fish, J. (1999). Questions as interventions: Perceptions of Socratic, solution focused, and diagnostic questioning styles. *Journal of Rational-Emotive and Cognitive-Behavior Therapy, 17*(2), 115–150.
Bluck, R. (1955). *Plato's* Phaedo. Indianapolis: Bobbs-Merrill.
Bono, G., & McCullough, M. (2006). Positive responses to benefit and harm: Bringing forgiveness and gratitude into cognitive psychotherapy. *Journal of Cognitive Psychotherapy, 20*(2), 147–158.
Bostock, D. (1986). *Plato's* Phaedo. New York: Oxford University Press.
Bransford, J., Sherwood, R., & Sturdevant, T. (1987). Teaching thinking and problem solving. In J. Baron & R. Sternberg (Eds.), *Teaching thinking skills: Theory and practice* (pp. 162–181). New York: Freeman.
Braun, J., Strunk, D., Sasso, K., & Cooper, A. (2015). Therapist use of Socratic questioning predicts session-to-session symptom change in cognitive therapy for depression. *Behaviour Research and Therapy, 70*(1), 30–37.
Breggin, P. (2016). Rational principles of psychopharmacology for therapists, healthcare providers and clients. *Journal of Contemporary Psychotherapy, 46*(1), 1–13.
Brickhouse, T., & Smith, N. (1983). The origin of Socrates' mission. *Journal of the History of Ideas, 44*, 657–666.
Brickhouse, T., & Smith, N. (1987). Socrates on goods, virtue, and happiness. *Oxford Studies in Ancient Philosophy, 5*, 1–27.
Brickhouse, T., & Smith, N. (1994). *Plato's Socrates*. New York: Oxford University Press.
Brickhouse, T., & Smith, N. (1997). Socrates and the unity of virtue. *Journal of Ethics, 1*, 311–324.
Briere, J. (2012). Working with trauma. In C. Germer & R. Siegel (Eds.), *Wisdom and compassion in psychotherapy* (pp. 265–279). New York: Guilford.

REFERENCES

Bright, D., Winn, B., & Kanov, J. (2014). Reconsidering virtue: Differences of perspective in virtue ethics and the positive social sciences. *Journal of Business Ethics, 119,* 445–460.

Brouwers, M., & Wiggum, C. (1993). Bulimia and perfectionism: Developing the courage to be imperfect. *Journal of Mental Health Counseling, 15*(2), 141–149.

Brown, M. (1967–68). Plato disapproves of the slave-boy's answer. *Review of Metaphysics, 21,* 57–93.

Brumbaugh, R. (1975). Plato's *Meno* as form and as content of secondary school courses in philosophy. *Teaching Philosophy, 1*(2), 107–115.

Burger, R. (1981). Belief, knowledge, and Socratic knowledge of ignorance. *Tulane Studies in Philosophy, 30,* 1–23.

Burnyeat, M. (1990). *The Theaetetus of Plato.* Indianapolis, IN: Hackett.

Calero-Elvira, A., Frojan-Parga, M., Ruiz-Sancho, E., & Alpanes-Freitag, M. (2013). Descriptive study of the Socratic method. *Behavior Therapy, 44,* 625–638.

Calogero, G. (1957). *Gorgias* and the Socratic principle. *Journal of Hellenic Studies, 77,* 12–17.

Caminada, M. (2008). A formal account of Socratic-style argumentation. *Journal of Applied Logic, 6*(1), 109–132.

Capaldi, N. (1969). *Human knowledge: A philosophical analysis of its meaning and scope.* New York: Pegasus.

Carey, T., & Mullan, R. (2004). What is Socratic questioning? *Psychotherapy, 41*(3), 217–226.

Carpenter, M., & Polansky, R. (2002). Variety of Socratic elenchi. In G. Scott (Ed.), *Does Socrates have a method?* (pp. 89–100). University Park: Pennsylvania State University Press.

Castonguay, L., Goldfried, M., Wiser, S., Raue, P., & Hayes, A. (1996). Predicting the effect of cognitive therapy for depression. *Journal of Consulting and Clinical Psychology, 64*(3), 497–504.

Cecchin, G. (1992). Constructing therapeutic possibilities. In S. McNamee & K. Gergen (Eds.), *Therapy as social construction* (pp. 86–95). New York: Sage.

Charlton, W. (1988). *Weakness of will.* New York: Blackwell.

Chessick, R. (1982). Socrates: First psychotherapy. *American Journal of Psychoanalysis, 42*(1), 71–83.

Chisholm, R. (1979). Socratic method and the theory of knowledge. *Ratio, 21,* 97–108.

Clark, G., & Egan, S. (2015). The Socratic method in cognitive-behavioural therapy. *Cognitive Therapy and Research, 39,* 863–879.

Clayton, V. (1982). Wisdom and intelligence. *International Journal of Aging and Human Development, 15*(4), 315–321.

Connor-Greene, P., & Greene, D. (2002). Science or snake oil? Teaching critical evaluation of "research" reports on the internet. *Teaching of Psychology, 29*(4), 321–324.

Cooper, J. M. (1977). The psychology of justice in Plato. *American Philosophical Quarterly, 14*(2), 151–157.

Cooper, J. M. (1999). *Reason and emotion: Essays on ancient moral psychology and ethical theory.* Princeton, NJ: Princeton University Press.

Copleston, F. (1946/1993). *A history of philosophy, Volume I: Greece and Rome.* New York: Doubleday.

REFERENCES

Cornford, F. (1932/1981). *Before and after Socrates*. New York: Cambridge University Press.
Crombie, I. M. (1962). *An examination of Plato's doctrines: I: Plato on man and society*. New York: Routledge & Kegan Paul.
Crombie, I. M. (1963). *An examination of Plato's doctrines: II: Plato on knowledge and reality*. New York: Routledge & Kegan Paul.
Crombie, I. M. (1964). *Plato: The midwife's apprentice*. New York: Barnes & Noble.
Cropsey, J. (1995). *Plato's world: Man's place in the cosmos*. Chicago: University of Chicago Press.
Cross, R., & Woozley, A. (1978). Knowledge, belief, and the forms. In *Plato: Metaphysics and epistemology* (pp. 70–96). Notre Dame, IN: University of Notre Dame Press.
Crossley, D., & Wilson, P. (1979). *How to argue: An introduction to logical thinking*. New York: Random House.
Csikszentmihalyi, M., & Rathunde, K. (1990). The psychology of wisdom. In R. Sternberg (Ed.), *Wisdom: Its nature, origins, and development* (pp. 25–51). New York: Cambridge University Press.
Curzer, H. (1991). Two varieties of temperance in the *Gorgias*. *International Philosophical Quarterly, 31,* 153–159.
Cushman, R. (1978). The Socratic-Platonic conception of philosophy as therapy. *Duke Divinity School Review, 43,* 152–168.
Dahlen, E. (2007). Cognitive therapy for clinically dysfunctional anger. *Clinical Case Studies, 6*(6), 493–507.
Davison, G. (1998). Being bolder with the Boulder model: The challenge of education and training in empirically-supported treatments. *Journal of Consulting and Clinical Psychology, 66*(1), 163–167.
Dawe, S., Rees, V., Mattick, R., Sitharthan, T., & Heather, N. (2002). Efficacy of moderation-oriented cue exposure for problem drinkers. *Journal of Consulting and Clinical Psychology, 70*(4), 1045–1050.
Day, J. (1994). Introduction. In J. Day (Ed.), *Plato's Meno* (pp. 1–34). New York: Routledge.
Dent, N. (1975). Virtues and actions. *Philosophical Quarterly, 25,* 318–335.
Dent, N. (1981). The value of courage. *Philosophy, 56,* 574–577.
Dent, N. (1984). *The moral psychology of the virtues*. New York: Cambridge University Press.
Despland, M. (1985). *The education of desire: Plato and the philosophy of religion*. Toronto: University of Toronto Press.
Devereux, D. (1977). Courage and wisdom in Plato's Laches. *Journal of the History of Philosophy, 15,* 129–141.
DeVogel, C. (1963). Who was Socrates? *Journal of the History of Philosophy, 1,* 143–161.
Dillon, J. T. (1990). *The practice of questioning*. New York: Routledge.
Dobbs, D. (1985, Nov.). The justice of Socrates' philosopher kings. *Journal of Political Science.* 809–826.
Dorter, K. (1994). *Form and good in Plato's eleatic dialogues*. Los Angeles: University of California Press.
Dorter, K. (1997). Knowledge and wisdom: Bypassing self-control. *Review of Metaphysics, 51*(2), 313–343.

REFERENCES

Drengson, A. (1981). The virtue of Socratic ignorance. *American Philosophical Quarterly, 18*(3), 237–242.

Duncan, R. (1978). Courage in Plato's Protagoras. *Phronesis: A Journal for Ancient Philosophy, 23*, 216–228.

Driver, J. (1989). The virtues of ignorance. *Journal of Philosophy, 86*, 373–384.

Edman, I. (1928/1956). *The works of Plato.* New York: Modern Library.

Efran, J., Lukens, M., & Lukens, R. (1990). *Language, structure, and change.* New York: Norton.

Elder, L., & Paul, R. (2007). Critical thinking: The art of Socratic questioning, part II. *Journal of Developmental Education, 31*(2), 32–33.

Ellis, A. (1962). *Reason and Emotion in Psychotherapy.* New York: Lyle Stuart.

Ellis, A. (1982). Must most psychotherapists remain as incompetent as they now are? *Journal of Contemporary Psychotherapy, 13*(1), 17–28.

Ellis, A. (1987). Self-control: The rational-emotive therapy method. *Southern Psychologist, 3*, 9–12.

Ellis, A. (1994). *Reason and emotion in psychotherapy* (Revised). New York: Birch Lane.

Ellis, A., & Dryden, W. (1987). *The practice of rational-emotive therapy (RET).* New York: Springer.

Ennis, R. (1982). Identifying implicit assumptions. *Synthese, 51*, 61–86.

Ericson, D. (2000). In Plato's cave: Philosophical counseling and philosophers of education. *Philosophy of Education Archive*, 81–89.

Ericsson, K. A. (2008). Deliberate practice and acquisition of expert performance. *Academic Emergency Medicine, 15*, 988–994.

Ericsson, K. A. (2014). Expertise. *Current Biology, 24*(11), R508–R510.

Ericsson, K. A., Krampe, R., & Tesch-Romer, C. (1993). The role of deliberate practice in the acquisition of expert performance. *Psychological Review, 100*(3), 363–406.

Ericsson, K. A., & Towne, T. (2010). Expertise. *Cognitive Science, 1*, 404–416.

Eskin, M., Ertekin, K., & Demir, H. (2008). Efficacy of a problem-solving therapy for depression and suicide potential in adolescents and young adults. *Cognitive Therapy and Research, 32*(2), 227–245.

Evans, J. (1989). *Bias in human reasoning.* London: Erlbaum.

Evans, J. (1990). Socratic ignorance—Socratic wisdom. *Modern Schoolman, 67*, 91–109.

Fagothey, A. (1976). *Right and reason: Ethics in theory and practice.* St. Louis, MO: Mosby.

Fine, G. (1992). Inquiry in the Meno. In R. Kraut (Ed.), *The Cambridge companion to Plato* (pp. 200–226). New York: Cambridge University Press.

Finfgeld, D. (1995). Becoming and being courageous in the chronically ill elderly. *Issues in Mental Health Nursing, 16*(1), 1–11.

Fitzpatrick, K., Witte, T., & Schmidt, N. (2005). Randomized controlled trial of a brief problem-orientation intervention for suicidal ideation. *Behavior Therapy, 36*(4), 323–333.

Fletcher, C. (1980a). Listening and talking to patients: The clinical interview. *British Medical Journal, 281*, 931–933.

Fletcher, C. (1980b). Listening and talking to patients: The exposition. *British Medical Journal, 281*, 994–996.

Foot, P. (1997). Virtues and vices. In R. Crisp & M. Slote (Eds.), *Virtue ethics* (pp. 163–177). New York: Oxford University Press.

REFERENCES

Fowers, B. (2005). *Virtue and psychology: Pursuing excellence in ordinary practices.* Washington, DC: American Psychological Association.

Franklin, M., Abramowitz, J., Bux, D., Zoellner, L., & Feeny, N. (2002). Cognitive-behavioral therapy with and without medication in the treatment of obsessive-compulsive disorder. *Professional Psychology: Research & Practice, 33*(2), 162–168.

Frede, D. (1986). The impossibility of perfection: Socrates' criticism of Simonides' poem in the *Protagoras. Review of Metaphysics, 39*(4), 729–753.

Frede, D. (1993). *Plato:* Philebus. Indianapolis & Cambridge.

Freedman, J., & Combs, G. (1993). Invitations to new stories: Using questions to explore alternative possibilities. In S. Gilligan & R. Price (Eds.), *Therapeutic Conversations* (pp. 291–303). New York: Norton.

Friedlander, P. (1969). *Plato: An introduction.* Princeton, NJ: Princeton University Press.

Frojan-Parga, M., Calero-Elvira, A., & Montano-Fidalgo, M. (2011). Study of the Socratic method during cognitive restructuring. *Clinical Psychology and Psychotherapy, 18,* 110–123.

Furedy, J., & Scher, H. (1985). The unexamined session is not worth attending. *Psychophysiology, 22*(3), 368–369.

Gadamer, H. (1980). *Dialogue and dialectic: Eight hermeneutical studies on Plato.* New Haven, CT: Yale University Press.

Gallagher, L., McAuley, J., & Moseley, L. (2013). A randomized-controlled trial of using a book of metaphors to reconceptualize pain and decreasing catastrophizing in people with chronic pain. *Clinical Journal of Pain, 29,* 20–25.

Gambrill, E. (1990). *Critical thinking in clinical practice.* New York: Wiley.

Gambrill, E. (1993). What critical thinking offers to clinicians and clients. *The Behavior Therapist, 16*(6), 141–147.

Gardner, E. (1995). *Justice and Christian ethics.* New York: Cambridge University Press.

Garrett, M. (2015). Understanding the experience of trauma in childhood: A Socratic ten factor model. *Journal of Education and Human Development, 4*(3), 9–19.

Garrett, R. (1996). Wisdom as the key to a better world. In J. Cautela & W. Ishaq (Eds.), *Contemporary issues in behavior therapy.* New York: Plenum.

Gericke, J. (1994). Courage and the unity of virtues in Plato's Laches. *South African Journal of Philosophy, 13*(1), 21–26.

Gerson, L. (1992). The ignorance of Socrates. *American Catholic Philosophical Association Proceedings, 66,* 123–135.

Godley, A. (1896). *Socrates and Athenian society in his day: A biographical sketch.* London: Seeley and Co.

Godlovitch, S. (1981). On wisdom. *Canadian Journal of Philosophy, 11*(1), 137–155.

Goldberg, C., & Simon, J. (1982). Toward a psychology of courage. *Journal of Contemporary Psychotherapy, 13*(2), 107–128.

Goldfried, M., & Eubanks-Carter, C. (2004). On the need for a new psychotherapy research paradigm. *Psychological Bulletin, 130*(4), 669–673.

Goldfried, M., & Wolfe, B. (1998). Toward a more clinically valid approach to therapy research. *Journal of Consulting and Clinical Psychology, 66*(1), 143–150.

Goldin, A., Pezzatti, L., Battro, A., & Sigman, M. (2011). From ancient Greece to modern education: Universality and lack of generalization of the Socratic dialogue. *Mind, Brain, and Education, 5*(4), 180–185.

REFERENCES

Goldman, A. (1986). *Epistemology and cognition.* Cambridge, MA: Harvard University Press.

Goldman, A. (1988). *Empirical knowledge.* Berkeley: University of California Press.

Gomez-Lobo, A. (1994). *The foundations of Socratic ethics.* Indianapolis, IN: Hackett.

Gordon, D. (1978). *Therapeutic metaphors.* Cupertino, CA: Meta.

Gosling, J. (1973). *Plato.* London: Routledge.

Goud, N. (2005). Courage: Its nature and development. *Journal of Humanistic Counseling, Education, and Development, 44,* 102–116.

Graesser, A., & Murachver, T. (1985). Symbolic procedures of question answering. In A. Graesser & J. Black (Eds.), *The psychology of questions* (pp. 15–88). Hillsdale, NJ: Erlbaum.

Graybar, S., & Leonard, L. (2005). In defense of listening. *American Journal of Psychotherapy, 59*(1), 1–18.

Green, L., & Glasgow, R. (2006). Evaluating the relevance, generalization, and applicability of research. *Evaluation & the Health Professions, 29*(1), 126–153.

Greenberg, G. (2010). *Manufacturing depression.* New York: Simon & Schuster.

Greenberg, L. (2012). Emotions, the great captains of our lives: Their role in the process of change in psychotherapy. *American Psychotherapist, 67*(8), 697–707.

Grey, S. (2007). A structured problem-solving group for psychiatric inpatients. *Groupwork, 17*(1), 20–33.

Griswold, C. (1986). *Self-knowledge in Plato's* Phaedrus. New Haven, CT: Yale University Press.

Grube, G. (1966). *Plato's thought.* Boston: Beacon.

Gruber, C. (2011). The psychology of courage: Modern research on an ancient virtue. *Integrative Psychological and Behavioral Science, 45,* 272–279.

Guidi, J., & Fava, F. (2014). Emerging trends in clinical psychology. *Riv. Psichiatr., 49*(6), 227.

Guisinger, S., & Blatt, S. (1994). Individuality and relatedness: Evolution of a fundamental dialectic. *American Psychologist, 49*(2), 104–111.

Guthrie, W. (1971). *Socrates.* New York: Cambridge University Press.

Guthrie, W. (1975a). *A history of Greek Philosophy: IV. Plato: The man and his dialogues, earlier period.* New York: Cambridge University Press.

Guthrie, W. (1975b). *The Greek philosophers: From Thales to Aristotle.* New York: Harper & Row.

Guthrie, W. (1978). *A history of Greek Philosophy: V. The later Plato and the Academy.* New York: Cambridge University Press.

Gyani, A., Shafran, R., Rose, S., & Lee, M. (2015). A qualitative investigation of therapists' attitudes toward research. *Behavioural and Cognitive Psychotherapy, 43,* 436–448.

Hackforth, R. (1933). Great thinkers: Socrates. *Journal of the British Institute of Philosophy, 8*(31), 259–272.

Haden, J. (1984). Socratic ignorance. In E. Kelly (Ed.), *New essays on Socrates* (pp. 17–28). Lanham, MD: University Press of America.

Hadot, I. (1986). The spiritual guide. In A. Armstrong (Ed.), *Classical Mediterranean spirituality* (pp. 436–459). New York: Crossroad.

Halberstam, J. (1982–83). The paradox of intolerance. *Philosophical Forum, 14*(2), 190–207.

REFERENCES

Halberstam, J. (1993). *Everyday ethics.* New York: Penguin.
Hampton, C. (1990). *Pleasure, knowledge, and being: An analysis of Plato's Philebus.* Albany: SUNY Press.
Hanna, F., Bemak, F., & Chung, R. (1999). Toward a new paradigm for multicultural counseling. *Journal of Counseling and Development, 77,* 125–134.
Hanna, F., & Ottens, A. (1995). The role of wisdom in psychotherapy. *Journal of Psychotherapy Integration, 5*(3), 195–219.
Hansen, D. (1988). Was Socrates a "Socratic teacher"? *Educational Theory, 38*(2), 213–224.
Harrah, D. (1982). What should we teach about questions? *Synthese, 51,* 21–38.
Hartshorne, C. (1987). *Wisdom as moderation: A philosophy of the middle way.* Albany: SUNY Press.
Hauck, P. (2001). When reason is not enough. *Journal of Rational Emotive and Cognitive-Behavioral Therapy, 19*(4), 245–257.
Hawtrey, R. (1972). Socrates and the acquisition of knowledge. *Antichthon, 6,* 109.
Hegel, M., Barrett, J., & Oxman, T. (2000). Training therapists in problem-solving treatment of depressive disorders in primary care: Lessons from the "treatment effectiveness project." *Families, Systems, & Health, 18*(4), 423–435.
Henrich, J., Heine, S., & Norenzayan, A. (2010). The weirdest people in the world? *Behavioral and Brain Sciences,* 1–75.
Hill, C. (2005). Therapist techniques, client involvement, and the therapeutic relationship. *Psychotherapy: Theory, Research, and Practice, 42*(4), 431–442.
Hoffart, A., Versland, S., & Sexton, H. (2002). Self-understanding, empathy, guided discovery, and schema belief in schema-focused cognitive therapy of personality problems. *Cognitive Therapy and Research, 26*(2), 199–219.
Hofmann, S. (2013). Bridging the theory-practice gap by getting even bolder with the Boulder model. *Behavior Therapy, 44*(4), 603–608.
Holland, J., Holyoak, K., Nisbett, R., & Thagard, P. (1986). *Induction: Processes of inference, learning, and discovery.* Cambridge, MA: MIT Press.
Holliday, S., & Chandler, M. (1986). *Wisdom: Explorations in adult competence.* Karger: Basel.
Howard, A. (2011). Socrates as a role model for counsellors. *Practical Philosophy, 2*(1), 15–17.
Howland, J. (1993). *The Republic: The odyssey of philosophy.* New York: Twayne.
Hoyt, M. (1996). Cognitive-behavioral treatment of post-traumatic stress disorder. In M. Hoyt (Ed.), *Constructive therapies.* New York: Guilford.
Hughen, R. (1982). Some arguments in support of the Socratic thesis that there is no such thing as weakness of the will. *Journal of Thought, 17,* 85–93.
Hunt, L. (1980). Courage and principle. *Canadian Journal of Philosophy, 10*(2), 281–293.
Irwin, T. (1974). Recollection and Plato's moral theory. *Review of Metaphysics, 27,* 752–772.
Irwin, T. (1977). *Plato's moral theory.* New York: Oxford University Press.
Irwin, T. (1986). Socrates the Epicurean. *Illinois Classical Studies, 11,* 85–112.
Irwin, T. (1992). Plato: The intellectual background. In R. Kraut (Ed.), *The Cambridge companion to Plato* (pp. 51–89). New York: Cambridge University Press.
Irwin, T. (1995). *Plato's ethics.* New York: Oxford University Press.

REFERENCES

Jacobs, T. (2008). On courage. *Psychoanalytic Psychology, 25*(3), 550–555.

James, I., & Moore, R. (2007). The use of questions in cognitive behaviour therapy. *Behavioural and Cognitive Psychotherapy, 35*, 507–511.

James, I., Morse, R., & Howarth, A. (2010). The science and art of asking questions in cognitive therapy. *Behavioural and Cognitive Psychotherapy, 38*, 83–93.

Johnsen, T., & Friborg, O. (2015). The effects of cognitive behavioral therapy as an anti-depressive treatment is falling: A meta-analysis. *Psychological Bulletin, 141*(4), 747–768.

Johnson, D., & Matross, R. (1975). Attitude modification methods. In F. Kanfer & A. Goldstein (Eds.), *Helping people change* (pp. 51–88). Elmsford, NY: Pergamon.

Jones, J., & Mehr, S. (2007). Foundations and assumptions of the scientist-practitioner model. *American Behavioral Scientist, 50*(6), 766–771.

Jordan, A., & Meara, N. (1990). Ethics and professional practice of psychologists: The role of virtues and principles. *Professional Psychology: Research and Practice, 21*(2), 107–114.

Jowett, B. (1892/1937). *The dialogues of Plato (Vol. 1 & 2)*. New York: Random House.

Joyce-Moniz, L. (1985). Epistemological therapy and constructivism. In *Cognition and psychotherapy* (pp. 143–179). New York: Springer.

Kachi, Y. (1983). Gods, forms, and Socratic piety. *Ancient Philosophy, 3*, 82–88.

Kaplan, A. (1977). *In pursuit of wisdom: The scope of philosophy*. Beverly Hills, CA: Glencoe.

Kashdan, T., & Rottenberg, J. (2010). Psychological flexibility as a functional aspect of health. *Clinical Psychology Review, 30*, 865–878.

Kazantzis, N., Fairburn, C., Padesky, C., Reinecke, M., & Teesson, M. (2014). Unresolved issues regarding the research and practice of cognitive behavior therapy: The case of guided discovery using Socratic questioning. *Behaviour Change, 31*(1), 1–17.

Kazantzis, N., Freeman, A., Fruzzetti, A., Persons, J., & Smucker, M. (2013). Unresolved issues regarding collaborative empiricism in cognitive behavioural therapies. *Behaviour Change, 30*(1), 1–11.

Kazdin, A. (2008). Evidence-based treatment and practice. *American Psychologist, 63*(3), 146–159.

Keitner, G., Posternak, M., & Ryan, C. (2003). How many subjects with major depressive disorder meet eligibility requirements on an antidepressant efficacy trial? *Journal of Clinical Psychiatry, 64*(9), 1091–1093.

Kekes, J. (1983). Wisdom. *American Philosophical Quarterly, 20*(3), 277–286.

Kekes, J. (1988). Understanding evil. *American Philosophical Quarterly, 25*(1), 13–24.

Kellerman, H., & Burry, A. (1988). *Psychopathology and differential diagnosis, Volume 1: History of psychopathology*. New York: Columbia University Press.

Kendall, P., & Beidas, R. (2007). Smoothing the trail for dissemination of evidence-based practices for youth: Flexibility with fidelity. *Professional Psychology: Research and Practice, 38*(1), 13–20.

Kennerly, H. (2007). *Socratic method*. Oxford: Oxford Cognitive Therapy Centre.

Kidd, I. (1992). Socratic questions. In B. Gower & M. Stokes (Eds.), *Socratic questions* (pp. 82–92). New York: Routledge.

Kierkegaard, S. (1841/1989). *The concept of irony with continual reference to Socrates*. Princeton, NJ: Princeton University Press.

REFERENCES

King, C. (2008). Wisdom, moderation, and elenchus in Plato's *Apology*. *Metaphilosophy*, 39(3), 346–362.

King, J. (1987). Elenchus, self-blame and the Socratic paradox. *Review of Metaphysics*, 41, 105–126.

Kinnier, R., Tribbensee, N., Rose, C., & Vaughan, S. (2001). In the final analysis: More wisdom from people who have faced death. *Journal of Counseling & Development*, 79, 171–177.

Kitchener, K., & Brenner, H. (1990). Wisdom and reflective judgment: Knowing in the face of uncertainty. In R. Sternberg (ed.), *Wisdom: Its nature, origins, and development* (pp. 212–229). New York: Cambridge University Press.

Klein, P. (1981). *Certainty: A refutation of skepticism*. Minneapolis: University of Minnesota Press.

Klein, S. (1986). Socratic dialectic in the *Meno*. *Southern Journal of Philosophy*, 24(3), 351–363.

Klerman, G., Weissman, M., Rounsaville, B., & Chevron, E. (1984). *Interpersonal psychotherapy of depression*. New York: Basic Books.

Kohak, E. (1960). The road to wisdom: Lessons on education from Plato's *Laches*. *Classical Journal*, 56, 123–132.

Kohlberg, L. (1970). Education for justice: A modern statement of the Platonic view. In N. Sizer & T. Sizer (Eds.), *Moral education* (pp. 57–83). Cambridge, MA: Harvard University Press.

Kramer, D. (1990). Conceptualizing wisdom: The primacy of affect-cognition relations. In R. Sternberg (Ed.), *Wisdom: Its nature, origins, and development* (pp. 279–313). New York: Cambridge University Press.

Kraut, R. (1984). *Socrates and the state*. Princeton, NJ: Princeton University Press.

Kraut, R. (1992a). Introduction to the study of Plato. In R. Kraut (Ed.), *The Cambridge companion to Plato* (pp. 1–50). New York: Cambridge University Press.

Kraut, R. (1992b). The defense of justice in Plato's *Republic*. In R. Kraut (Ed.), *The Cambridge companion to Plato* (pp. 311–337). New York: Cambridge University Press.

Kraut, R., Olson, J., Banaji, M., Bruckman, A., Cohen, J., & Couper, M. (2004). Psychological research online: Report of Board of Scientific Affairs' Advisory Group on the conduct of research on the internet. *American Psychologist*, 59(2), 105–117.

Kristeva, J. (1995). *New maladies of the soul*. New York: Columbia University Press.

Krupnick, J., Sotsky, S., Elkin, I., Watkins, J., & Pilkonis, P. (1996). The role of the therapeutic alliance in psychotherapy and pharmacotherapy outcome. *Journal of Consulting and Clinical Psychology*, 64(3), 532–539.

Kupperman, J. (2005). Morality, ethics, and wisdom. In R. Sternberg & J. Jordan (Eds.), *A handbook of wisdom* (pp. 245–271). New York: Cambridge University Press.

Lageman, A. (1989). Socrates and psychotherapy. *Journal of Religion and Health*, 28(3), 219–223.

Lake, L. (1957). *How to cross-examine witnesses successfully*. Englewood Cliffs, NJ: Prentice-Hall.

Lane, C. (2016, Jan. 22). The problem with heroizing Robert Spitzer. *Psychology Today*.

Legomsky-Abel, D. (1989). The transformative function of Socratic dialectic. *Journal of Religion and Psychical Research*, 12, 159–166.

Lehrer, K. (1971). Why not skepticism? *Philosophical Forum*, 2, 283–298.

REFERENCES

Leigh, F. (2007). Platonic dialogue, maieutic method and critical thinking. *Journal of Philosophy of Education*, 41(3), 309–323.

Lesher, J. (1987). Socrates' disavowal of knowledge. *Journal of the History of Philosophy*, 25(2), 275–288.

Lesher, J. (2002). Parmenidean elenchus. In G. Scott (Ed.), *Does Socrates have a method?* (pp. 19–35). University Park: Pennsylvania State University Press.

Livingstone, R. (1938). *Portrait of Socrates*. New York: Oxford University Press.

Lopez, S., Rasmussen, H., Skorupski, W., Koetting, K., Petersen, S., & Yang, Y. (2010). Folk conceptualizations of courage. In C. Pury & S. Lopez (Eds.), *The psychology of courage* (pp. 23–45). Washington, DC: American Psychological Association.

Louden, R. (1997). On some vices of virtue ethics. In R. Crip & M. Slote (Eds.), *Virtue ethics* (pp. 201–216). Oxford: Oxford University Press.

Lutz, M. J. (1998). *Socrates' education to virtue: Learning the love of the noble*. Albany: SUNY Press.

Lycos, K. (1987). *Plato on justice and power*. Albany: SUNY Press.

Macintyre, A. (1997). The nature of the virtues. In R. Crip & M. Slote (Eds.), *Virtue ethics* (pp. 118–140). Oxford: Oxford University Press.

Mackenzie, M. (1981). *Plato on punishment*. Berkeley: University of California Press.

Mackenzie, M. (1988). The virtues of Socratic ignorance. *Classical Quarterly*, 38(2), 331–350.

Malouff, J., Thorsteinsson, E., & Schutte, N. (2007). The efficacy of problem solving therapy in reducing mental and physical health problems: A meta-analysis. *Clinical Psychology Review*, 27, 46–57.

Marinoff, R. (1999). *Plato, not Prozac: Applying philosophy to everyday problems*. New York: Harper-Collins.

Marshall, W., Bristol, D., & Barbaree, H. (1992). Cognitions and courage in the avoidance behavior of acrophobics. *Behavior Research and Therapy*, 30(5), 463–470.

Mason, R., & Wakefield, H. (1955). *Socrates: The man and his teaching*. London: Oxford University Press.

Matthews, G. (1972). *Plato's epistemology*. New York: Humanities Press.

Mathieson, F., Jordan, J., Carter, J., & Stubbe, M. (2016). Nailing down metaphors in CBT. *Behavioural and Cognitive Psychotherapy*, 44, 236–248.

Maxwell, N. (1984). *From knowledge to wisdom: A revolution in the aims and methods of science*. Oxford: Basil Blackwell.

McClaren, R. (1989). *Solving moral problems: A strategy for practical inquiry*. Mountain View, CA: Mayfield.

McCracken, S., & Marsh, J. (2008). Practitioner expertise in evidence-based practice decision making. *Research on Social Work Practice*, 18(4), 301–310.

McDaniel, M., & Schlager, M. (1990). Discovery learning and transfer of problem-solving skills. *Cognition and Instruction*, 7(2), 129–159.

McDowell, J. (1997). Virtue and reason. In R. Crip & M. Slote (Eds.), *Virtue ethics* (pp. 141–162). Oxford: Oxford University Press.

McFall, R. (2006). Doctoral training in clinical psychology. *Annual Review of Clinical Psychology*, 2, 21–49.

McKee, P., & Barber, C. (1999). On defining wisdom. *International Journal of Aging and Human Development*, 49(2), 149–164.

REFERENCES

McKim, R. (1988). Shame and truth in Plato's *Gorgias*. In C. Griswold (Ed.), *Platonic writings, Platonic readings* (pp. 34–48). New York: Routledge.

McKinney, R. (1983). The origins of modern dialectics. *Journal of the History of Ideas*, 44, 179–190.

McMurran, M., Neza, A., & Nezu, C. (2008). Problem-solving therapy for people with personality disorders. *Mental Health Review Journal*, 13(2), 35–39.

McPherran, M. (1985). Socratic piety in the *Euthyphro*. *Journal of the History of Philosophy*, 23, 283–310.

McPherran, M. (1996). *The religion of Socrates*. University Park: Pennsylvania State University Press.

McPherran, M. (2011). Socratic religion. In D. Morrison (Ed.), *The Cambridge companion to Socrates* (pp. 111–137). Cambridge: Cambridge University Press.

Meacham, J. (1983). Wisdom and the context of knowledge: Knowing that one doesn't know. *Contributions to Human Development*, 8, 111–134.

Meacham, J. (1990). The loss of wisdom. In R. Sternberg (Ed.), *Wisdom: Its nature, origins, and development* (pp. 181–211). New York: Cambridge University Press.

Meara, N., Schmidt, L., & Day, J. (1996). Principles and virtues: A foundation for ethical decisions, policies, and character. *Counseling Psychologist*, 24, 4–77.

Medina, M. (2008). Everyday courage. *Existential Analysis*, 19(2), 280–298.

Meichenbaum, D. (2003). *A clinical handbook/practical therapist manual for assessing and treating adults with post-traumatic stress disorder (PTSD)*. Institute Press.

Mele, A. (1987). *Irrationality: An essay on akrasia, self-deception, and self-control*. New York: Oxford University Press.

Melling, D. (1987). *Understanding Plato*. New York: Oxford University Press.

Meyer, M. (1980). Dialectic and questioning: Socrates and Plato. *American Philosophical Quarterly*, 17(4), 281–289.

Mikula, G. (1980). Main issues in the psychological research on justice. In G. Mikula (Ed.), *Justice and social interaction*. New York: Springer-Verlag.

Miller, J. (1971). The Socratic meaning of virtue. *Southern Journal of Philosophy*, 9, 141–150.

Milliren, A., Milliren, M., & Eckstein, D. (2007). Combining Socratic questions with the "ADAPT" problem-solving model. *Family Journal*, 15(4), 415–419.

Minuchin, S., & Fishman, H. C. (1981). *Family therapy techniques*. Cambridge, MA: Harvard University Press.

Mitchell, S. (2006). Socratic dialogue, the humanities, and the art of the question. *Arts & Humanities in Higher Education*, 5(2), 181–197.

Moravcsik, J. (1994). Learning as recollection. In J. Day (Ed.), *Plato's* Meno (pp. 112–128). New York: Routledge.

More, P. E. (1928). *The religion of Plato*. Princeton, NJ: Princeton University Press.

Morgan, M. (1990). *Platonic piety: Philosophy and ritual in fourth-century Athens*. New Haven, CT: Yale University Press.

Moss, D. (1992). Cognitive therapy, phenomenology, and the struggle for meaning. *Journal of Phenomenological Psychology*, 23(1), 87–102.

Moynihan, R., & Cassels, A. (2005). *Selling sickness*. New York: Nation.

Mulder, J., House, J., & Gregory, D. (2000). Transforming experience into wisdom: Healing amidst suffering. *Journal of Palliative Care*, 16(2), 25–29.

REFERENCES

Nash, R. (1988). *Faith and reason*. Grand Rapids, MI: Zondervan.

Nasser, E. H., & Overholser, J. C. (2005). Recovery from major depression: The role of support from family, friends, and spiritual beliefs. *Acta Psychiatrica Scandinavica, 111*(2), 125–132.

Navia, L. (1985). *Socrates: The man and his philosophy*. Lanham, MD: University Press of America.

Neenan, M. (2009). Using Socratic questioning in coaching. *Journal of Rational-Emotive and Cognitive-Behavioral Therapy, 27*, 249–264.

Neenan, M. (2009). Using Socratic questioning in coaching. *Journal of Rational-Emotive and Cognitive-Behavioral Therapy, 27*, 249–264.

Nehamas, A. (1985). Meno's paradox and Socrates as a teacher. *Oxford Studies in Ancient Philosophy, 3*, 1–30.

Nehamas, A. (1986). Socratic intellectualism. *Proceedings of the Boston Area Colloquium in Ancient Philosophy, 2*, 275–316.

Nehamas, A. (1994). Meno's paradox and Socrates as a teacher. In J. Day (Ed.), *Plato's Meno* (pp. 221–248). New York. Routledge.

Nehamas, A. (1999). *Virtues of authenticity: Essays on Plato and Socrates*. Princeton, NJ: Princeton University Press.

Nelson, L. (1949). *Socratic method and critical philosophy* (Trans. T. Brown). New Haven, CT: Yale University Press.

Nelson, L. (1980). The Socratic method. *Thinking, 2*, 34–38.

Nezu, A., & Nezu, C. (2001). Problem solving therapy. *Journal of Psychotherapy Integration, 11*(2), 187–205.

Norman, R. (1983). *The moral philosophers*. Oxford: Clarendon.

Norton, P., & Weiss, B. (2009). The role of courage on behavioral approach in a fear-eliciting situation. *Journal of Anxiety Disorders, 23*, 212–227.

Nussbaum, M. (1986). *The fragility of goodness*. New York: Cambridge University Press.

Odegard, D. (1982). *Knowledge and skepticism*. Totowa, NJ: Rowman & Littlefield.

Orford, J. (1985). *Excessive appetites: A psychological view of addictions*. New York: Wiley.

Osbeck, L., & Robinson, D. (2005). Philosophical theories of wisdom. In R. Sternberg & J. Jordan (Eds.), *A handbook of wisdom* (pp. 61–83). New York: Cambridge University Press.

Overholser, J. C. (1987). Facilitating autonomy in passive-dependent persons: An integrative model. *Journal of Contemporary Psychotherapy, 17*, 250–269.

Overholser, J. C. (1988). Clinical utility of the Socratic method. In C. Stout (Ed.), *Annals of clinical research* (pp. 1–7). Des Plaines, IL: Forest Institute.

Overholser, J. C. (1991). The Socratic method as a technique in psychotherapy supervision. *Professional Psychology: Research and Practice, 22*(1), 68–74.

Overholser, J. C. (1992). Socrates in the classroom. *College Teaching, 40*(1), 14–19.

Overholser, J. C. (1993a). Elements of the Socratic method: I. Systematic questioning. *Psychotherapy, 30*, 67–74.

Overholser, J. C. (1993b). Elements of the Socratic method: II. Inductive reasoning. *Psychotherapy, 30*, 75–85.

Overholser, J. C. (1994a). Elements of the Socratic method: III. Universal definitions. *Psychotherapy, 31*, 286–293.

REFERENCES

Overholser, J. C. (1995). Elements of the Socratic method: IV. Disavowal of knowledge. *Psychotherapy, 32*, 283–292.

Overholser, J. C. (1996). Elements of the Socratic method: V. Self-Improvement. *Psychotherapy, 33*, 549–559.

Overholser, J. C. (1997). Treatment of excessive interpersonal dependency: A cognitive-behavioral model. *Journal of Contemporary Psychotherapy, 27*, 283–301.

Overholser, J. C. (1999a). Elements of the Socratic method: VI. Promoting virtue in everyday life. *Psychotherapy, 36*, 137–145.

Overholser, J. C. (1999b). Courage and the Socratic method of psychotherapy. *Voices: Journal of the American Academy of Psychotherapists, 35*(3), 6–14.

Overholser, J. C. (2002). Treatments for depression: Wisdom imparted from treatments discarded. *International Journal of Psychiatry in Medicine, 32*(4), 317–336.

Overholser, J. C. (2003a). Where has all the psyche gone: Searching for treatments that focus on psychological issues. *Journal of Contemporary Psychotherapy, 33*(1), 49–61.

Overholser, J. C. (2003b). Cognitive-behavioral treatment of depression: A three-stage model to guide treatment planning. *Cognitive and Behavioral Practice, 10*, 231–239.

Overholser, J. C. (2005a). The four pillars of psychotherapy supervision. *Clinical Supervisor, 23*(1), 1–13.

Overholser, J. C. (2005b). Group psychotherapy and existential concerns: An interview with Irvin Yalom. *Journal of Contemporary Psychotherapy, 35*(2), 185–197.

Overholser, J. C. (2007a). The Boulder model in academia: Struggling to integrate the science and practice of psychology. *Journal of Contemporary Psychotherapy, 37*, 205–211.

Overholser, J. C. (2007b). The central role of the therapeutic alliance: A simulated interview with Carl Rogers. *Journal of Contemporary Psychotherapy, 37*(2), 71–78.

Overholser, J. C. (2008). Advancing the field of psychotherapy through innovation and integration in scholarly works. *Journal of Contemporary Psychotherapy, 38*(2), 97–104.

Overholser, J. C. (2010a). Psychotherapy according to the Socratic Method: Integrating ancient philosophy with contemporary cognitive therapy. *Journal of Cognitive Psychotherapy, 24*(4), 355–364.

Overholser, J. C. (2010b). Clinical expertise: A preliminary attempt to clarify its core elements. *Journal of Contemporary Psychotherapy, 40*(3), 131–139.

Overholser, J. C. (2010c). Ten criteria to qualify as a scientist-practitioner in clinical psychology: An immodest proposal for objective standards. *Journal of Contemporary Psychotherapy, 40*(1), 51–59.

Overholser, J. C. (2010d). Psychotherapy that strives to encourage social interest: A simulated interview with Alfred Adler. *Journal of Psychotherapy Integration, 20*(4), 347–363.

Overholser, J. C. (2011). Collaborative empiricism, guided discovery, and the Socratic method: Core processes for effective cognitive therapy. *Clinical Psychology: Science and Practice, 18*(1), 62–66.

Overholser, J. C. (2012a). Behind a thin veneer: What lurks beneath the scientist-practitioner label? *Journal of Contemporary Psychotherapy, 42*(4), 271–279.

Overholser, J. C. (2012b). Guiding clients through difficult situations and complicated decisions. *Ohio State Journal of Criminal Law, 10*(1), 229–236.

Overholser, J. C. (2013). Guided discovery: Problem-solving therapy integrated within the Socratic method. *Journal of Contemporary Psychotherapy, 43*(2), 73–82.

Overholser, J. C. (2015a). Positive psychotherapy according to the Socratic method. *Journal of Contemporary Psychotherapy, 45*(2), 137–142.

Overholser, J. C. (2015b). Protesting the decline but predicting the demise of clinical psychology: Can we avoid a total collapse? *Journal of Contemporary Psychotherapy, 44*(4), 273–281.

Overholser, J. C. (2017a). Guided discovery: A clinical strategy derived from the Socratic method. *International Journal of Cognitive Therapy*.

Overholser, J. C. (2017b). From Puddles to Potholes: The Role of Overvalued Beliefs in Emotional Problems. *Journal of Contemporary Psychotherapy*, 1–10.

Overholser, J. C., Braden, A., & Fisher, L. (2010). You've got to believe: Core beliefs that underlie effective psychotherapy. *Journal of Contemporary Psychotherapy, 40*(4), 185–194.

Overholser, J. C., & Fine, M. (1994b). Cognitive-behavioral treatment of excessive interpersonal dependency: A four-stage psychotherapy model. *Journal of Cognitive Psychotherapy, 8*, 55–70.

Packer, M. (1985). Hermeneutic inquiry in the study of human conduct. *American Psychologist, 40*(10), 1081–1093.

Padesky, C. (1993). Socratic questioning: Changing minds or guiding discovery? Presented at the European Congress of Behavioral and Cognitive Therapies, London. http://www.padesky.com.

Padesky, C., & Beck, A. T. (2003). Science and philosophy: Comparison of cognitive therapy and rational-emotive behavior therapy. *Journal of Cognitive Psychotherapy, 17*(3), 211–224.

Padesky, C., & Mooney, K. (2012). Strengths-based cognitive-behavioural therapy. *Clinical Psychology and Psychotherapy, 19*, 283–290.

Pappas, N. (1995). *Plato and the Republic*. New York: Routledge.

Parker, M. (1979). *Socrates: The wisest and most just?* London: Cambridge University Press.

Parry, R. (1996). *Plato's craft of justice*. Albany: SUNY Press.

Patterson, R. (1965). *Plato on immortality*. University Park: Pennsylvania State University Press.

Paul, R., & Elder, L. (2007). Critical thinking: The art of Socratic questioning. *Journal of Developmental Education, 31*(1), 36–37.

Paul, R., & Elder, L. (2008). Critical thinking: The art of Socratic questioning, part III. *Journal of Developmental Education, 31*(3), 34–35.

Penner, T. (1971). Thought and desire in Plato. In G. Vlastos (Ed.), *Plato II: Ethics, politics, and philosophy of art and religion* (pp. 96–118). Notre Dame: University of Notre Dame Press.

Penner, T. (1992). What Laches and Nicias miss—and whether Socrates thinks courage merely a part of virtue. *Ancient Philosophy, 12*, 1–27.

Peterson, C., & Seligman, M. (2004). *Character strengths and virtues: A handbook and classification*. Washington, D.C.: American Psychological Association.

REFERENCES

Pincoffs, E. (1986). *Quandaries and virtues: Against reductivism in ethics.* Lawrence: University Press of Kansas.

Poland, W. (2008). "The best thing in me": The analyst's courage in clinical practice. *Psychoanalytic Psychology, 25*(3), 556–559.

Popper, K. (1979). *Objective knowledge: An evolutionary approach* (2nd ed.). Oxford: Clarendon.

Prasinos, S. (1992). Spiritual aspects of psychotherapy. *Journal of Religion and Health, 31*(1), 41–52.

Prest, L., & Keller, J. (1993). Spirituality and family therapy. *Journal of Marital and Family Therapy, 19*(2), 137–148.

Prior, W. (1985). *Unity and development in Plato's metaphysics.* La Salle, IN: Open Court.

Prior, W. (1991). *Virtue and knowledge: An introduction to ancient Greek ethics.* New York: Routledge.

Pury, C., Lopez, S., & Key-Roberts, M. (2010). The future of courage research. In C. Pury & S. Lopez, *The psychology of courage* (pp. 229–235). Washington, DC: American Psychological Association.

Pury, C., & Starkey, C. (2010). Is courage an accolade or a process? In C. Pury & S. Lopez, *The psychology of courage* (pp. 67–87). Washington, DC: American Psychological Association.

Putnam, D. (1997). Psychological courage. *Philosophy, Psychiatry, & Psychology, 4*(1), 1–11.

Putnam, D. (2010). Philosophical roots of the concept of courage. In C. Pury & S. Lopez, *The psychology of courage* (pp. 9–22). Washington, DC: American Psychological Association.

Rachman, S. (1976). A theoretical analysis of high and low therapeutic demands. *Behavior Research and Therapy, 14,* 301–302.

Raimy, V. (1950). *Training in clinical psychology.* New York: Prentice-Hall.

Rate, C. (2010). Defining the features of courage. In C. Pury & S. Lopez, *The psychology of courage* (pp. 47–66). Washington, DC: American Psychological Association.

Rawls, J. (1971). *A theory of justice.* Cambridge, MA: Harvard University Press.

Rawls, J. (2001). *Justice as fairness: A restatement.* Cambridge, MA: Harvard University Press.

Reale, G. (1987). *A history of ancient philosophy: I. From the origins to Socrates.* Buffalo: State University of New York Press.

Regan, D. (1973). An adaptation of the Socratic method. *Proceedings of the American Catholic Philosophical Association, 47,* 87–91.

Reeve, C. (1988). *Philosopher-kings: The argument of Plato's Republic.* Princeton, NJ: Princeton University Press.

Reeve, C. (1989). *Socrates in the Apology.* Indianapolis, IN: Hackett.

Reiman, J. (1990). *Justice and modern moral philosophy.* New Haven, CT: Yale University Press.

Renaud, F. (2002). Humbling as upbringing: The ethical dimension of the elenchus in the *Lysis.* In G. Scott (Ed.), *Does Socrates have a method?* (pp. 183–198). University Park: Pennsylvania State University Press.

Richmond, W. K. (1955). *Socrates and the western world.* New York: Citadel.

Robinson, D. (1990). Wisdom through the ages. In R. Sternberg (Ed.), *Wisdom: Its nature, origins, and development* (pp. 13–24). New York: Cambridge University Press.

REFERENCES

Robinson, R. (1941). *Plato's earlier dialectic*. Ithaca, NY; Cornell University Press.
Robinson, R. (1971a). Elenchus. In G. Vlastos (Ed.), *The philosophy of Socrates* (pp. 78–93). Notre Dame, IN: University of Notre Dame Press.
Robinson, R. (1971b). Elenchus: Direct and indirect. In G. Vlastos (Ed.), *The philosophy of Socrates* (pp. 94–109). Notre Dame, IN: University of Notre Dame Press.
Robinson, R. (1971c). Socratic definition. In G. Vlastos (Ed.), *The philosophy of Socrates* (pp. 110–124). Notre Dame, IN: University of Notre Dame Press.
Robinson, T. (1995). *Plato's psychology* (2nd ed.). Toronto: University of Toronto Press.
Rocklin, T. (1987). Defining learning: Two classroom activities. *Teaching of Psychology*, 14(4), 228–229.
Roemer, L., & Orsillo, S. (2012). Anxiety disorders: Acceptance, compassion, and wisdom. In C. Germer & R. Siegel (Eds.), *Wisdom and compassion in psychotherapy* (pp. 234–248). New York: Guilford.
Rogers, A. (1933). *The Socratic problem*. New Haven, CT: Yale University Press.
Roochnik, D. (1990). *The tragedy of reason: Toward a Platonic conception of logos*. New York: Routledge.
Roochnik, D. (1996). *Of art and wisdom: Plato's understanding of techne*. University Park: Pennsylvania State University Press.
Rorty, A. (1986). The two faces of courage. *Philosophy*, 61, 151–171.
Rosen, N., & Wyer, R. (1972). Some further evidence for the "Socratic effect" using a subjective probability model of cognitive organization. *Journal of Personality and Social Psychology*, 24(3), 420–424.
Rosenbaum, M. (1993). The three functions of self-control behaviour: Redressive, reformative, and experiential. *Work & Stress*, 7(1), 35–46.
Rosenberg, H. (1993). Prediction of controlled drinking by alcoholics and problem drinkers. *Psychological Bulletin*, 113, 129–139.
Rotenstreich, N. (1998). *On faith*. Chicago: University of Chicago Press.
Rothwell, P. (2005). External validity of randomised controlled trials. *Lancet*, 365, 82–93.
Rud, A. (1994). Intuition and the Socratic method: Two opposed ways of knowing? *Studies in Philosophy and Education*, 13, 65–75.
Rudebusch, G. (1999). *Socrates, pleasure, and value*. New York: Oxford University Press.
Rutter, J., & Friedberg, R. (1999). Guidelines for the effective use of Socratic dialogue in cognitive therapy. *Innovations in Clinical Practice*, 17, 481–490.
Ryan, R., & Deci, E. (2008). A self-determination theory approach to psychotherapy: The motivational basis for effective change. *Canadian Psychology*, 49(3), 186–193.
Ryan, R., Huta, V., & Deci, E. (2008). Living well: A self-determination theory perspective in eudaimonia. *Journal of Happiness Studies*, 9, 139–170.
Ryff, C., & Singer, B. (2008). Know thyself and become what you are: A eudaimonic approach to psychological well-being. *Journal of Happiness Studies*, 9, 13–39.
Sallis, J. (1986). *Being and logos: The way of Platonic dialogue*. Atlantic Highlands, NJ: Humanities Press International.
Santas, G. (1969). Socrates at work on virtue and knowledge in Plato's *Laches*. *Review of Metaphysics*, 22, 433–460.
Santas, G. (1974). The Socratic fallacy. *Journal of the History of Philosophy*, 10, 127–141.
Santas, G. (1979). *Socrates: Philosophy in Plato's early dialogues*. London: Routledge.

REFERENCES

Sayers, S. (1999). *Plato's* Republic: *An introduction*. Edinburgh: Edinburgh University Press.

Schmid, W. (1983). Socratic moderation and self-knowledge. *Journal of the History of Philosophy, 21*, 339–348.

Schmid, W. (1985). The Socratic conception of courage. *History of Philosophy Quarterly, 2*(2), 113–129.

Schmid, W. (1992). *On manly courage: A study of Plato's* Laches. Carbondale: Southern Illinois University Press.

Schmid, W. (2002). Socratic dialectic in the *Charmides*. In G. Scott (Ed.), *Does Socrates have a method?* (pp. 235–251). University Park: Pennsylvania State University Press.

Schulte, D., & Eifert, G. (2002). What to do when manuals fail? The dual model of psychotherapy. *Clinical Psychology: Science and Practice, 9*, 312–328.

Scott, G. (2002). Introduction. In G. Scott (Ed.), *Does Socrates have a method?* (pp. 1–16). University Park: Pennsylvania State University Press.

Scott, J., & Freeman, A. (2010). Beck's cognitive therapy. In N. Kazantzis, M. Reinecke, & A. Freeman (Eds.), *Cognitive and behavioral theories in clinical practice* (pp. 28–75). New York: Guilford.

Scraper, R. (2000). The art and science of maieutic questioning within the Socratic method. *International Forum for Logotherapy, 23*(1), 14–16.

Seeskin, K. (1976). Courage and knowledge: A perspective on the Socratic paradox. *Southern Journal of Philosophy, 14*, 511–521.

Seeskin, K. (1987). *Dialogue and discovery: A study in Socratic method*. Albany: SUNY Press.

Seiple, G. (1985). The Socratic method of inquiry. *Dialogue, 28*, 16–22.

Seligman, M., Parks, A., & Steen, T. (2004). A balanced psychology and a full life. *Philosophical Transactions of the Royal Society for Biological Sciences, 359*(1449), 1379–1381.

Sesonske, A., & Fleming, N. (1965). *Plato's* Meno. Belmont, CA: Wadsworth.

Shklar, J. (1984). *Ordinary vices*. Cambridge, MA: Harvard University Press.

Siemonsma, P., Stuive, I., Roorda, L., Vollebregt, J., Walker, M., Lankhorst, G., & Lettinga, A. (2013). Cognitive treatment of illness perceptions in patients with chronic low back pain. *Physical Therapy, 93*(4), 435–438.

Simon, B. (1978). *Mind and madness in ancient Greece: The classical roots of modern psychiatry*. Ithaca, NY: Cornell University Press.

Sitharthan, T., Sitharthan, G., Hough, M., & Kavanagh, D. (1997). Cue exposure in moderation drinking. *Journal of Consulting and Clinical Psychology, 65*(5), 878–882.

Sitharthan, T., Sitharthan, G., & Kavanagh, D. (2001). Emotional cue exposure for alcohol abuse. *Clinical Psychology and Psychotherapy, 8*, 73–78.

Skemp, J. (1986). The spirituality of Socrates and Plato. In A. Armstrong (Ed.), *Classical Mediterranean spirituality* (pp. 102–120). New York: Crossroad.

Skovholt, T., Ronnestad, M., & Jennings, L. (1997). Searching for expertise in counseling, psychotherapy, and professional psychology. *Educational Psychology Review, 9*(4), 361–369.

Slote, M. (1992). *From morality to virtue*. New York: Oxford University Press.

Slote, M. (1997). Agent-based virtue ethics. In R. Crip & M. Slote (Eds.), *Virtue ethics* (pp. 239–262). Oxford: Oxford University Press.

REFERENCES

Smith, J., & Baltes, P. (1990). Wisdom-related knowledge. *Developmental Psychology, 26*(3), 494–505.

Stalley, R. (1986). The responsibility of Socrates. *Polis, 6,* 2–30.

Stauffer, D. (2001). *Plato's introduction to the question of justice.* Albany: SUNY Press.

Steger, M., Kashdan, T., & Oishi, S. (2008). Being good by doing good: Daily eudaimonic activity and well-being. *Journal of Research in Personality, 42,* 22–42.

Stein, H. (1991). Adler and Socrates: Similarities and differences. *Individual Psychology, 47*(2), 241–246.

Sternberg, R. (1998a). A balance theory of wisdom. *Review of General Psychology, 2*(4), 347–365.

Sternberg, R. (2003). Intelligence: Can one have too much of a good thing? In E. Chang & L. Sanna (Eds.), *Virtue, vice, and personality* (pp. 39–51). Washington, DC: American Psychological Association.

Stokes, M. (1986). *Plato's Socratic conversations.* Baltimore, MD: Johns Hopkins University Press.

Stephenson, G., Maggi, P., Lefever, R., & Morojele, N. (1995). Excessive behaviors: An archival study of behavioural tendencies reported by 471 patients admitted to an addiction treatment centre. *Addiction Research, 3,* 245–265.

Strohmer, D., Moilanen, D., & Barry, L. (1988). Personal hypothesis testing. *Journal of Counseling Psychology, 35,* 56–65.

Strycker, E. (1966). The unity of knowledge and love in Socrates' conception of virtue. *International Philosophical Quarterly, 6,* 428–444.

Swain, M. (1981). *Reasons and knowledge.* Ithaca, NY: Cornell University Press.

Szasz, T. (1960). The myth of mental illness. *American Psychologist, 15,* 113–118.

Szasz, T. (1970). *The manufacture of madness.* New York: Harper & Row.

Taran, L. (1985). Platonism and Socratic ignorance. *Studies in Philosophy and the History of Philosophy, 13,* 85–109.

Taranto, M. (1989). Facets of wisdom: A theoretical synthesis. *International Journal of Aging and Human Development, 29*(1), 1–21.

Taylor, A. E. (1953). *Socrates: The man and his thought.* New York: Doubleday.

Taylor, A. E. (1956). *Plato: The man and his work.* New York: Meridian.

Taylor, C. (1992). Socratic ethics. In B. Gower & M. Stokes (Eds.), *Socratic questions* (pp. 137–152. New York: Routledge.

Taylor, R. (2002). *Virtue ethics.* Amherst, NY: Prometheus.

Tee, J., & Kazantzis, N. (2011). Collaborative empiricism in cognitive therapy: A definition and theory for the relationship construct. *Clinical Psychology: Science and Practice, 18*(1), 47–61.

Tillich, P. (1952). *The courage to be.* New Haven, CT: Yale University Press.

Tomm, K. (1987). Interventive interviewing: Reflexive questioning as a means to enable self-healing. *Family Process, 26,* 167–183.

Tomm, K. (1988). Interventive interviewing: Intending to ask lineal, circular, strategic, or reflexive questions? *Family Process, 27*(1), 1–15.

Toulmin, S. (1950/1986). *The place for reason in ethics.* Chicago: University of Chicago Press.

Tredennick, H. (1969). *Plato: The last days of Socrates.* London: Penguin.

REFERENCES

Tredennick, H., & Waterfield, R. (1990). *Xenophon: Conversations of Socrates*. New York: Penguin.

Trianosky, G. (1987). Virtue, action, and the good life: Toward a theory of the virtues. *Pacific Philosophical Quarterly*, 124–147.

Trianosky, G. (1988). Rightly ordered appetites: How to live morally and live well. *American Philosophical Quarterly, 25*, 1–12.

Turkcapar, M. H., Kahraman, M. S., & Sargin, A. E. (2015). Guided discovery with Socratic questioning. *Journal of Cognitive Behavioral Psychotherapy and Research, 1*, 47–53.

Unger, P. (1975). *Ignorance: A case for skepticism*. Oxford: Clarendon.

Vannicelli, M. (2001). Moderation training for problem drinkers. *Cognitive and Behavioral Practice, 8*, 53–61.

VanRossem, K. (2014). Meeting Socrates: How to do Socratic consultations. *Philosophical Practice, 9*(1), 1344–1351.

Vernezze, P. (2008). Moderation or the middle way: Two approaches to anger. *Philosophy East & West, 58*(1), 2–16.

Versenyi, L. (1963). *Socratic humanism*. New Haven, CT: Yale University Press.

Versenyi, L. (1982). *Holiness and justice: An interpretation of Plato's* Euthyphro. Washington, DC: University Press of America.

Vitiello, M. (2005). Professor Kingsfield: The most misunderstood character in literature. *Hofstra Law Review, 33*, 955–966.

Vitousek, K., Watson, S., & Wilson, G. T. (1998). Enhancing motivation for change in treatment-resistant eating disorders. *Clinical Psychology Review, 18*(4), 391–420.

Vlastos, G. (1971). Justice and happiness in the *Republic*. In G. Vlastos (Ed.), *Plato II: Ethics, politics, and philosophy of art and religion* (pp. 66–95). Notre Dame, IN: University of Notre Dame Press.

Vlastos, G. (1983). The Socratic elenchus. *Oxford Studies in Ancient Philosophy, 1*, 27–58.

Vlastos, G. (1985). Socrates' disavowal of knowledge. *Philosophical Quarterly, 35*(138), 1–31.

Vlastos, G. (1987). Socratic irony. *Classical Quarterly, 37*(1), 79–96.

Vlastos, G. (1989). Socratic piety. *Boston Area Colloquium in Ancient Philosophy, 5*, 213–237.

Vlastos, G. (1991). *Socrates: Ironist and moral philosopher*. Ithaca, NY: Cornell University Press.

Vlastos, G. (1992). Elenchus and mathematics: A turning point in Plato's philosophical development. In H. Benson (Ed.), *Essays on the philosophy of Socrates* (pp. 137–161). New York: Oxford University Press.

Vlastos, G. (1994). *Socratic studies*. London: Cambridge University Press.

Walitzer, K., & Connors, G. (2007). Thirty-month follow-up of drinking moderation training for women. *Journal of Consulting and Clinical Psychology, 75*(3), 501–507.

Wallace, J. (1978). *Virtues and vices*. Ithaca, NY: Cornell University Press.

Waterfield, R. (1990). *Conversations of Socrates*. London: Penguin.

Waterfield, R. (1994). *Plato: Gorgias*. Oxford: Oxford University Press.

Waterfield, R. (1995). Plato's *Euthydemus*. *Ancient Philosophy, 15*(1), 191–198.

Waterfield, R. (2009). *Why Socrates died*. Toronto: McClelland & Stewart.

REFERENCES

Watson, G. (1985). Plato and the story. *Studies in Philosophy and the History of Philosophy, 13,* 35–52.

Weber, S., & Pargament, K. (2014). The role of religion and spirituality in mental health. *Current Opinion in Psychiatry, 27*(5), 358–363.

Weeks, G. (1977). Toward a dialectical approach to intervention. *Human Development, 20,* 277–292.

Weiner, N. (1993). *The harmony of the soul.* Albany: SUNY Press.

Weiss, R. (1994). Virtue without knowledge: Socrates conception of holiness in Plato's *Euthyphro. Ancient Philosophy, 14,* 263–282.

Westen, D., Novotny, C., & Thompson-Brenner, H. (2004). The empirical status of empirically supported psychotherapies. *Psychological Bulletin, 130*(4), 631–663.

White, N. (1976). *Plato on knowledge and reality.* Indianapolis, IN: Hackett.

White, N. (1979). *A companion to Plato's* Republic. Indianapolis, IN: Hackett.

White, N. (1994). Inquiry. In J. Day (Ed.), *Plato's* Meno (pp. 152–171). New York. Routledge.

Whiteley, T. R. (2014). Using the Socratic method and Bloom's taxonomy of the cognitive domain to enhance online discussion, critical thinking, and student learning. *Developments in Business Simulation and Experiential Learning, 33,* 65–70.

Wilbur, J., & Allen, H. (1979). *The worlds of Plato and Aristotle.* Buffalo, NY: Prometheus.

Williams, D., & Levitt, H. (2007). A qualitative investigation of eminent therapists' values within psychotherapy. *Journal of Psychotherapy Integration, 17*(2), 159–184.

Wilson, J. (1984). *The politics of moderation: An interpretation of Plato's* Republic. Lanham, MD: University Press of America.

Wink, P., & Helson, R. (1997). Practical and transcendent wisdom. *Journal of Adult Development, 4,* 1–15.

Wolpe, J. (1958). *Psychotherapy by Reciprocal Inhibition.* Stanford, CA: Stanford University Press.

Wolz, H. (1974). The paradox of piety in Plato's *Euthyphro* in the light of Heidegger's conception of authenticity. *Southern Journal of Philosophy, 12,* 493–511.

Woolfolk, R. (2015). *The value of psychotherapy: The talking cure in an age of clinical science.* New York: Guilford.

Zare, P., & Mukundan, J. (2015). The use of Socratic method as a teaching/learning tool to develop students' critical thinking. *Language in India, 15*(6), 256–263.

Zimmerman, M. (1980). Socratic ignorance and authenticity. *Tulane Studies in Philosophy, 29,* 133–150.

Zimmerman, M., Chelminski, I., & Posternak, M. (2004). Exclusion criteria used in antidepressant efficacy trials. *Journal of Nervous and Mental Disease, 192*(2), 87–94.

Index

abandonment, pervasive fear of, 193
abstract ideas, 162
abusiveness, verbal, 110
academic performance, excessive devotion to, 177
Academus, 8
Academy, the, 8
accuracy, therapist's questions for, 52
action, and virtue ethics, 142
action-oriented therapies, 116–117
action plan, preparing, 45–46
adaptive behavior skills, 228
adaptive perspective, 158
addiction: disease models of, 175; psychosocial factors in, 175
adjustment, of clients, 13
Adler, Alfred, 13, 19, 116, 187, 217, 220
adolescents, Socratic method with, 227
afterlife: client's beliefs in, 200; faith in, 203
age, wisdom and, 153
akrasia, 122
alcohol: in moderation, 179; and self-control, 122
alcohol abuse, treatment for, 175
Alexander the Great, 9
Alice in Wonderland (Carroll), 69

alliance, in psychotherapy, 215
altruism, 122
Amazon MTurk system, 21
ambiguity, of terminology, 69
American Psychological Assoc. (APA), 1947 Detroit meeting of, 25
analogical reasoning, 53
analogies: client's, 63; using, 62–63, 64
analogue research, 31
analogue samples, 220
anger, feelings of: interfering with logical reasoning, 184; middle ground for, 196
anger management, 184, 186, 191
anhedonia, persistent, 183
anticipatory guilt, 142, 143, 181–184
antidepressant drug trials, eligibility for, 24
antidepressant medication, expanding sales of, 12
anxiety, chronic social, 163
anxiety disorders, treatments for, 163
Apology (Plato), 7
aporetic state, 136
aporia, 2, 136–137
appearance, physical, evaluation of, 108–109

INDEX

appetites: guided, 177; healthy gratification of normal, 185; suppressed by reason, 184
archetypes, Jung's notion of, 225
Aristotle, 9, 58, 150
art, personal expressions through, 116
assertiveness, focus on, 186
assertiveness training, 191
attitude modification methods, ix
attitudes, 159; adaptive, 104; changes in, 19; changing clients', 210; and emotions, 158; as hypotheses to be tested, 98
attraction, quality of, 77
attributions, in cognitive intervention, 10, 11
authority: and justice, 189; questioning, 228

balanced lifestyle: goal of, 175; importance of, 124
beauty, 29; client's view of, 84
Beck, Aaron, ix, 1, 10, 11, 23, 102, 217, 220
beginner's mind, Zen principle of, 89
behavior: potential consistency in, 134; rationalization of, 134; virtuous, 144
behavioral activities, 106–107
behavioral rehearsal, 41
behavior change, role of, x
behavior therapy, ix, 19
beliefs: acceptable, 98; avoiding self-contradicting, 53; challenging, 98, 99; and definitions, 81; dominant role of, 91; erroneous, 97; evaluating consistency across, 48; evidence to support client's, 100; examining, 54, 100, 101f; exploring client's, 65–67; fallibility of, 89–91; false trust in one's, 92; found to be true, 100; inconsistent, 73; information that conforms to, 92; justification of, 97; vs. knowledge, 47–48; and learning major ideas, 95; nihilistic, 55; problematic, 86; reliance on unsupported, 99; removing false and incompatible, 217; testing, 99; trusted, 100; truth value of, 104; upgrading, 212
Benson, H., 14
Beutler, L., 3
Bible study classes, 208
biological urges, satisfying, 122
bipolar, use of term, 77
blame: among depressed clients, 60–61; attributions of, 11
Boulder conference (1950), 25
Boulder model, 221
bravado, vs. courage, 164
bravery, acts of, 171
breadth, therapist's questions for, 52

Callicles, 204
career paths, 22, 81, 117, 119; choosing, 118–119
case examples, xi
case material, for professional presentation, xi–xii
catastrophe, definition of, 77–78
caught, getting, 191–192
causal attributions, clarification of, 56–61
causal reasoning, and self-blame, 61
CBT. See cognitive behavioral therapy
Chaerephon, 88
change, 133; courage to, 170; and long-term satisfactions, 128; with self-improvement, 123; strategies for, 229
character, use of term, 131–132
character traits, 131
Charcot, Jean-Martin, 19, 220
chariot analogy, 184
childhood trauma, 216
Chisholm, R., 49
choice: virtue as, 144; and virtue ethics, 142
church activities, 208
church services, 201
classroom discussions, xiv, 221
classroom settings, Socrates in, 105
cleaning, compulsive, 181–182

INDEX

clients, xiii; accurate definitions for, 86; appropriate for therapy, 227; changes made by, 138; decision-making of, 49–51; deriving own answers, 38–39; encouraged to listen, 31; failure felt by, 56–57; focus on future of, 112; interpersonal conflict of, 36; learning from, 24; new perspective for, 49; original definition of, 79; psychotherapy sessions adapted to, 214; questions of, 34–35; research in, 25, 26; and role of therapist, 17–18; and Socratic approach, 221–222; validity of belief of, 48; value of objects for, 140–141

client scenarios, using, xi

clinical experience, for successful therapy, 23, 31

clinical expertise: acquiring, 18; and clinical practice, 23

clinical guidelines, vagueness of, 28

clinical practice, 221; and research, 27; subtle nuances of, 17

clinical psychology: empirical foundation for, 20; lack of ongoing clinical experience in, 26

clinical settings, well-controlled studies in, 29

clinical technique, abstract ideals in, xi

clinical training, scientist-practitioner model in, 25–26

cognitive-behavioral therapy (CBT), 9; effectiveness of, 22; foundations of, 220; for OCD, 19; reduced potency of, 23

cognitive change, 15

cognitive psychotherapy, evolved from behavior therapy, 19

cognitive therapy, 9–10; erroneous beliefs in, 98; guided discovery in, 112–113; and Socratic method, 10

collaboration: promotion of, 97; in therapy sessions, 225

collaborative empiricism, 52

collaborative exploration: in guided discovery, 109; reliance of therapy on, 140–141

collaborator, therapist as, 96

community, feeling of, 187

comorbidity, diagnostic, 24

compassion, compared with religion, 207

competence: clinical, 23; professional, 92

confession, encouraging honest, 194

confidentiality: client, xii; maintaining, xi

confirmation bias, 91–92

conflicts, resolving, 197

conflict with authority, of adolescents, 227

confrontation, fear of, 166

consistency, potential, 134

constructive therapy, and Socratic method, 10

consumption, excessive, 176

contentment, reliance on virtue of, 135–136

control groups, 17

conversations, Socratic, 70, 115

cooperation: and justice, 189; Socratic questions in, 41

coping role model, value of, 168

coping strategies, 42; of clients, 13; in lack of moderation, 183; questions exploring, 43–44

corrupting youth of Athens, Socrates accused of, 7

counterexample, using, 73

courage, 130, 162, 163–164; to be sincere and authentic, 167; to change, 170; and conflicts, 197; definition for, 68; development of, 166; explaining, 88; in family dynamics, 167; in justice, 195; lack of, 166, 171; in modern society, 163, 214; needed in therapy, 167; and risk of harm, 165–167; Socrates on, 162; in therapeutic dialogue, 167–171; in treatment of debilitating anxiety disorders, 163; understanding nature of, 163–165; and wisdom, 171

[255]

INDEX

courageous acts, 165
creativity, wisdom and, 147
critical thinking: skills, 101; in Socratic method, 52
Crito (Socrates), dialogue of, 192
cultural differences, 34
curiosity: for therapists, 96; wisdom and, 147

daily events, focus on, 149
daily reminders, 141
dance, personal expressions through, 116
danger, courage in, 164, 172. *See also* courage
death: clients' views on, 202, 206; fear of, 202; impending, 202; near-death experience, 203; Socrates on, 203; by suicide, 204
death sentence, Socrates's, 7
decision making: independent, 114; and justice, 190; responsible, 125; wisdom in, 155
decisions, just, 188
definitions: accurate, 86; to clarify behavior labels, 85; clarifying, 78f; collaborative, 71–72; and counterexamples, 73; evaluative standards for, 81–86; vs. examples, 71, 72; focus on, 76, 86; inadequate, 80; and knowledge, 72; priority of, 70–72; refuting incorrect, 80–81; related to evaluations, 72; search for, 14, 68–69, 71; testing, 73; true, 70; universal, 70–71, 76–80. *See also* terminology
dependent personality disorder, x
depression, 179; client with, 123; interpersonal psychotherapy of, 28; lack of wisdom associated with, 152; research-based treatment of, 24; and self-acceptance, 120; and Socratic method, 11, 226; and suicidal urges, 202; and view of afterlife, 204
depth, therapist's questions for, 52

depth perception, in therapeutic dialogue, 213
desensitization, systematic, 19
desires: adjusting, 177; excessive, 174, 175; healthy gratification of normal, 185; moderation of, 178; necessary vs. unnecessary, 177; personal, 148–149; physical, 123; reducing or eliminating excessive, 185; self-awareness of, 115; self-control over, 173
Detroit meeting (APA, 1947), 25
diagnostic comorbidity, 24
dialectic: defined, 14; discussion in, 9; Socratic, 8
dialogue: collaborative, 72, 127; exploration in, 48; guiding therapeutic, 46; in self-awareness process, 118; self-contemplative, 173; Socratic, x, 6–7, 89; in therapy sessions, 229; value of spoken, 6. *See also* Socratic dialogue
Dialogues of Plato, The (Jowett), 2
disagreements, appearing trivial, 192
discipline, personal, training for, 122
discovery, guided, 4, 102, 212; collaborative empiricism in, 106–110; dialogue of, 105; examined, 103–104, 103f; goal of, 103, 103f, 104, 107–108; process of, 103, 103f, 105; questions in, 110
distance, maintaining professional, 16
distractions: bodily urges as, 145; from eternal peace, 200; of modern society, 129
divorce, surviving, 151
documentation, age of, 6
drama therapy, 120
dreams, 116
drinkers, problem, 179
drug addiction, logic behind, 181–182
Dubois, Paul, 19, 220
dysthymic disorder, research in, 24

eating disorders, 77, 216
effectiveness and efficacy research, 210

INDEX

Einstein, Albert, 87, 160, 223
"elenchus," the: explained, 2–3; Socratic, 5, 8–9, 89; steps in, 48–49
elimination, in inductive reasoning, 53
Ellis, Albert, ix, 1, 11, 14, 23, 119, 210, 217, 220
emotional reactions: emphasis on, 123; excessive, 183; transcending, 151
emotions: and attitudes, 158; in construction of reality, 226–227; in moderation, 184; negative, 79; rational control over, 191; suppressed by reason, 184
empathy: cultivating, 192; questions grounded in, 33; in therapy sessions, 225
empirical research, limitations of, 29
empiricism, 4
empiricism, collaborative, 106–110, 212
endurance, and courage, 165
enumeration, in inductive reasoning, 53
episteme, explained, 1–2
equality, 29; and justice, 197
essential analysis, 159
ethical issues, 128
ethical relativism, 144
ethics: situational, 137; virtue, 128; virtue vs. situational, 143. *See also* virtue ethics
evaluation, questions for, 46
event-coping efforts, 46
evidence: and contemporary psychotherapy, 223; in examining beliefs, 100–101, 101f
evi: acts, 148; behavior, 129; vs. good, 133
examples, definition constructed by, 73
excess: exploring periods of, 180; forms of, 173; negative consequences of, 182; problems caused by, 180; taming tendency for, 177–178
exercise, and virtue ethics, 141
existential analysis, 199
expectations: changes in, 19; changing clients', 210; in cognitive intervention, 10, 11; of parents, 81, 119; pessimistic, 47
experimental therapists, 116
expert, avoiding role of, 204
expertise, 92
exposure therapy, 19
extremes, finding balance between, 178–181

faculty members, psychology, 21; career path of, 22; in clinical practice, 26
fad ideas, and wisdom, 150
failures: client's view of, 83–84; definition of, 73–74; meaning of, 72
fairness, 186; and justice, 197; nature of, 187
faith: as appropriate topic, 200–201; in psychotherapy, 201; use of term, 199. *See also* piety
fame: compared with virtue, 148; value of, 147
family conflict, 169–170
family therapist, training for, 27
fear, and courage, 165, 171–172
Fishman, H. C., 27
flexibility, cultivating, 224
foolhardiness, vs. courage, 164
forgiveness, 186, 191; promotion of, 208
fortitude, 165
Frankl, Viktor, 13, 159, 199, 217, 220
freedom, personal, 138
free will, 138
Freud, Sigmund, 13, 19, 127, 217, 220, 225, 226
friendship, definition for, 68
fulfillment, 138

gadfly, Socrates considered as, 104–105
gambling, excessive, 185
gardening metaphor, in age of short-term therapy, 14
gender differences, 34
generalizations: helping clients form new, 54–57; inductive, 56
Glasser, William, 217, 220

INDEX

gluttony, tendencies for, 174
goals: and contentment, 116; process of understanding, 117–118
Golden Rule, the, 208
good, vs. evil, 133
good person, Platonic ideals of, 132
goods, distribution of, and justice, 186–187, 189
graduate training in psychology, 16–17, 22
gratification, delayed, 182
gratitude, feelings of, 213
greed, 176
group therapy, structured, 41
guided discovery, 10, 102. *See also* discovery, guided
guilt, anticipatory, 142–143, 181, 184

habit, and virtue ethics, 141
handouts, 41
hangover, memories of severe, 182
happiness, 144–145; aligned with virtue, 148; and moral character, 130; searching for, 150–153; wisdom and, 148
harm: to one's moral character, 203–204; situations that pose risk of, 165–167
harmony, personal, 127
hedonism, short-term, 144
hemlock poison, 7
hermeneutics, 4
high-risk situation, evaluation of, 109
holiness, use of term, 199
homework assignments, 41
human nature, positive view of, 133
humility, compared with modesty, 93
hypothesis testing, 4, 17, 53–54, 58–59

identity, pious, 205. *See also* piety
identity issues, for adolescents, 227
ignorance: acceptance of, 88, 100, 115, 212; and evil behavior, 129, 148; expressions of, 89; and goals and values, 101; helping clients accept their own, 97–99; as part of wisdom, 149–150; Socrates on, 87, 88, 204; usefulness of, 95; and wisdom, 150
ignorance, Socratic, 87, 91, 93; and role of therapist, 96
immoral actions, involuntary nature of, 152
impiety, Socrates accused of, 7, 198
inconsistencies, dealing with, 73
inductive reasoning, 4, 14, 53; causal attributions clarified in, 56–61; causal factors in, 61; definitions in, 68; general conclusions in, 54; via generalization, 56; goal of, 54; learning in, 62–67; limitations of, 55, 58; and past failures, 59–60; in psychotherapeutic process, 28; rational approach in, 67; reliance on, 58; used by Socratic therapist, 211–212
information: as beliefs, 90; biased ways of processing, 118; obtained through senses, 158
injustice, 191; committing acts of, 193–194, 195; and punishment, 194
inner reserves, Socratic view of, 82–83
insight-oriented therapies, 116
insulting words, 196
insurance coverage, curtailment of sessions due to, 13
integrity, 119; cultivating, 224
intellect, in Socratic approach, 217
intellectual modesty, 92, 93, 96, 150, 199; in collaborative exploration, 140; of therapist, 100
intelligence, compared with wisdom, 146–147
intentional behaviors, 127
intentions, 139; in virtue, 135
interactions, spontaneous, 27
interlocutor, in historic dialogues of Plato, 3
interpersonal conflict, 36
interpretations, in cognitive intervention, 10–11
interventions, highly structured, 220
interviewing, motivational, 34

INDEX

intimacy, avoiding, 177
intimate relationships conflict in, 84
introspection, 118

Janet, Pierre, 19, 220
job, characteristics of, 75
job stress, 153, 196
Jung, Carl, 13, 19, 220
justice, 29; centrality of, 190; combined with wisdom, 195–196; conflated with punishment, 193; and conflicts, 197; definition for, 68; explaining, 88; external appearance of, 190; focus of, 189; lacking, 187; meaning of, 130; middle ground for, 196; nature of, 188; in position of authority, 197; relevance of, 186–187; revenge compared with, 190–194

key terms, client's implicit definition of, 137
knowledge: Aristotle on, 150; vs. belief, 47–48; beliefs as, 90; benefits of, 123; errors of false, 90; examining, 54; expansion of, 160; fallibility of, 149; false, 89, 94; innate, 225; limits of, 4, 154; necessity of, 72–76; vs. opinion, 53; searching for, 141; seeking, 88–89; Socrates on, 87; in Socratic method, xii; technical, 147; true, 91, 159; of virtue, 148
"know thyself," 115

labeling, limits of, 13
labels, use of various evaluative, 78
labor, division of, and justice, 187, 189
Laches (Athenian general), 162
Laws (Plato), 8
leadership decisions, and justice, 187
learning, 6; from client's life experiences, 212; fundamental impediment to, 96–97; openness to, 149–150; role of ignorance in, 89; wisdom and, 147
learning by discovery, 113

legal proceedings, justice in, 187
life, examination of, 132
life decisions, 106
life events: example of major, 153; importance of, 153–157; negative, 153; reviewing, 156, 183; thoughtful review of, 158
life goals, 71, 224; in cognitive therapy, 10; and cultivating wisdom, 158; identification of, 114; primary, 207; and self-control, 124; in Socratic method, 128
life meaning, 217
life review, personal, 152
life satisfaction, lasting sources of, 179
lifestyle changes, 15, 174
listening, effective, 109
living, effective, 135
living well, 144–145
logic: and justice, 188; for rational dialogue, 67
loneliness, pervasive fear of, 193
loss, and wisdom, 151
love, 117; definition of, 76, 77, 107–108; explaining, 88
luxuries, unnecessary, 177

managed-care corporations, 224
manuals, structured therapy, 23, 221; "gap" created by, 223; to guide psychotherapy, 18; usefulness of, 224; well-designed, 224–225
marriage, topic of, 180–181
maturity, cultivating, 224
Maxwell, N., 223
meaning, in cognitive therapy, 10
meanings: idiographic, 85; search for, 213
medical model, for mental illness, 12
meditation, peaceful, 208
Meichenbaum, Donald, 11, 217, 220
Meno (Socrates), 95, 108; dialogue of, 133, 160
mental health: research on, 29; role of spirituality in, 198
mental health counseling, 4

INDEX

mental health professionals, 90; Socratic style adopted by, 329
mental illness: international manufacture of, 12; medical model for, 12
metaphors, client's, 63
Meteora, Greece, monks of, 201
midwife, intellectual, Socrates as, 105
midwife metaphor, 5
Mill, John Stuart, 58
mind: obstacles to open, 91–93; psychology of, 9
mindfulness strategies, 116
Minuchin, Salvador, 27, 220
miracles, worksheet on everyday, 160–161
misbehaviors: common, 134; as learning opportunities, 133
moderation: definition for, 68, 178; development of, 173; in justice, 195; lack of, 176; promoting, 180; reason in, 185; therapeutic focus on, 175; wisdom required for, 173–174
moderation training, 179
modesty, 176; compared with humility, 93. See also intellectual modesty
moral character, 131, 144, 145
moral development, 131
moral health, 130
moral ideals, universal relevance of, 144
moral issues, 128; and therapeutic process, 69
morality, 130; and life goals, 147
moral problems, 139
mortality, client's views on, 200
motivation, individual's, 139
My Lai massacre, 139
mythology, Greek gods of, 7

narrative therapy, and Socratic method, 10
Nazi Germany, 139
near-death experience, 154, 203
negative moods, 123–124
negotiation, justice in, 187

Nelson, Leonard, 13
new analogies, learning from, 62–67
news feeds, 114
nocebo reactions, 29
normal: meaning of, 72; notion of, 80

obesity, 174
objectivity: maintaining professional, 16; in Socratic approach, 30
obsessive-compulsive disorder (OCD), CBT for, 19
occupational productivity, excessive devotion to, 177
openness, in collaborative exploration, 140
opinions: confronting, 91; definition of, 89–90; fallibility of, 89–91; as hypotheses to be tested, 98; vs. knowledge, 53; views as, 90
Oracle of Delphi, 88, 115
overeating, and self-control, 122
overgeneralization, refuting, 56
overindulgence, 123
overstatements, 47

pain: personal restraint over, 121; and wisdom, 151
painting metaphor, 27–28
panic attack, definition of, 77
Pascal, Blaise, 141
passions, self-control over, 173
patience: in application of psychotherapy, 227; promotion of, 208
peer pressure, 166; confronting, 168
peer relationships, for adolescents, 227
peer-review process, 20
Penn, William, 188
perfection, pursuit of, 175–178
Perfect Storm, The (film), 168–169
"perfect storm" metaphor, 168–169
Perls, Fritz, 13, 220
personality, Socrates's theory of, 225
personality development, 17
personality disorder, 128; and guided discovery, 113

INDEX

personality traits, of skilled psychotherapist, 17
personal tendencies, self-awareness of, 115
person-centered therapy, 34
perspectives, stimulating new, 63
persuasion, 158
Phaenarete, 5
pharmaceutical industry, 12
phenomenology, 14
philosophy: ancient, 137, 222; psychology vs., 2
phrases, to avoid, 85t, 86
phronesis, 2, 146
physical desires, 177
physical health, 131
piety, 200, 205, 207, 208; as appropriate topic, 200–201; as controversial topic, 200; definition for, 68; discussions about, 205–206, 208; personal sense of, 201; in Plato's dialogues, 209; in psychotherapy sessions, 198; Socratic notion of, 199, 201, 209; therapeutic discussions of, 199–200; use of term, 198–199
placebo effect, 29, 30
plan for action, questions identifying, 44–45
Plato, x, xiii, 58; and independent thinking, 108; intuitive and experiential approach of, 30; Socrates's dialogues recorded by, 7–8; on wisdom, 147
Plato, "dialogues" of, xiii, 8, 87, 88, 162, 225; historical foundation for, 2; search for universal definition of virtues in, 136; soul in, 199
pleasures: aligned with virtue, 148; and desire, 174, 185; excessive pursuit of, 176; personal restraint over, 121; physical vs. intellectual, 145; pursuit of, 175–178; short- compared with long-term, 182; short-term, 122
politics, topics of, 97
Polus, discussion with, 194

popular opinion: reversals in, 93–94; and wisdom, 150
pornography, reliance on, 142–143
Positive Attitudes, Worksheet on, 218
positive moods, 124
possessions: excessive focus on, 176; personal, 140; pursuit of, 175–178
poverty, and courage, 166
power: and justice, 189; value of, 147
practice: in clinical psychology, 9; and developing expert skills, 18; in effective psychotherapy, 16; integrating science and, 25–27
practicum settings, 17
prayer: isolated, 201; solitary, 208
precision, questions for, 52
prestige: desire for, 185; pursuit of, 175–178
probabilities, 94
"problems of living," 13
problem solving, 113; questions guiding, 34; rational, 41–42; stages of, 46; with variety of questions, 41
problem-solving strategies, in psychotherapy, 75
problem-solving therapy, effectiveness of, 41
process issues, 216; in contemporary psychotherapy, 210; in therapy, 230
professional skills, 92
profit, desire for, 185
proper motives, 127
Protagoras, 6
psyche: psychotherapy treatment for, 11–12; tripartite model of, 225–226
psychiatric diagnosis, financial basis of, 12–13
psychiatric labels, artificial creation of, 12
psychiatry, lack of ongoing clinical experience in, 26
psychological assessment, 17

INDEX

psychological intervention, research support for, xii
psychological treatments, in clinical settings, 220
psychology, philosophy *vs.*, 2
psychosexual problems, 77
psychotherapist: effective, 18–19, 224; making of, 16–18; professional competence as, 92
psychotherapy, 219; from ancient dialogue to, 9–14; contemporary, 9–14; creativity in, 26–27; to cultivate wisdom, 159; dependent on secondary sources about, 26; effective, 168; empirical approach to, 30; evolution of, 19; focus on symptoms management of, 31; goals of, 63, 127, 211, 224; informed by Socratic method, 210; manual-driven, 96; philosophical foundations for, 29–30; pioneers of, 19; processes of, 15; pseudomedical format for, 24; research on, 24; scientific foundation for, 18–25; search for definitions in, 69; Socratic method of, 4; standard diagnostic nomenclature of, 130; time-limited, 75; topic areas for, 15; using Socratic method, 213; wisdom as focus for, 158–159
psychotherapy, schools of, 220
psychotherapy sessions: interactional nature of, 25; problem-solving strategies in, 75; process within, 110–112; Socratic method in, 1; structure of, 27–28
psychotropic medication, 13
punishment: beneficial effects of, 194–195; threats of, 196
purchasing, overemphasis on, 176

questioning: collaborative style of, 41; internalization of, 211; Socratic, 96
questioning, systematic, 32; process of, 47–51; for Socratic therapist, 211; therapeutic use of, 33–34
questions: for action plan, 45–46; bifurcated format for, 36; change of behavior encouraged by, 40; collaborative approach to, 35; content of, 41–47; customizing, 47; and effective listening, 109; to enhance self-awareness, 118; to evaluate consistency of beliefs, 48; to examine client's understanding, 65–67; exploratory, 36; exploring coping strategies, 43–44; factual, 36; format of useful, 35–40; goal of, 42; to identify causal factors, 61; to identify plan of action, 44–45; importance of, 205–208; and justice, 188; leading, 36, 37; multiple purposes of, 75; with no correct answer, 98; open-ended, 35, 36; options provided by, 35; packaging, 51; phrased openly, 35; in psychotherapeutic process, 28; shifting client's time perspective, 39–40; simple yes/no, 36; to stimulate creative thinking, 104; to structure guided discovery, 113; thought-provoking, 124; use of "why," 49
questions, Socratic, 36, 37, 41, 50–51, 104; effective use of, 33
questions, systematic, 37–38, 39, 42, 43, 44–45, 46
quotes, inspirational, 141

racial differences, 34
rapport, of psychotherapy, 215
rational analysis, 4
rational-emotive behavior therapy (REBT), 10, 23
rationalizations, self-serving, 148
"rational uncertainty," 93
rational views, cultivation of, 56
Rawls, John, 189
reality, 14; perceived, 15
reason: and dialectic, 29; in justice, 195–196; in Socratic approach, 217
reasonableness, in therapy, 100

INDEX

reasoning: analogical, 64; and justice, 188; and treatment, 31
rebuilding, using metaphor of, 63–64
reciprocal inhibition therapy, 19
reflection, personal, and virtue ethics, 142
regret, value of anticipatory, 181–184
relationship, intimate, role of past in, 108
relationship problems, 40
relevance, questions for, 52
religion: compared with compassion, 207; personal beliefs about, 205; in psychotherapeutic circles, 199; topics of, 97; use of term, 198
religious beliefs, 201
religious views, inappropriate, 200
remedy, punishment as, 195
reporting, anonymous, 191
Republic (Plato), 8
Republic (Socrates), 120
reputation: compared with character, 132; compared with virtue, 148; pursuit of, 129
research, 221; aim of, 21–22; anonymous online surveys, 21; applied, 22; with clients as participants, 26; and clinical practice, 27; with college-student samples, 21–22; fallibility of, 90; limitations of, 21; samples used in, 20–21; value of, 20
research design, 17
research project, aborted, 24
research protocols, and treatment, 24–25
resentment, 186
resilience, personal, 113
responsibility, cultivating, 224
restitution, justice in, 187
restraint, lack of, 177
revenge, 186; client's planning for, 192–193; justice and, 190–194
review, questions for, 46
reviews, online, 191
ridicule, facing risk of, 168

risk: courage in, 164; and responsible behavior, 134; of self-fulfilling prophecy, 99; in situations that pose harm, 165–167; suicide, 202
Rogers, Carl, 217, 220, 229–230
romance, 117; overgeneralized views of, 55
romantic relationship: as clients' problem, 63–64; end of, 192–193; goals and motivation of, 123; person's view of, 76

samples, 20–21; college students as, 21–22; in treatment-outcome research, 219–220
satisfaction: lasting, 122; long-term, 144, 182
science: in clinical psychology, 9; in effective psychotherapy, 16; fallibility of, 90; integrating practice and, 25–27; and practice of psychology, 221; reversals in, 94
scientific inquiry, 223
scientific methods, 17
scientist-practitioner, 20
scientist-practitioner model, 25–26
self-acceptance, 114–115, 213; developing sincere, 120; goal of, 120; from self-evaluation, 119–121; unconditional, 119
self-actualized, becoming, 118
self-awareness, 40, 128, 223; objectivity in, 116; process of, 117; pursuit of, 115–119
self-control, 121–126, 124, 126f; facilitating, 173; focus on, 127; goal of, 121; issues related to, 128; lack of, 121, 122; and moderation, 178; training for, 122
self-determination, client, 126
self-direction, 119, 191
self-discipline, 121, 128
self-discovery, 119
self-esteem, 176
self-esteem, low, and self-acceptance, 120

INDEX

self-evaluation, 114; process of, 121; self-acceptance from, 119–121
self-examination, 115
self-exploration, goal of, 117
self-fulfilling prophecy, risk of, 99
self-ignorance, 115
self-improvement, 115, 123, 226; facilitating, 173; focus on, 213; lifelong goal of, 15; notion of ongoing, 135; for pious individual, 199; primary ingredients of, 114; proper motives for, 127; and psychotherapy sessions, 28; in therapeutic dialogue, 211
self-indulgence, 177
self-knowledge, 119; extent of, 116; lack of, 115; pursuit of, 115
self-monitoring form, 59, 59f, 117
self-reflection, 114, 118
self-regulation, 115, 121–126, 122, 126f, 128, 213
self-restraint, 180, 181
self-statements, positive, 167–168
self-understanding, 116
senses, information obtained through, 29
sensory experiences, Socrates on, 29
sensory perception, 158
shaping process, in psychotherapy, 112–113, 212
shopping, and self-control, 122
short-term care, emphasis on, 224
short-term therapy, 13
sickness, selling, 12
similarities, using observed, 64
"Sir Grantsalot," 26
situational ethics, 143
skepticism, attitude of, 93–94
sleep disorders, 77
social anxiety disorder, 12
social injustice, 171
social interest, 187; as goal, 116
social-media postings, 114
social norms, opposing, 168
social pressure, courage to confront, 166
social status, pursuit of, 129

Socrates: death sentence for, 228; definitions sought by, 68; on experts, 23–24; lack of diplomacy of, 228; leading questions used by, 36; life and philosophy of, 5; on sensory experiences, 29; sentenced to death, 7; trial of, 127
Socratic approach, vii; intent of, 222; limitations of, 217; therapist in, 117
Socratic dialogue, 1, 62; collaborative exploration in, 140; common goal of, 130; elements of, 33; and ethical behavior, 131; and exploring client's beliefs, 48; inconsistencies uncovered in, 57; primary components of, 211; refuting false beliefs in, 98–99; steps in, 73; success of, 113; systematic questioning in, 32; use of, 159–160
Socratic exploration, 159
Socratic fallacy, 139
Socratic method, ix, 5, 8, 9, 14; acceptance of one's ignorance in, 100; and adult clients, 227; applications and limitations of, 226; appropriateness of, 228; central goal of, 157; choosing, 229; clinical examples vs. statistical significance in, 11; as cognitive intervention, 227; collaborative exploration in, 1; components of, 28; conceptual shift required by, 3–4; in contemporary psychotherapy, 28; core of, 142; critical evaluation in, 81; and desirable behavior, 127; discussions about piety and, 203; empiricism of, 212; examining beliefs in, 54; focus on, xi; as form of psychotherapy, xii; framework provided by, 229; fully adopting, 228–229; goals of, 10, 15, 127–128, 222; for guiding psychotherapy sessions, 221; history for, 14; and human functioning, 226; inductive reasoning in, 55; integrated with other forms of psychotherapy, 229; key components

of, ix; lack of empirical support for, 30; logical and rational approach of, 149; "mutant form" of, 34; over time, 113; philosophical foundation for, 3, 30; philosophical foundation underlying, 133; practical application of, 28; psychotherapy according to, 210, 223, 225; question-and-answer exchanges in, 49; role of therapist in, 134; role of wisdom in, 137–139; theoretical foundations of, xiii; for therapy sessions, 214; and unsupported beliefs, 49; widespread utility of, 102
Socratic style, for chronic problems, 228
sophia, explained, 1
Sophist (Plato), 8
Sophists, 6, 137
Sophronicus, 5
soul: in death experience, 202; nature of, 191; Socrates's view of, 225; use of term, 131–132; virtues of, 130
spiritual beliefs, in psychotherapy sessions, 198
spiritual faith, focus on, 206
spirituality: client's beliefs in, 200; personal beliefs about, 205; in psychotherapeutic circles, 199; use of term, 198, 199. *See also* piety
standards, evaluative, 79, 81–86
statements, empty, 94
Statesman (Plato), 8
strengths, identifying potential, 169–170
success: client's view of, 82; exploring definition of, 74–75; external indicators of, 143; person's view of, 76
suffering: and courage, 172; and wisdom, 151
suicidal crisis, piety and faith and, 201–202
suicidal ideation, quick response to, 228
"surrogate outcomes," 20

survivors, changed views of, 205
symbols, 116
Szasz, Thomas, 13

teacher: avoiding role of, 204; vs. life of philosopher, 6
teammate, client aligned with therapist as, 216
teamwork, promotion of, 212
techne, 2
technical skills, 27; and philosophical wisdom, 131
technology: reliance on, 150; in therapeutic practice, 18
temptations: potentially harmful effects of, 174; self-control over, 173
terminal disease, 202
terminology: ambiguity in, 69; in CBT, 220; clarification of, 73–74; core essence of, 72; emotional connotations of, 77; emotionally loaded, 76; evaluative, 79; problematic, 77; testing utility of definition of, 80; use of common, 77; use of moral, 71. *See also* definitions
Theaetetus (Socrates), 76
therapeutic activities, 75–76
therapeutic alliance, 125, 215–216
therapeutic dialogue: beliefs in, 99; components of, 4; depth perception in, 213; for exploring consequences, 180; focal points for, 213; and improvements in physical health, 182; promoting brave actions through, 167–171; promoting self-control in, 184; questions in, 98; substantive content for, 211
therapeutic relationship, 19
therapeutic sessions, focus for, 84
therapist: beginning, 106–107; and collaborative empiricism, 106–107; competency of, 22–23; effective, 27, 95, 149; novice, 27, 28; optimal role of, 222; Socratic, 80–81, 105; theoretical orientation of, 95; use of term, 3

INDEX

therapist questions, 52
therapy: analogies in, 63; cognitive-based theories of, 11; collaborative nature of, 102–103; as collaborative process, 229; converting theory into, 28; effective, 71, 131, 155, 170, 182, 215, 217, 219, 223; goal of, 52, 114, 123, 130; individualized approach for, 168; intentional goals of, 18; interpersonal style in, 13; overall plan for, 214; wisdom as central goal for, 159
therapy sessions: and acceptance of ignorance, 95; collaborative and exploratory nature of, 221; direct and rapid approach to, 102; discussion of justice in, 186; focus of, 213; guidelines for, 224; improper use of terminology in, 80; moving through, 79; optimal structure of, 223
third-person phrasing, 92
thoughts, words influencing, 86
thrill seeking, vs. courage, 164
time-limited therapy, 216; and Socratic method, 224, 227–228
tolerance: cultivating, 224; promotion of, 208
tracking form, 126, 126f
trauma: childhood, 216; and wisdom, 152
treatment: prescriptive approaches to, 129–130; value of research to, 31
treatment manuals, 23, 31, 216. *See also* manuals
treatment-outcome studies, 25; problems with, 219
treatment strategies, innovative, 30
trivialities, 149; daily, 154
turf wars, 220

uncertainty: attitude of, 93–94; in Socratic approach, 117; value of, 94
understanding, human, fallibility of, 154
universal definitions, 4, 56; for Socratic therapist, 212. *See also* definitions

universal meanings, search for, 69–70. *See also* meanings
urges, deviant, fending off, 184

values: and contentment, 116; personal, 71; process of understanding, 117–118; in therapeutic sessions, 128; and wisdom, 152
vice: act of, 132; punishment as treatment for, 195; and virtue, 133–134
virtue, 129; based in wisdom, 137–139; confronting, 132; contentment and, 135–136; core aspects of, 134; cultivating, 224; in daily habits, 141–143; definition of, 71; development of, 142; discussion of, 135, 213; evaluation of, 139; ideal of, 138; knowledge of, 148; lack of, 143; learning about, 133, 134; and life goals, 128, 147; motivation for, 135; nature of, 149; promotion of, 213; as proper behavior, 138; in search for happiness, 150; testing of, 132; and vice, 133–134
virtue ethics, 129, 131, 143, 217, 223, 226; action in, 141; choices in, 138; focus on, 132–133, 144, 213; intentions in, 139; and psychotherapy sessions, 28; in therapeutic dialogue, 211. *See also* character traits
virtues, the, 130; *aporia* for, 136–137; cardinal, 144; compared with pleasures, 174; definitions for, 136–137; importance of, 130; of soul, 130; unity of, 195–196
virtuous behavior, cultivation of, 142
virtuous person, 189

wealth: pursuit of, 129; value of, 147
weight-loss programs, 174
well-being, and financial gain, 131
wicked people, death for, 206
Wilde, Oscar, 153
will, weakness of, 122
wind-eggs, 105

wisdom: barriers to, 148; beneficial impact of, 157–158; as cardinal virtue, 152; compared with intelligence, 146–147; and courage, 164, 165, 171; development of, 153, 160; factors involved in, 146; as focus for psychotherapy, 158–159; focus on, 209; ignorance as part of, 149–150; and justice, 188, 195, 196; as life-long quest, 147; and making changes, 157; and moderation, 173–174; in modern society, 152–153; nature of, 146, 149, 150, 151, 160; Plato's view of, 147; practical, 146; psychotherapy to cultivate, 159; pursuit of, 160; search for, 150, 158; sincere pursuit of, 156; Socrates on, 87, 89; and Socratic dialogue, 48; usefulness of, 151; virtue based in, 137–139

Wolpe, Joseph, 19

Wooden, John, 132

words: adaptive alternatives for hazardous, 85t; to avoid, 85t, 86

workaholic habits, 179

working alliance, effective, 215–216

workplace conflicts, 189. *See also* job

worksheets: on everyday miracles, 160–161; on positive attitudes, 218

writing projects, between sessions, 216

written documents, Socratic view of, 6

wrong, doing, 194

Xenophon, 8

Yalom, Irv, 220

GPSR Authorized Representative: Easy Access System Europe, Mustamäe tee 50, 10621 Tallinn, Estonia, gpsr.requests@easproject.com

www.ingramcontent.com/pod-product-compliance
Lightning Source LLC
Chambersburg PA
CBHW021938290426
44108CB00012B/884